T0324487

Theory and Practice of
Computation

Theory and Practice of
Computation

Proceedings of Workshop on Computation: Theory and Practice WCTP2013

University of the Philippines Diliman, Philippines
30 September – 1 October 2013

Editors

Shin-ya Nishizaki
Tokyo Institute of Technology, Japan

Masayuki Numao
Osaka University, Japan

Jaime D L Caro
University of the Philippines Diliman, Philippines

Merlin Teodosia C Suarez
De La Salle University, Philippines

 **World Scientific**

NEW JERSEY · LONDON · SINGAPORE · BEIJING · SHANGHAI · HONG KONG · TAIPEI · CHENNAI

Published by

World Scientific Publishing Co. Pte. Ltd.

5 Toh Tuck Link, Singapore 596224

USA office: 27 Warren Street, Suite 401-402, Hackensack, NJ 07601

UK office: 57 Shelton Street, Covent Garden, London WC2H 9HE

British Library Cataloguing-in-Publication Data
A catalogue record for this book is available from the British Library.

THEORY AND PRACTICE OF COMPUTATION
Proceedings of Workshop on Computation: Theory and Practice (WCTP2013)

ISBN 978-981-4612-87-6

Printed in Singapore

CONTENTS

PREFACE

Computation should be a good blend of theory and practice. Researchers in the field should create algorithms to address real world problems putting equal weight to analysis and implementation. Experimentation and simulation can be viewed as yielding to refined theories or improved applications. WCTP2013 is the third workshop organized by the Tokyo Institute of Technology, The Institute of Scientific and Industrial Research-Osaka University, University of the Philippines-Diliman and De La Salle University-Manila that is devoted to theoretical and practical approaches to computation. It aims to present the latest developments by theoreticians and practitioners in academe and industry working to address computational problems that can directly impact the way we live in society. Following the success of the Workshop on Computation: Theory and Practice 2011 (WCTP 2011), held in University of the Philippines Diliman, Quezon City, on September 2011, and of WCTP 2012, held in De La Salle University–Manila, on September 2012, the main and satellite conferences of WCTP 2013 are held both in University of the Philippines Diliman, on September 30 and October 1, 2013 and in University of San Jose-Recoletos, Cebu, on September 28 and 29, 2013.

This post-proceedings is the collection of the selected papers that were presented at WCTP 2013.

The program of WCTP 2013 was a combination of an invited talk given by Prof. Takashi Washio (Osaka University), and selected research contributions. It included the most recent visions and researches of the invited talk and 18 contributions. We collected the original contributions after their presentation at the workshop and began a review procedure that resulted in the selection of the papers in this volume. They appear here in the final form.

WCTP 2013 required a lot of work that was heavily dependent on members of the program committee, and lastly, we owe a great debt of gratitude to the Tokyo Institute of Technology, specifically, its Philippines Office, which is managed by Ronaldo Gallardo, for sponsoring the workhop.

December, 2013

Shin-ya Nishizaki
Masayuki Numao
Jaime Caro
Merlin Teodosia Suarez

PROGRAM CO-CHAIRS

Shin-ya Nishizaki   Tokyo Insitute of Technology, Tokyo, Japan
Masayuki Numao   Osaka University, Osaka, Japan
Jaime Caro   Univeristy of the Philippines – Diliman,
         the Philippines
Merlin Teodosia Suarez   De La Salle Univeristy – Manila,
         the Philippines

PROGRAM COMMITTEES

Tobias Mömke   – Saarland University, Germany
Miguel A. Gutiérrez-Naranjo   – University Seville, Spain
Gabrial Ciobanu   – the Romanian Academy of Science,
         Romania
Satoshi Kurihara, Koichi Moriyama, Ken-ichi Fukui,
         – Osaka University, Japan
Ryutaro Ichise   – National Institute of Technology,
         Japan
Mitsuharu Yamamoto   – Chiba University, Japan
Hiroyuki Tominaga   – Kagawa University, Japan
Naoki Yonezaki, Takuo Watanabe, Shigeki Hagihara
         – Tokyo Institute of Technology, Japan
Raymund Sison, Jocelynn Cu, Gregory Cu, Rhia Trogo,
Judith Azcarraga, Ethel Ong, Charibeth Cheng
         – De La Salle University,
         the Philippines
Rommel Feria, Henry Adorna, Prospero Naval
         – University of the Philippines,
         the Philippines

John Paul Vergara, Mercedes Rodrigo
  – Ateneo De Manila University, the Philippines

Allan A. Sioson Ateneo de Naga University, the Philippines

Randy S. Gamboa Univeristy of Southeastern Philippines, the Philippines

GENERAL CO-CHAIRS

Hirofumi Hinode Tokyo Tech Philippines Office, Tokyo Institute of Technology, Japan

Kazuhiko Matsumoto International Collaboration Center, The Institute of Scientific and Industrial Research, Osaka University, Japan

ORGANIZING COMMITTEES

Greg Gabison University of San Jose Recoletos, the Philippines

Cherry Lyn Sta. Romana Cebu Institute of Technology, the Philippines

SECRETARIAT

UP Information Technology Development Center

CALL-BY-NAME EVALUATION OF RPC AND RMI CALCULI

Shota Araki and Shin-ya Nishizaki

Department of Computer Science, Tokyo Institute of Technology,
Tokyo, 152-8552, Japan
E-mail: nisizaki@cs.titech.ac.jp

Object-oriented programming is one of the fundamental notions in every phase of software development. Several kinds of theoretical frameworks for formalizing object-oriented programming languages have been proposed. The object calculus, proposed by Abadi and Cardelli, formulates various styles of object-oriented programming languages such as prototype-based and class-based programming languages. The sigma calculus is the simplest among the various systems of object calculus.

Distributed computation is a fundamental technology in information technology. The remote procedure call (RPC) is a widely used technology for programming in distributed computation. The remote procedure call is known as the remote method invocation in object-oriented programming. Cooper and Wadler proposed the RPC calculus, which is a formal system for modeling remote procedure calls.

Matumoto and Nishizaki proposed the RMI calculus, which is based on the sigma calculus and incorporated with remote method invocations. In their work, they studied the relationship between the RPC and RMI calculi. They found a correspondence between all-by-value evaluations of the two calculi. In this paper, we investigate call-by-name evaluation for the calculi.

Keywords: Lambda Calculus; Remort Procedure Call; RPC Calculus; Evaluation Strategy; Call-by-name Evaluation.

1. Introduction

1.1. *Evaluation Strategies*

An *evaluation strategy* is a set of rules for evaluating expressions in a programming language. This defines in what order the arguments of a function are evaluated and when they are substituted into the function. The most common evaluation strategy is *call-by-value* evaluation, which is used in various programming languages such as C, Java, and Scheme. In this, the actual parameter expression is evaluated and then the resulting value is bound to the corresponding formal parameter variable of the function. In lambda calculus, the call-by-value evaluation is formulated as an evaluation relation ($\langle$Expression$\rangle$) $\Downarrow$ ($\langle$Resulting Value$\rangle$), and is inductively defined by the following rule.

$$\frac{M \Downarrow \lambda x.M' \quad N \Downarrow W \quad M'\{x \leftarrow W\} \Downarrow V}{(MN) \Downarrow V}$$

$$\overline{x \Downarrow x}, \quad \overline{\lambda x.M \Downarrow \lambda x.M}, \quad \frac{M \Downarrow V}{(xM) \Downarrow (xV)}$$

where the expressions of the lambda calculus — variables, lambda abstractions and function applications — are defined inductively by

$$M ::= x \mid \lambda x.M \mid (MN),$$

respectively.

On the other hand, in *call-by-name* evaluation, an actual parameter expression is bound to the corresponding formal parameter variable before it is evaluated. In the lambda calculus, call-by-name evaluation is formulated as follow.

$$\frac{M \Downarrow \lambda x.M' \quad M'\{x \leftarrow N\} \Downarrow V}{(MN) \Downarrow V}$$

$$\overline{x \Downarrow x}, \quad \overline{\lambda x.M \Downarrow \lambda x.M}, \quad \frac{M \Downarrow V}{(xM) \Downarrow (xV)}.$$

Call-by-name evaluation is occasionally preferable to call-by-value evaluation, since if a formal parameter is not used in a function body, then its actual parameter expression is not evaluated.

It is known that call-by-value evaluation is dual to call-by-name with respect to linear negation of Girard's linear logic.[1–3]

1.2. *The RPC Calculi*

The *remote procedure call* (RPC)[4] is one of the programming constructs for distributed computation, which is an inter-process communication and allows a program to cause a procedure to be executed on another computer in the same manner as the usual procedure call.

Cooper and Wadler[5] formulated the remote procedure call in the framework of the lambda calculus. They proposed the RPC calculus (λrpc), which is an extension of the lambda calculus with call-by-value evaluation incorporated with the concepts of computing location and the remote procedure call.

The syntax of λrpc-calculus is defined as follows.

Definition 1.1 (Terms of λrpc). Terms *of λrpc-calculus are defined inductively by the following grammar:*

$$M ::= x \mid \lambda^m x.M \mid (MN)$$

where m is a location, which is either a client location c *or a server location* s. *The terms* x, $\lambda^m x.M$, *and M represent a* variable, *a* function application, *and a* lambda application *respectively, similarly to the λ-calculus.*

The syntax of the lambda abstraction in λrpc-calculus is slightly different from that in the λ-calculus: the location in which the lambda abstraction $\lambda^a x$. is evaluated is explicitly designated as m. Names of locations correspond to network addresses in calling RPC.

The operational semantics of λrpc-calculus are defined as big-step semantics of the call-by-value evaluation.

Definition 1.2 (Call-by-value Operational Semantics of λrpc-calculus). *An* call-by-value operational semantics *of the λrpc-calculus is a ternary relation* $M \Downarrow_a^{CBV} V$ *among a term M, a location m, and a value V inductively defined by the following rules.*

$$\frac{}{V \Downarrow_m^{CBV} V} \; \text{Value}$$

$$\frac{L \Downarrow_m^{CBV} \lambda^l x.N \quad M \Downarrow_m^{CBV} W \quad N\{x \leftarrow W\} \Downarrow_l^{CBV} V}{(LM) \Downarrow_m^{CBV} V} \; \text{Beta}$$

If there is the danger of ambiguity between the call-by-value operational semantics of λrpc-calculus and the other calculus', we write $\Downarrow_m^{CBV}$ as $\Downarrow_m^{\lambda \text{rpc-CBV}}$.

We write the λrpc-calculus as λ_{rpc}^{CBV}-calculus, if we study λrpc-calculus with the call-by-value operational semantics.

1.3. *The RMI Calculi*

The RMI calculus was proposed by Matsumoto and Nishizaki[6] in order to formalize the remote message invocation in the framework of ς-calculus, which is one of the fragments of the object calculus.[7] In the RMI calculus, locations are introduced into the syntax and they are attached to each self parameter binding. We define a calculus ςrmi^{let}-calculus extended with let-binding, which is utilized in order to translate the λrpc-calculus into the RMI calculus. If we restrict the usage of let-bindings, the calculus is considered as the ςrmi-calculus.

Definition 1.3 (Terms of ςrmi- and ςrmi^{let}-calculi). *Terms of* ςrmi^{let}-*calculus are defined inductively by the following grammar:*

$$
\begin{array}{lll}
a, b, c ::= & & term \\
\mid & x & variable \\
\mid & [l_i = \varsigma(m_i, x_i)b_i]^{i \in 1..n} & object \\
\mid & a.l & method\ invocation \\
\mid & a.l \Leftarrow \varsigma(m, x)b & method\ override \\
\mid & \mathsf{let}^m\ x = a\ \mathsf{in}\ b & let\text{-}binding\ with\ location
\end{array}
$$

The subsystem which does not include the let-binding with locaion is called ςrmi-*calculus.*

The self parameter binding $\varsigma(m, x)$ corresponds to $\varsigma(x)$ in the σ-calculus. The binder designates a self parameter x and a location where its body should be evaluated. The notation $[l_i = \varsigma(m_i, x_i)b_i]^{i \in 1..n}$ is an abbreviation of

$$[l_1 = \varsigma(m_1, x_1)b_1, l_2 = \varsigma(m_2, x_2)b_2, \ldots, l_n = \varsigma(m_n, x_n)b_n].$$

If n is 0, then the notation $[\,]$ means the empty object. In a method override $a.l \Leftarrow \varsigma(m, x)b$, if a self parameter x does not appear in its body b, we write it as $a.l :=^m b$. Similarly, if a self parameter x_i does not appear in an entry $l_i = \varsigma(m_i, x_i)b_i$ of an object, we write it as $l_i =^{m_i} b_i$.

In the previous work of Matsumoto and Nishizaki,[6] we give a call-by-value evaluation in the style of big-step semantics to the ςrmi- and ςrmi^{let}-calculi.

Definition 1.4 (Call-by-value Evaluation of ςrmi- and ςrmi^{let}-calculi). *Call-by-value evaluation of* ςrmi- *and* ςrmi^{let}-*calculi is defined by a ternary relation* $a \Downarrow_m^{CBV} v$.

$$\frac{}{v \Downarrow_m^{CBV} v}\ \text{Value}$$

$$\frac{a \Downarrow_m^{CBV} o \quad b_j\{x_j \leftarrow o\} \Downarrow_{m_j}^{CBV} v}{a.l_j \Downarrow_m^{CBV} v}\ \text{Select}$$

$$\frac{a \Downarrow_m^{CBV} o}{a.l_j \Leftarrow \varsigma(m', x)b \Downarrow_m^{CBV} \left[l_j = \varsigma(m', x)b,\ l_i = \varsigma(m_i, x_i)b_i^{i \in 1..n - \{j\}}\right]}\ \text{Override}$$

$$\frac{a \Downarrow_l^{\mathrm{CBV}} w \quad b\{x \leftarrow w\} \Downarrow_l^{\mathrm{CBV}} v}{\mathsf{let}^l \; x = a \; \mathsf{in} \; b \Downarrow_m^{\mathrm{CBV}} v} \; \mathsf{Let}$$

In the definition of the evaluation, the meta-variables v and w means values defined as follows.

Definition 1.5 (Values of ςrmi- and ςrmi^let-calculi). *Values of ςrmi- and ςrmi^let-calculi are defined by the following grammar:*

$$v, w ::= c \mid x \mid [l_i = \varsigma(m_i, x_i)b_i]^{i \in 1..n}$$

If there is the danger of confusion between the call-by-value operational semantics of ςrmi^let-calculus and the other calculus, we write $\Downarrow_m^{\mathrm{CBV}}$ as $\Downarrow_m^{\mathrm{\varsigma rmi\text{-}CBV}}$.

1.4. *Research Purpose*

In the previous work of Matsumoto and Nishizaki,[6] they studied the relationship between the RPC and RMI calculi, but, only call-by-value evaluations of the two calculi were considered. In this paper, we introduce call-by-name evaluation into the RMI calculus. We also show the correspondence of the evaluation strategies between the two kinds of calculus.

2. Call-by-name Evaluation of the RPC Calculus

Before making a definition of the call-by-value evaluation of the RMI calculus, we introduce call-by-name evaluation into the RPC calculus, based on call-by-value evaluation of the lambda calculus. Definition 2.1, 2.2, and 2.3 presents the terms, values, and operational semantics of the $\lambda_{\mathrm{rpc}}^{\mathrm{CBN}}$-calculus, respectively.

Definition 2.1 (Terms of $\lambda_{\mathrm{rpc}}^{\mathrm{CBN}}$-calculus). *The Terms of $\lambda_{\mathrm{rpc}}^{\mathrm{CBN}}$-calculus is defined inductively by the following grammar:*

$$
\begin{array}{lll}
M ::= & x & terms \\
\mid & \lambda^m x.M & lambda \; abstraction \\
\mid & (MN) & funciton \; application \\
\mid & \mathsf{eval}^m(M) & eval
\end{array}
$$

where m is called a location, *which is either a* client location *c or a* server location *s.*

Definition 2.2 (Values of $\lambda_{\mathrm{rpc}}^{\mathrm{CBN}}$-calculus). *The value of $\lambda_{\mathrm{rpc}}^{\mathrm{CBN}}$-calculi is either a variable x or a lambda abstraction $\lambda^a x.M$.*

Definition 2.3 (Operational Semantics of $\lambda_{\mathrm{rpc}}^{\mathrm{CBN}}$-calculus). *An call-by-name operational semantics of the λrpc-calculus is a ternary relation*

$M \Downarrow_a^{CBN} V$ among a term M, a location m, and a value V inductively defined by the following rules.

$$\frac{}{V \Downarrow_m^{CBN} V} \text{ Value}$$

$$\frac{L \Downarrow_m^{CBN} \lambda^l x.N \quad N\{x \leftarrow \text{eval}^m(M)\} \Downarrow_l^{CBN} V}{(LM) \Downarrow_m^{CBN} V} \text{ Beta}$$

$$\frac{M \Downarrow_l^{CBN} V}{\text{eval}^l(M) \Downarrow_m^{CBN} V} \text{ Eval}$$

If there is the danger of ambiguity between the call-by-name operational semantics of λrpc-calculus and the other calculus', we write $\Downarrow_m^{CBN}$ as $\Downarrow_m^{\lambda CBN}$.

We next show an example of call-by-name evaluation.

Example 2.1 (Example of call-by-name evaluation). *Consider a term*

$$(\lambda^s x.x(\lambda^s y.y))((\lambda^s z.z)(\lambda^c w.w)),$$

which is assumed to be evaluated at a location c. *Then*

$$\frac{\overline{(\lambda^s x.x(\lambda^s y.y)) \Downarrow_c^{\lambda CBN} (\lambda^s x.x(\lambda^s y.y))} \quad \overset{\vdots \ \Sigma}{(\text{eval}^c((\lambda^s z.z)(\lambda^c w.w)))(\lambda^s y.y) \Downarrow_s^{\lambda CBN} \lambda^s y.y}}{(\lambda^s x.x(\lambda^s y.y))((\lambda^s z.z)(\lambda^c w.w)) \Downarrow_c^{\lambda CBN} \lambda^s y.y}$$

where the subtree Σ is as follows:

$$\frac{\dfrac{\dfrac{\dfrac{}{\lambda^s z.z \Downarrow_c^{\lambda CBN} \lambda^s z.z} \quad \dfrac{\dfrac{}{\lambda^c w.w \Downarrow_c^{\lambda CBN} \lambda^c w.w}}{\text{eval}^c(\lambda^c w.w) \Downarrow_s^{\lambda CBN} \lambda^c w.w}}{((\lambda^s z.z)(\lambda^c w.w)) \Downarrow_c^{\lambda CBN} \lambda^c w.w}}{\text{eval}^c(((\lambda^s z.z)(\lambda^c w.w))) \Downarrow_s^{\lambda CBN} \lambda^c w.w} \quad \dfrac{\dfrac{}{\lambda^s y.y \Downarrow_c^{\lambda CBN} \lambda^s y.y}}{\text{eval}^s(\lambda^s y.y) \Downarrow_c^{\lambda CBN} \lambda^s y.y}}{(\text{eval}^c((\lambda^s z.z)(\lambda^c w.w)))(\lambda^s y.y) \Downarrow_s^{\lambda CBN} \lambda^s y.y}$$

In the rest of the paper, proofs will be presented in the style of indented lines rather than in the Gentzen's long-bar style as follows.

$$
\begin{aligned}
&(\lambda^s x.x(\lambda^s y.y))((\lambda^s z.z)(\lambda^c w.w)) \Downarrow_c^{\lambda CBN} \lambda^s y.y && (1) \\
&\quad (\lambda^s x.x(\lambda^s y.y)) \Downarrow_c^{\lambda CBN} (\lambda^s x.x(\lambda^s y.y)) && (1.1) \\
&\quad (\text{eval}^c((\lambda^s z.z)(\lambda^c w.w)))(\lambda^s y.y) \Downarrow_s^{\lambda CBN} \lambda^s y.y && (1.2) \\
&\qquad \text{eval}^c(((\lambda^s z.z)(\lambda^c w.w))) \Downarrow_s^{\lambda CBN} \lambda^c w.w && (1.2.1) \\
&\qquad\quad ((\lambda^s z.z)(\lambda^c w.w)) \Downarrow_c^{\lambda CBN} \lambda^c w.w && (1.2.1.1) \\
&\qquad\qquad \lambda^s z.z \Downarrow_c^{\lambda CBN} \lambda^s z.z && (1.2.1.1.1)
\end{aligned}
$$

$$\mathsf{eval}^\mathsf{r}(\lambda^\mathsf{c}w.w) \Downarrow_\mathsf{s}^{\lambda\mathsf{CBN}} \lambda^\mathsf{L}w.w \quad (1.2.1.1.2)$$
$$\lambda^\mathsf{c}w.w \Downarrow_\mathsf{c}^{\lambda\mathsf{CBN}} \lambda^\mathsf{c}w.w \quad (1.2.1.1.2.1)$$
$$\mathsf{eval}^\mathsf{s}(\lambda^\mathsf{s}y.y) \Downarrow_\mathsf{c}^{\lambda\mathsf{CBN}} \lambda^\mathsf{s}y.y \quad (1.2.2)$$
$$\lambda^\mathsf{s}y.y \Downarrow_\mathsf{s}^{\lambda\mathsf{CBN}} \lambda^\mathsf{s}y.y \quad (1.2.2.1)$$

3. Call-by-name Evaluation of the RMI Calculus

We next add a call-by-name evaluation strategy to the ςrmi-calculus. After this section, we will add a translation of the call-by-name ςrmi-calculus into the call-by-name λrpc-calculus, in order to give a justification that the evaluation of the ςrmi-calculus is really call-by-name in the traditional sense.

Definition 3.1 (Terms of ςrmi$^\mathbf{CBN}$-calculi). Terms *of* ςrmi$^\mathrm{CBN}$-*calculus are defined inductively by the following grammar:*

$$
\begin{array}{lll}
a, b, c ::= & & term \\
\quad | \quad x & & variable \\
\quad | \quad [l_i = \varsigma(m_i, x_i)b_i]^{i \in 1..n} & & object \\
\quad | \quad a.l & & method\ invocation \\
\quad | \quad a.l \Leftarrow \varsigma(m, x)b & & method\ override \\
\quad | \quad \mathsf{let}^m\ x = v.l\ \mathsf{in}\ b & & let\text{-}binding\ with\ location \\
\quad | \quad \mathsf{eval}^m(a) & & evaluation\ with\ location,
\end{array}
$$

where v is a value, *which is either a variable or an object.*

In a method override $a.l \Leftarrow \varsigma(m, x)b$, if a self parameter x does not appear in its body b, we write it as $a.l :=^m b$. Similarly, if a self parameter x_i does not appear in an entry $l_i = \varsigma(m_i, x_i)b_i$ of an object, we write it as $l_i =^{m_i} b_i$.

Before giving call-by-name evaluation to the RMI calculus, we define values of the calculus.

Definition 3.2 (Values of the ςrmi$^\mathbf{CBN}$-calculus). *A* value *of the* ςrmi$^\mathrm{CBN}$-*calculus is given by either a variable x or an object* $[l_i = \varsigma(m_i, x_i)b_i]^{i \in 1..n}$.

Definition 3.3 (Call-by-name Operational Semantics of the ςrmi$^\mathbf{CBN}$-calculus). *The operational semantics of the* ςrmi$^\mathrm{CBN}$-*calculus is given by the following rules.*

$$\frac{}{v \Downarrow_m^{\mathrm{CBN}} v} \ \mathsf{Value}$$

$$\frac{a \Downarrow_m^{\mathrm{CBV}} o \quad b_j\{x_j \leftarrow o\} \Downarrow_{m_j}^{\mathrm{CBV}} v}{a.l_j \Downarrow_m^{\mathrm{CBV}} v} \ \mathsf{Select}$$

$$\frac{a \Downarrow_m^{\text{CBN}} o}{a.l_j \Leftarrow \varsigma(m',x)b \Downarrow_m^{\text{CBN}} \left[l_j = \varsigma(m',x)b, \; l_i = \varsigma(m_i,x_i)b_i^{i \in 1..n-\{j\}}\right]} \text{ Override}$$

$$\frac{b\{x \leftarrow \text{eval}^{m_j}(b_j\{x_j \leftarrow o\})\} \Downarrow_m^{\text{CBN}} v}{\text{let}^m \; x = o.l_j \text{ in } b \Downarrow_m^{\text{CBV}} v} \text{ Let}$$

$$\frac{a \Downarrow_n^{\text{CBN}} v}{\text{eval}^n(a) \Downarrow_v^{\text{CBN}}} \text{ Eval}$$

We then show an example of call-by-name evaluation of the ςrmi^{CBN}-calculus below.

Example 3.1. We consider a term to be evaluated as

$$(o.\textit{arg} :=^c ([\textit{one} =^c 1, \textit{two} =^c 2].\textit{two})).\textit{getArg}$$

where o is $[\textit{arg} =^s 0, \textit{getArg} = \varsigma(s,x) \text{ let}^s \; x = x.\textit{arg} \text{ in } x]$. Numerals 1 and 2 are formulated as *variables* which does not occur in any binders such as $\varsigma(m,1)$ nor let^1. We might define them as constants, but we avoid introducing the notion of a constant into the calculus for sake of simplicity. The derivation tree of the call-by-name evaluation is as follows.

$(o.\textit{arg} :=^c ([\textit{one} =^c 1, \textit{two} =^c 2].\textit{two})).\textit{getArg} \Downarrow_c^{\text{CBN}} 2$ (1)

   $o.\textit{arg} :=^c ([\textit{one} =^c 1, \textit{two} =^c 2].\textit{two}) \Downarrow_c^{\text{CBN}} o'$ (1.1)

    $o \Downarrow_c^{\text{CBN}} o$ (1.1.1)

   $\text{let}^s \; x = o'.\textit{arg} \text{ in } x \Downarrow_s^{\text{CBN}} 2$ (1.2)

    $\text{eval}^c([\textit{one} =^c 1, \textit{two} =^c 2].\textit{two}) \Downarrow_s^{\text{CBN}} 2$ (1.2.1)

     $[\textit{one} =^c 1, \textit{two} =^c 2].\textit{two} \Downarrow_c^{\text{CBN}} 2$ (1.2.1.1)

      $[\textit{one} =^c 1, \textit{two} =^c 2] \Downarrow_c^{\text{CBN}} [\textit{one} =^c 1, \textit{two} =^c 2]$ (1.2.1.1.1)

      $2 \Downarrow_c^{\text{CBN}} 2$ (1.2.1.1.2)

where o' is supposed to be

$$[\textit{arg} =^c [\textit{one} =^c 1, \textit{two} =^c 2].\textit{two}, \textit{getArg} = \varsigma(s,x) \text{ let}^s \; x = x.\textit{arg} \text{ in } x].$$

This derivation tree can be depicted in Gentzen's style as

$$\cfrac{\cfrac{\cfrac{\overline{(1.2.1.1.1)} \text{ Value} \quad \overline{(1.2.1.1.2)} \text{ Value}}{(1.2.1.1)} \text{ Select}}{\cfrac{\cfrac{\overline{(1.1.1)} \text{ Value}}{(1.1)} \text{ Override} \qquad \cfrac{(1.2.1)}{(1.2)} \text{ LetLoc}}{(1.2.1)} \text{ Eval}}}{(1)} \text{ Select}$$

3.1. Translation of the Call-by-Name RPC Calculus into the Call-by-Name RMI Calculus

Next, we give a translation of $\lambda_{\mathrm{rpc}}^{\mathrm{CBN}}$-calculus into the $\varsigma\mathrm{rmi}^{\mathrm{CBN}}$-calculus and study correspondence between these two calculi.

Definition 3.4 (Translation $\langle M \rangle_m^{\mathrm{CBN}}$). *We define a translation*

$$\langle M \rangle_m^{\mathrm{CBN}}$$

of a $\lambda_{\mathrm{rpc}}^{\mathrm{CBN}}$-term M into a $\varsigma\mathrm{rmi}^{\mathrm{CBN}}$-term with respect to a location m is defined by the following equations.

$$\langle x \rangle_m^{\mathrm{CBN}} = x,$$
$$\langle (MN) \rangle_m^{\mathrm{CBN}} = (\langle M \rangle_m^{\mathrm{CBN}}.arg :=^m \langle N \rangle_m^{\mathrm{CBN}}).val,$$
$$\langle \lambda^n x.N \rangle_m^{\mathrm{CBN}} = [arg = \varsigma(n,x)x.arg, \; val = \varsigma(n,x) \; \mathsf{let}^n \; x = x.arg \; \mathsf{in} \; \langle N \rangle_n^{\mathrm{CBN}}],$$
$$\langle \mathsf{eval}^n(M) \rangle_m^{\mathrm{CBN}} = \mathsf{eval}^n\left(\langle M \rangle_n^{\mathrm{CBN}} \right).$$

The following is examples of the translation.

Example 3.2 (Translation $\langle M \rangle_m^{\mathrm{CBN}}$).

$$\langle \lambda^c x.x \rangle_c^{\mathrm{CBN}} = [arg = \varsigma(c,x)x.arg, val = \varsigma(c,x) \; \mathsf{let}^c \; x = x.arg \; \mathsf{in} \; x]$$

$$\langle (\lambda^c x.x)(\lambda^s y.y) \rangle_c^{\mathrm{CBN}} = (\langle \lambda^c x.x \rangle_c^{\mathrm{CBN}}.arg :=^c \langle \lambda^s y.y \rangle_c^{\mathrm{CBN}}).val,$$
$$= ([arg = \varsigma(c,x)x.arg, \; val = \varsigma(c,x) \; \mathsf{let}^c \; x = x.arg \; \mathsf{in} \; x]$$
$$.arg :=^c [arg = \varsigma(s,y)y.arg,$$
$$val = \varsigma(s,y) \; \mathsf{let}^s \; y = y.arg \; \mathsf{in} \; y]).val$$

We next show correspondence of the $\lambda_{\mathrm{rpc}}^{\mathrm{CBN}}$-calculus to the $\varsigma\mathrm{rmi}^{\mathrm{CBN}}$-calculus, in other words, the soundness of translation $\langle (-) \rangle_{(-)}^{\mathrm{CBN}}$ with respect to the $\lambda_{\mathrm{rpc}}^{\mathrm{CBV}}$-calculus. Before proving the correspondence, we demonstrate the substitution lemma for the translation $\langle M \rangle_m^{\mathrm{CBN}}$.

Lemma 3.1 (Substitution Lemma for Translation $\langle M \rangle_m^{\mathrm{CBN}}$). *For $\lambda_{\mathrm{rpc}}^{\mathrm{CBN}}$-terms M and N, locations m and n, it holds that*

$$\langle M \rangle_m^{\mathrm{CBN}}\{x \leftarrow \mathsf{eval}^n(\langle N \rangle_n^{\mathrm{CBN}})\} = \langle M\{x \leftarrow \mathsf{eval}^n(N)\} \rangle_m^{\mathrm{CBN}}.$$

Proof. We prove the lemma by induction on structure of term M.
Case $M = x$:

$$\langle M \rangle_m^{\mathrm{CBN}}\{x \leftarrow \mathsf{eval}^n(\langle N \rangle_n^{\mathrm{CBN}})\} = \langle x \rangle_m^{\mathrm{CBN}}\{x \leftarrow \mathsf{eval}^n \langle N \rangle_n^{\mathrm{CBN}}\}$$
$$= \mathsf{eval}^n \langle N \rangle_n^{\mathrm{CBN}}$$
$$= \langle x\{x \leftarrow \mathsf{eval}^n(N)\} \rangle_m^{\mathrm{CBN}}$$
$$= \langle M\{x \leftarrow \mathsf{eval}^n(N)\} \rangle_m^{\mathrm{CBN}}.$$

Case $M = y(\neq x)$:

$$\langle M \rangle_m^{\mathrm{CBN}} \{x \leftarrow \mathsf{eval}^n(\langle N \rangle_n^{\mathrm{CBN}})\} = \langle y \rangle_m^{\mathrm{CBN}} \{x \leftarrow \mathsf{eval}^n \langle N \rangle_n^{\mathrm{CBN}}\}$$
$$= y$$
$$= \langle y\{x \leftarrow \mathsf{eval}^n(N)\} \rangle_m^{\mathrm{CBN}}$$
$$= \langle M\{x \leftarrow \mathsf{eval}^n(N)\} \rangle_m^{\mathrm{CBN}}.$$

Case $M = \lambda^l y.K$: The induction hypothesis of the case is

$$\langle K \rangle_l^{\mathrm{CBN}} \{y \leftarrow y'''\}\{x \leftarrow \mathsf{eval}^n(\langle N \rangle_n^{\mathrm{CBN}})\}$$
$$= \langle K\{y \leftarrow y'''\} \rangle_l^{\mathrm{CBN}} \{x \leftarrow \mathsf{eval}^n(\langle N \rangle_n^{\mathrm{CBN}})\}$$
$$= \langle K\{y \leftarrow y'''\}\{x \leftarrow \mathsf{eval}^n(N)\} \rangle_l^{\mathrm{CBN}}.$$

Using this equality, we know that

$$\langle \lambda^l y.K \rangle_m^{\mathrm{CBN}} \{x \leftarrow \mathsf{eval}^n(\langle N \rangle_n^{\mathrm{CBN}})\}$$
$$= [arg = \varsigma(l, y)y.arg,$$
$$\quad val = \varsigma(l, y) \,\mathsf{let}^l\, y = y.arg \,\mathsf{in}\, \langle K \rangle_l^{\mathrm{CBN}}]\{x \leftarrow \mathsf{eval}^n(\langle N \rangle_n^{\mathrm{CBN}})\}$$
$$= [arg = \varsigma(l, y')y'.arg,$$
$$\quad val = \varsigma(l, y')(\mathsf{let}^l\, y = y.arg \,\mathsf{in}\, \langle K \rangle_l^{\mathrm{CBN}})\{y \leftarrow y'\}\{x \leftarrow \mathsf{eval}^n(\langle N \rangle_n^{\mathrm{CBN}})\}]$$
$$\quad (\text{where } y' \notin \mathsf{FV}(\langle K \rangle_l^{\mathrm{CBN}}) \cup \mathsf{FV}(\langle N \rangle_n^{\mathrm{CBN}}) \cup \{x\})$$
$$= [arg = \varsigma(l, y')y'.arg,$$
$$\quad val = \varsigma(l, y')\,(\mathsf{let}^l\, y'' = y'.arg \,\mathsf{in}\, \langle K \rangle_l^{\mathrm{CBN}}\{y \leftarrow y''\}\{y \leftarrow y'\})$$
$$\qquad\qquad \{x \leftarrow \mathsf{eval}^n(\langle N \rangle_n^{\mathrm{CBN}})\}]$$
$$\quad (\text{where } y'' \notin \mathsf{FV}(\langle K \rangle_l^{\mathrm{CBN}}) \cup \{y'\} \cup \{y\})$$
$$= [arg = \varsigma(l, y')y'.arg,$$
$$\quad val = \varsigma(l, y')(\mathsf{let}^l\, y''' = y'.arg \,\mathsf{in}$$
$$\qquad\qquad \langle K \rangle_l^{\mathrm{CBN}}\{y \leftarrow y''\}\{y'' \leftarrow y'''\}\{x \leftarrow \mathsf{eval}^n(\langle N \rangle_n^{\mathrm{CBN}})\}])$$
$$\quad (\text{where } y''' \notin \mathsf{FV}(\langle K \rangle_l^{\mathrm{CBN}}) \cup \mathsf{FV}(\langle N \rangle_n^{\mathrm{CBN}}) \cup \{x\})$$
$$= [arg = \varsigma(l, y')y'.arg,$$
$$\quad val = \varsigma(l, y')(\mathsf{let}^l\, y''' = y'.arg \,\mathsf{in}\, \langle K \rangle_l^{\mathrm{CBN}}\{y \leftarrow y'''\}\{x \leftarrow \mathsf{eval}^n(\langle N \rangle_n^{\mathrm{CBN}})\}])$$

On the other hand, we know that

$$\langle (\lambda^l y.K)\{x \leftarrow \mathsf{eval}^n(N)\} \rangle_m^{\mathrm{CBN}}$$
$$= \langle \lambda^l y'.(K\{y \leftarrow y'\}\{x \leftarrow \mathsf{eval}^n(N)\}) \rangle_m^{\mathrm{CBN}}$$
$$\quad (\text{where } y' \notin \mathsf{FV}(K) \cup \mathsf{FV}(N) \cup \{x\})$$

$$= [arg = \varsigma(l, y').y'.arg,$$
$$val = \varsigma(l, y')(\text{let}^l \ y' = y'.arg \text{ in } \langle K\{y \leftarrow y'\}\{x \leftarrow \text{eval}^n(N)\}\rangle_l^{\text{CBN}}])$$

By the induction hypothesis, it is obtained that

$$\langle \lambda^l y.K\rangle_m^{\text{CBN}}\{x \leftarrow \text{eval}^n(\langle N\rangle_n^{\text{CBN}})\} = \langle (\lambda^l y.K)\{x \leftarrow \text{eval}^n(N)\}\rangle_m^{\text{CBN}},$$

assuming that $y' = y'''$ without loss of generality.

Case $M = (L\ K)$: The induction hypothesis of the case is

$$\langle L\rangle_m^{\text{CBN}}\{x \leftarrow \text{eval}^n(\langle N\rangle_n^{\text{CBN}})\} = \langle L\{x \leftarrow \text{eval}^n(N)\}\rangle_m^{\text{CBN}}$$
$$\langle K\rangle_m^{\text{CBN}}\{x \leftarrow \text{eval}^n(\langle N\rangle_n^{\text{CBN}})\} = \langle K\{x \leftarrow \text{eval}^n(N)\}\rangle_m^{\text{CBN}}.$$

We therefore have that

$$\langle (LK)\rangle_m^{\text{CBN}}\{x \leftarrow \text{eval}^n(\langle N\rangle_n^{\text{CBN}})\}$$
$$= ((\langle L\rangle_m^{\text{CBN}}.arg :=^m \langle K\rangle_m^{\text{CBN}}).val)\{x \leftarrow \text{eval}^n(\langle N\rangle_n^{\text{CBN}})\}$$
$$= ((((\langle L\rangle_m^{\text{CBN}}\{x \leftarrow \text{eval}^n(\langle N\rangle_n^{\text{CBN}})\}).arg :=^m \langle K\rangle_m^{\text{CBN}}\{x \leftarrow \text{eval}^n(\langle N\rangle_n^{\text{CBN}})\}).val)$$
$$= (\langle L\{x \leftarrow \text{eval}^n(N)\}\rangle_m^{\text{CBN}}.arg :=^m \langle K\{x \leftarrow \text{eval}^n(N)\}\rangle_m^{\text{CBN}}.val)$$
$$= \langle (L\{x \leftarrow \text{eval}^n(N)\} \ K\{x \leftarrow \text{eval}^n(N)\})\rangle_m^{\text{CBN}}$$
$$= \langle (LK)\{x \leftarrow \text{eval}^n(N)\}\rangle_m^{\text{CBN}}.$$

Case $M = \text{eval}^l(K)$: The induction hypothesis of th case is

$$\langle K\rangle_l^{\text{CBN}}\{x \leftarrow \text{eval}^n(N)\} = \langle K\{x \leftarrow \text{eval}^n(N)\}\rangle_l^{\text{CBN}}.$$

We therefore obtain that

$$\langle \text{eval}^l(K)\rangle_m^{\text{CBN}}\{x \leftarrow \text{eval}^n\langle N\rangle_n^{\text{CBN}}\}$$
$$= (\text{eval}^l(\langle K\rangle_l^{\text{CBN}}))\{x \leftarrow \text{eval}^n(\langle N\rangle_n^{\text{CBN}})\}$$
$$= \text{eval}^l(\langle K\rangle_l^{\text{CBN}}\{x \leftarrow \text{eval}^n(\langle N\rangle_n^{\text{CBN}})\})$$
$$= \text{eval}^l(\langle K\{x \leftarrow \text{eval}^n(N)\}\rangle_l^{\text{CBN}})$$
$$= \langle \text{eval}^l(K\{x \leftarrow \text{eval}^n(N)\})\rangle_l^{\text{CBN}}. \qquad \square$$

Next, we show the soundness of the translation.

Theorem 3.1 (Soundness of Translation $\langle - \rangle^{\text{CBN}}$). *For a term M, value V, and location m, if $M \Downarrow_m^{\text{CBN}} V$, then there is a location n satisfying that*

$$\langle M\rangle_m^{\text{CBN}} \Downarrow_m^{\text{CBN}} \langle V\rangle_n^{\text{CBN}}.$$

Proof. We prove the theorem by induction on structure of $\Downarrow_m^{\mathrm{CBN}}$.

Case of Rule Value: In this case, we have $M = V$ and therefore we have

$$\frac{}{\langle V \rangle_m^{\mathrm{CBN}} \Downarrow_m^{\mathrm{CBN}} \langle V \rangle_m^{\mathrm{CBN}}} \text{ Value}.$$

Case of Rule Beta: We assume that $M = (KL)$ and

$$\frac{K \Downarrow_m^{\mathrm{CBN}} \lambda^n x.N \quad N\{x \leftarrow \mathsf{eval}^m(L)\} \Downarrow_n^{\mathrm{CBN}} V}{(KL) \Downarrow_m^{\mathrm{CBN}} V} \text{ Beta}.$$

By the induction hypothesis, we have

$$\langle K \rangle_m^{\mathrm{CBN}} \Downarrow_m^{\mathrm{CBN}} \langle \lambda^n x.N \rangle_{m'}^{\mathrm{CBN}}$$

for some m'. Then,

$$\langle K \rangle_m^{\mathrm{CBN}} \Downarrow_m^{\mathrm{CBN}} [arg = \varsigma(n,x)x.arg, val = \varsigma(n,x) \ \mathsf{let}^n \ x = x.arg \ \mathsf{in} \ \langle N \rangle_n^{\mathrm{CBN}}].$$

By Rule Override, we have

$$\frac{\langle K \rangle_m^{\mathrm{CBN}} \Downarrow_m^{\mathrm{CBN}} [arg = \varsigma(n,x)x.arg, val = \varsigma(n,x) \ \mathsf{let}^n \ x = x.arg \ \mathsf{in} \ \langle N \rangle_n^{\mathrm{CBN}}].}{\langle K \rangle_m^{\mathrm{CBN}}.arg :=^m \langle L \rangle_m^{\mathrm{CBN}} \Downarrow_m^{\mathrm{CBN}} o.} \text{ Override}$$

where o is $[arg = \langle L \rangle_m^{\mathrm{CBN}}, val = \varsigma(n,x) \ \mathsf{let}^n \ x = x.arg \ \mathsf{in} \ \langle N \rangle_n^{\mathrm{CBN}}]$. We call the derivation tree which derives $\langle K \rangle_m^{\mathrm{CBN}}.arg :=^m \langle L \rangle_m^{\mathrm{CBN}} \Downarrow_m^{\mathrm{CBN}} o$, Σ_1.

By the induction hypothesis,

$$\langle N\{x \leftarrow \mathsf{eval}^m(L)\} \rangle_n^{\mathrm{CBN}} \Downarrow_n^{\mathrm{CBN}} \langle V \rangle_n^{\mathrm{CBN}}.$$

By the substitution lemma, we have

$$\langle N \rangle_n^{\mathrm{CBN}}\{x \leftarrow \mathsf{eval}^m(L)\} \Downarrow_n^{\mathrm{CBN}} \langle V \rangle_{n'}^{\mathrm{CBN}}.$$

By Rule Let,

$$\frac{\langle N \rangle_n^{\mathrm{CBN}}\{x \leftarrow \mathsf{eval}^m(L)\} \Downarrow_n^{\mathrm{CBN}} \langle V \rangle_{n'}^{\mathrm{CBN}}}{\mathsf{let}^n \ x = o.arg \ \mathsf{in} \ \langle N \rangle_n^{\mathrm{CBN}} \Downarrow_n^{\mathrm{CBN}} \langle V \rangle_{n'}^{\mathrm{CBN}}} \text{ Let}$$

We call the derivation tree which derives $\mathsf{let}^n \ x = o.arg \ \mathsf{in} \ \langle N \rangle_{n'}^{\mathrm{CBN}} \Downarrow_n^{\mathrm{CBN}} \langle V \rangle_{n'}^{\mathrm{CBN}}$, Σ_2. Applying Rule Select to Σ_1 and Σ_2, we have

$$\frac{\begin{array}{cc} \vdots \ \Sigma_1 & \vdots \ \Sigma_2 \\ \langle K \rangle_m^{\mathrm{CBN}}.arg :=^m \langle L \rangle_m^{\mathrm{CBN}} \Downarrow_m^{\mathrm{CBN}} o & \mathsf{let}^n \ x = o.arg \ \mathsf{in} \ \langle N \rangle_n^{\mathrm{CBN}} \Downarrow_n^{\mathrm{CBN}} \langle V \rangle_{n'}^{\mathrm{CBN}} \end{array}}{(\langle K \rangle_m^{\mathrm{CBN}}.arg :=^m \langle L \rangle_m^{\mathrm{CBN}}).val \Downarrow_m^{\mathrm{CBN}} \langle V \rangle_{n'}^{\mathrm{CBN}}} \text{ Select}$$

Since $(\langle K\rangle_m^{\text{CBN}}, arg \cdot=^m \langle L\rangle_m^{\text{CBN}}).val$ equals to $\langle(KL)\rangle_m^{\text{CBN}}$, it derives

$$\langle(KL)\rangle_m^{\text{CBN}} \Downarrow_n^{\text{CBN}} \langle V\rangle_{n'}^{\text{CBN}}$$

Case of Rule Eval: Assume that $M = \text{eval}^n(K)$. Then, we have

$$\frac{\vdots \\ K \Downarrow_n^{\text{CBN}} V}{\text{eval}^n(K) \Downarrow_m^{\text{CBN}} V} \text{ Eval.}$$

By the induction hypothesis, we have $\langle K\rangle_n^{\text{CBN}} \Downarrow_n^{\text{CBN}} \langle V\rangle_{n'}^{\text{CBN}}$ and therefore

$$\frac{\langle K\rangle_n^{\text{CBN}} \Downarrow_m^{\text{CBN}} \langle V\rangle_{n'}^{\text{CBN}}}{\text{eval}^n(K) \Downarrow_m^{\text{CBN}} \langle V\rangle_{n'}^{\text{CBN}}} \text{ Eval}$$

Since $\langle \text{eval}^n(K)\rangle_m^{\text{CBN}} = \text{eval}^n\langle K\rangle_n^{\text{CBN}}$, we have $\langle \text{eval}^n(K)\rangle_m^{\text{CBN}} \Downarrow_m^{\text{CBN}} \langle V\rangle_{n'}^{\text{CBN}}$.

$\square$

4. Concluding Remarks

We defined the call-by-name RPC calculus, $\lambda_{\text{rpc}}^{\text{CBN}}$, extending the RPC calculus. We then proposed the call-by-name RMI calculus, $\varsigma\text{rmi}^{\text{CBN}}$, extending the RMI calculus. We showed the correspondence of $\lambda_{\text{rpc}}^{\text{CBN}}$ with $\varsigma\text{rmi}^{\text{CBN}}$ by giving the translation $\langle M\rangle_m^{\text{CBN}}$.

The call-by-name evaluation of $\varsigma\text{rmi}^{\text{CBN}}$-calculus gives us an insight into the design of the lazy object-oriented programming language. The evaluation strategy that formalizes lazy functional languages more precisely is call-by-need evaluation, which was proposed by Ariola et al.[8] We should extend our work to call-by-need evaluation, and study the design of an object-oriented programming language.

References

1. P. Wadler, Call-by-value is dual to call-by-name – reloaded, in *Proceedings of the 16th RTA 2005*, (Springer-Verlag Berlin Heidelberg, 2005).
2. S. Nishizaki, Programs with continuations and linear logic, *Science of Computer Programming* **21**, 165 (1993).
3. J.-Y. Girard, Linear logic, *Theoretical Computer Science* **50**, 1 (1987).
4. A. D. Birrell and B. J. Nelson, Implementing remote procedure calls, *ACM Transactions on Computer Systems* **2**, 39 (1984).
5. E. Cooper and P. Wadler, The RPC calculus, in *Proceedings of the 11th ACM SIGPLAN Conference on Principles and Practice of Declarative Programming, PPDP 2009*, (ACM Press, 2009).

6. S. Matsumoto and S. Nishizaki, An object calculus with remote method invocation, *Proceedings of the Second Workshop on Computation: Theory and Practice, WCTP2012, Proceedings in Information and Communication Technology* **7**, 34 (2013).
7. M. Abadi and L. Cardelli, *A Theory of Objects* (Springer-Verlag,Berlin, 1996).
8. Z. M. Ariola, J. Maraist, M. Odersky, M. Felleisen and P. Wadler, The call-by-need lambda calculus, in *Proceedings of the 22nd ACM SIGPLAN-SIGACT symposium on Principles of programming languages*, (ACM Press, 1995).

NOTES IN DELAYS AND BISIMULATIONS OF SPIKING NEURAL P SYSTEMS USING SNP ALGEBRA

Henry N. Adorna, Kelvin C. Buño

and Francis George C. Cabarle

Department of Computer Science, University of the Philippines Diliman,
Quezon City, 1101, Philippines
E-mail: hnadorna@dcs.upd.edu.ph, kcbuno@up.edu.ph,
fccabarle@up.edu.ph

Spiking Neural P Systems (SNP systems in short) are Turing complete computing models inspired by biological spiking neurons. In this work we relate SNP Systems with delay and those without delay using SNP algebra, a type of process algebra specifically for SNP systems. Given an initial configuration where only the *initial neuron(s)* fires a spike, i.e. the first set of neuron(s) to fire, we focus on four SNP system modules performing four spike routings: sequential, join, split, and iteration. We show that there exist bisimulations between the respective four modules of SNP systems with delays and the four modules without delays. We then use these modules (both with and without delays) to create larger SNP systems such that bisimulations also exist between them.

Keywords: Membrane Computing; Spiking Neural P systems; SNP algebra; structural operational semantics; labeled transition systems; bisimulation.

1. Introduction

Membrane computing is a recently added branch of Natural computing, aiming to abstract and obtain ideas (e.g. data structures, data and control operations, models) from the structure and functioning of biological cells.[1] In 2003 Membrane computing was considered by ISI as a "fast-emerging research area in computer science" (see http://esi-topics.com). Membrane or P systems are the computing models in membrane computing and are parallel, distributed, nondeterministic models. P systems are able to solve hard problems in polynomial to linear time, with the usual trade-off of exponential space.[2] More recently, the idea of spiking in biological neurons have been introduced in the framework of Membrane computing as Spiking Neural P systems (SNP systems in short).[3]

In spiking neurons as well as in SNP systems, the indistinct signals known as *spikes* do not encode the information. Instead, information is derived from the time difference between two spikes, or the number of spikes sent (received) per time step. Time therefore is an information support in spiking neurons, and not just a background for performing computations. SNP systems can be thought of as a network of multiset processors, processing spike objects and sending these to other neurons. Essentially, SNP systems are directed graphs where nodes are neurons (often drawn as ovals) and edges between neurons are synapses. Neurons use spiking rules within them in order to send spikes (represented as the symbol a) to one another via synapses between neurons.

We denote by Π an SNP system with delay (the firing or sending of spikes from a neuron can come after the time of rule application in the neuron), and by $\overline{\Pi}$ an SNP system without delay (the time of rule application in a neuron is the same time as the time a spike is sent from the neuron). Both SNP systems with delays and without delays are known to be Turing complete[3,4] so we are not interested with the languages that they compute. Instead, we are interested with their behavioral equivalence, where in systems interact with their environment. This concept of behavioral equivalence, or simply equivalence if there is no confusion, that we consider in this work is well established in literature e.g. Ref. 5 and a survey in Ref. 6. A system A is said to be equivalent to system B if A interacts in the same way with the environment of B for every computation step. In this manner we can replace B with A and we will still obtain the same results from the computations.

SNP systems where each neuron has exactly one rule are called *simple*, while the systems that have the same set of rules are called *homogeneous*.[7] In this work, if SNP systems only have rules of the restricted form $(a^k)^+/a^k \rightarrow a$ where k is a natural number, we refer to them as *semi-homogeneous*. We only consider restricted forms of SNP systems Π and $\overline{\Pi}$ that are simple and semi-homogeneous, such that there is one spike in the initial neuron (we clarify this in the next section) only and no spike in every other neuron in the initial configurations of both systems. We make no restrictions on the values of the delays in a (rule of a) neuron in Π. The objective is to *route* or move the single spike in the initial neuron through the system, towards the output neuron, and eventually to the environment.

Another objective is to contribute towards the goal of realizing ways in order to use SNP systems for modeling and verification. SNP systems and other P systems have been related to other modeling tools such as process algebra and Petri nets as in Ref. 8 to 14 to name a few. For example, workflow systems are systems that describe the flow of business or organizational processes, and have been successfully modeled, analyzed, and verified using a subclass of Petri nets known as workflow nets.[15,16] To be able to perform modeling, analysis, and verifications of such or similar systems on SNP systems is one of our main interests.

The paper is organized as follows: In section 2 we provide preliminaries for SNP systems, the SNP algebra which will be used for our results, as well as the definitions for labeled transition systems, simulation, and types of labels. Section 3 provides our main results. Finally, we provide concluding remarks and future research directions in section 4.

2. Preliminaries

It is assumed that the readers are familiar with the basics of Membrane Computing (a good introduction is Ref. 2 with recent results and information in the P systems webpage at http://ppage.psystems.eu/ and a recent handbook in Ref. 17) and formal language theory. We only briefly mention notions and notations which will be useful throughout the paper.

We denote the set of natural numbers as $\mathbb{N}$. Let V be an alphabet, V^* is the free monoid over V with respect to concatenation and the identity element λ (the empty string). The set of all non-empty strings over V is denoted as V^+ so $V^+ = V^* \setminus \{\lambda\}$. We call V a *singleton* if $V = \{a\}$ and simply write a^* and a^+ instead of $\{a^*\}$ and $\{a^+\}$. The length of a string $w \in V^*$ is denoted by $|w|$. If a is a symbol in V, $a^0 = \lambda$. A language $L \subseteq V^*$ is regular if there is a regular expression E over V such that $L(E) = L$. A regular expression over an alphabet V is constructed starting from λ and the symbols of V using the operations union, concatenation, and +, using parentheses when necessary to specify the order of operations. Specifically, (i) λ and each $a \in V$ are regular expressions, (ii) if E_1 and E_2 are regular expressions over V then $(E_1 \cup E_2)$, $E_1 E_2$, and E_1^+ are regular expressions over V, and (iii) nothing else is a regular expression over V. With each expression E we associate a language $L(E)$ defined in the following way: (i) $L(\lambda) = \{\lambda\}$ and $L(a) = \{a\}$ for all $a \in V$, (ii) $L(E_1 \cup E_2) = L(E_1) \cup L(E_2)$, $L(E_1 E_2) = L(E_1)L(E_2)$, and $L(E_1^+) = L(E_1)^+$, for all regular expressions E_1, E_2 over V. Unnecessary parentheses are omitted when writing regular expressions, and $E^+ \cup \{\lambda\}$ is written as E^*. Next we have the definition for an SNP system,[3,18] with a preprint of Ref. 3 at http://psystems.disco.unimib.it/download/spikingf.pdf.

Definition 2.1 (SNP system). *A Spiking Neural P system (SNP system) of a finite degree $m \geq 1$ is a construct of the form $\Pi = (O, \sigma_1, \ldots, \sigma_m, syn, out)$, where:*

1. $O = \{a\}$ *is the singleton alphabet (a is called spike).*
2. $\sigma_1, \ldots, \sigma_m$ *are pairs $\sigma_i = (n_i, \mathcal{R}_i), 1 \leq i \leq m$, called neurons, where $n_i \geq 0$ and $n_i \in \mathbb{N} \cup \{0\}$ represents the initial spikes in σ_i, $\mathcal{R}_i$ is a finite set of rules of the form $E/a^c \rightarrow a^b; d$ where E is a regular expression over O, $c \geq 1$, if $b = 1$ then $d \geq 0$ and $c \geq b$, else if $b = 0$ then $d = 0$.*
3. *syn, is the synapse set, a nonreflexive relation on $\{1, \ldots, m\} \times \{1, \ldots, m\}$*
4. *$out \in \{1, 2, \ldots, m\}$ is the index of the output neuron.*

A *spiking rule* is where $b \geq 1$. A *forgetting rule* is where $b = 0$ and is written as $E/a^c \rightarrow \lambda$. If $L(E) = \{a^c\}$ then spiking and forgetting rules are simply written as $a^c \rightarrow a^b$ and $a^c \rightarrow \lambda$, respectively. Applications of rules are as follows: if neuron σ_i contains k spikes, $a^k \in L(E)$ and $k \geq c$, then the rule $E/a^c \rightarrow a^b \in \mathcal{R}_i$ must be applied. If $b = 1$, the application of this rule consumes or removes c spikes from σ_i, so that only $k - c$ spikes remain in σ_i. The neuron sends a spike to every σ_j such that $(i, j) \in syn$. The output neuron has a synapse not directed to any other neuron, only to the environment. The neuron σ_1 (or the first in the defined order) is referred to as the *initial neuron*.

A delay is a $d \in \mathbb{N} \cup \{0\}$. If a spiking rule has delay $d = 0$ (forgetting rules do not have delays) then d is omitted from writing, and a spike is sent immediately i.e. in the same time step as the application of the rule. If $d \geq 1$ and the spiking rule was applied at time t, then the spike is sent at time $t + d$. From time t to $t + d - 1$ the neuron is said to be *closed* (inspired by the *refractory period* of the neuron in biology) and cannot receive spikes. Any spikes sent to the neuron when the neuron is closed are *lost* or removed from the system. At time $t + d$ the neuron becomes *open* and can then receive spikes again. The neuron can then apply another rule at time $t + d + 1$.

For a forgetting rule, no spikes are produced (they are forgotten or removed from the system). SNP systems assume a global clock, so the application of rules and the sending of spikes by neurons are all synchronized. The *nondeterminism* in SNP systems occurs when, given two rules $E_1/a^{c_1} \rightarrow a^{b_1}$ and $E_2/a^{c_2} \rightarrow a^{b_2}$, it is possible to have $L(E_1) \cap L(E_2) \neq \emptyset$. In this situation, only one rule will be nondeterministically chosen and applied.

SNP systems are *globally parallel* (neurons operate in parallel) but are *locally sequential* (at most one rule per neuron is used). Note that if a spiking rule can be applied, then there is no forgetting rule that can be applied, and vice versa i.e. if a spiking and forgetting rule have regular expressions E_{spik} and E_{forg} respectively in a neuron, then $L(E_{spik}) \cap L(E_{forg}) = \emptyset$.

A configuration of the system at time k is denoted as $C_k = \langle r_1/t_1, \ldots, r_m/t_m, r_e \rangle$, where each element of the vector (except for r_e, representing the spikes in the environment) represents the number of the symbol a (spikes) in neuron σ_i, with $r_i \geq 0, r_i \in \mathbb{N}$ and neuron i is open after $t_i \geq 0$ steps. When a rule in a neuron with delay $d = t_i$ is fired, t_i is decreased by one every time step until the neuron fires when $t_i = 0$. An initial configuration C_0 is therefore $\langle n_1/0, \ldots, n_m/0, 0 \rangle$ since no rules whether with or without delay, have yet been applied and the environment is initially empty. A *computation* is a sequence of transitions from an initial configuration. A computation may halt (no more rules can be applied for a given configuration) or not. If an SNP system does halt, all neurons should be open. Computation result in this work is obtained by checking the number of spikes in the environment once the system halts. A *path* exists between σ_i and σ_m if there exist a series of neurons $\sigma_j, \sigma_k, \ldots, \sigma_l$ and a series of synapses $(i,j), (j,k), \ldots, (l,m)$ between them, leading from σ_i to σ_m.

As in Ref. 19, we focus on four routing constructs for SNP systems in this work, and we provide four $\overline{\Pi}$ modules for them (we refer to Fig. 1): $\overline{\Pi}_{seq}$ module for *sequential* routing, where, given at least two neurons σ_1, σ_2 such that σ_2 spikes only after σ_1 spikes and there is a path from σ_1 to σ_2; $\overline{\Pi}_{iter}$ module for *iteration* routing, where at least two neurons spike multiple (possibly an infinite) number of times and a loop is formed e.g. adding a synapse $(2,1)$ which creates a loop between σ_1 and σ_2; $\overline{\Pi}_{split}$ module for *split* routing, where a spike from a neuron σ_3 is sent to at least two output neurons σ_4 and σ_5, and that $(3,4), (3,5) \in syn$; $\overline{\Pi}_{join}$ module for *join*, where spikes from at least two input neurons σ_6, σ_7 are sent to a neuron σ_8, where $(6,8), (7,8) \in syn$, so that σ_8 produces a spike only after accumulating spikes from σ_7 and σ_8. Without loss of generality, we may assume that the initial neurons do not have delays. Adding delays to any of the non-initial neurons of the modules in Fig. 1 transforms them into their Π counterpart modules.

Prior to,[19] relating Π and $\overline{\Pi}$ started in Ref. 20. In Ref. 19 the idea of *simulation* is such that two requirements must be satisfied: (i) halting time t_h of Π modules coincide with the halting time t'_h of $\overline{\Pi}$ modules, (ii) number of spikes in the environment of Π modules at t_h is equal to the number of

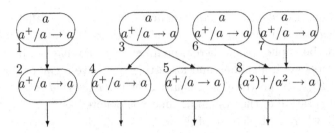

Fig. 1. Routing constructs as $\overline{\Pi}$ modules (from left to right): $\overline{\Pi}_{seq}$, $\overline{\Pi}_{split}$, and $\overline{\Pi}_{join}$ respectively. A $\overline{\Pi}_{iter}$ module can be formed if for example we add a synapse from neuron σ_2 to neuron σ_1.

spikes in the environment of $\overline{\Pi}$ modules at t'_h. It was shown in Ref. 19 that for any Π module that performs any of the four routing constructs, we can construct a $\overline{\Pi}$ module performing the same routing such that $\overline{\Pi}$ satisfies (**i**) and (**ii**) with respect to the computations of Π.

For the next set of definitions and discussions we follow those from Ref. 14 for the SNP algebra, labeled transition systems, and their semantics. We denote with $\mathcal{L}$ the set of all possible neuron labels, and denote the union of two sets (or multisets) s_1, s_2 as $s_1 s_2$ (we omit the $\cup$ operator).

Definition 2.2 (SNP algebra). *The abstract syntax of neuron contents c and spiking neural system sns is given by the following grammar:*

$$c ::= (\emptyset, \emptyset, 0) \mid (\emptyset, a, 0) \mid (E/a^c \to a^b; d, \emptyset, t) \mid (a^c \to \lambda, \emptyset, 0) \mid c \cup c,$$
$$sns ::= [c]_l^L \mid sns \mid sns \mid (l)sns,$$

where d, t range over $\mathbb{N} \cup \{0\}$, $t \leq d$, l ranges over $\mathcal{L}$, L ranges over $2^{\mathcal{L}}$ (the power set of $\mathcal{L}$).

Neuron content c (the computation state of a neuron) is a triple $(\mathcal{R}, u, t)$ where $\mathcal{R}$ is a finite set of spiking and forgetting rules, t is a countdown timer before spiking, and u is a multiset of spikes inside a neuron. Given neuron contents $(\mathcal{R}_1, u_1, t_1) \cup (\mathcal{R}_2, u_2, t_2)$ we represent this as $(\mathcal{R}_1 \mathcal{R}_2, u_1 u_2, \max(t_1, t_2))$ since semantic rules of the SNP algebra require us that *at most one* timer in each neuron content will have a positive value, while the rest are zero. A neuron content is open if $t = 0$, and is closed if $t > 0$. We represent a neuron σ_l from neuron contents using the $[\ \_\ ]_l^L$ operator, where l is the neuron label and L is a set of labels such that given neuron label $i \in L$ implies $(i, l) \in syn$ i.e. there is a synapse for every neuron σ_i to σ_l. An SNP system of degree m can thus be represented as a juxtaposition of terms $[c_1]_1^{L_1} \mid \cdots \mid [c_m]_m^{L_m}$, where each $L_i \subseteq \{1, \ldots, m\}$, $1 \leq i \leq m$.

The outgoing synapses are the output interfaces of an SNP system while incoming synapses are the input interfaces (the set L in neuron $[c]_t^L$). The restriction operation $(l)sns$ restricts σ_l to sending spikes (i.e. restricting outgoing synapses) to sns alone, thus making σ_l "invisible" to succeeding juxtapositions. Restriction therefore allows us to *modularize* our systems, and select which input or output interfaces to reveal to or hide from an external system. Now we recall labeled transition systems (LTS) and their semantics.

Definition 2.3 (LTS). *A labeled transition system (LTS) is a construct* $(S, \mathcal{L}, \{\stackrel{\ell}{\to} | \ell \in \mathcal{L}\})$, *where S is a set of states, $\mathcal{L}$ is a set of labels, and* $\stackrel{\ell}{\to} \subseteq S \times S$ *is a transition relation for each $\ell \in \mathcal{L}$.*

We write $s \stackrel{\ell}{\to} s'$ for $(s, s') \in \stackrel{\ell}{\to}$. SNP algebra semantics are given in terms of an LTS where a state is a syntactically correct term, obtained from semantic rules describing the individual behavior of spiking and forgetting rules. A labeled transition corresponds to one computation step. Labels in the SNP algebra LTS take the following forms, given a neuron content c:

(1) (U, E, u, v, v', I, O), describes a computation step done if c is open, where:

- U is a set of regular expressions so that for each rule in c with regular expression E, whether spiking or forgetting, we have $E \in U$;
- E is either the regular expression of the rule fired, or $\emptyset$ (no rule is fired);
- u is either the multiset of consumed spikes in c after a rule is fired (whether spiking or forgetting), or $\emptyset$ (no rule is fired);
- v is obtained from semantic rules of individual spikes in c. v is checked with u if $v = u$ when c is inserted to $[c]_t^L$ and transitions having a label with $u \neq v$ are removed, ensuring that spikes consumed by any rule are present in $[c]_t^L$ and are then removed from $[c]_t^L$;
- v' is the multiset of spikes in c that are not consumed;
- I is either the multiset of spikes received from other neurons, $\emptyset$ (no spike received), or $\perp$ meaning the neuron is closed;
- O is either the multiset of spikes sent to other neurons, or $\emptyset$ (no output spike).

(2) $(1, I, O)$, describes a computation step done if c is closed, where 1 indicates that the transition decreases the timer by one, and I, O are as in the previous case.

(3) $(\mathcal{I}, \mathcal{O})$, describes a computation step done by an *sns* where $\mathcal{I}$ is a set of pairs (l, I) such that $\sigma_l, l \notin sns$, and some neurons in *sns* receive a multiset of spikes I, and $\mathcal{O}$ is a set of pairs (l, O) such that $\sigma_l, l \in sns$, sends a multiset of spikes $\mathcal{O}$.

As in Ref. 14, we write transitions with labels of the first form with the first five elements of the label (i.e. U, E, u, v, v') under the transition arrow, and the last two elements (i.e. I, O) above the arrow, for the sake of legibility. For the second form, we write 1 and (I, O) under and over the arrow, respectively. We rely on a standard way of associating a set of transitions with a set of transition rules. Structural operational semantic transition rules allow us to infer the movement of SNP algebra terms with the movement of their subterms. For the sake of brevity we do not present in this work the inference rules presented in Ref. 14 about open and closed neuron contents, unions of neuron contents, and spiking neural systems rules. Instead, we direct the reader to consult Ref. 14 and we immediately apply these rules in this work, based on the semantics of LTS and SNP algebra previously defined.

Now we present an idea of simulation (a behavioral equivalence) in terms of LTS. We write as $s \not\xrightarrow{\ell}$ if $s \xrightarrow{\ell} s'$ holds for no s', and $s \not\rightarrow$ if $s \not\xrightarrow{\ell}$ for all $\ell \in \mathcal{L}$.

Definition 2.4. Let $(S, \mathcal{L}, \{\xrightarrow{\ell} | \ell \in \mathcal{L}\})$ be an LTS. A relation $R \subseteq S \times S$ is a *simulation* if, for each pair $s_1 R s_2$, if $s_1 \xrightarrow{\ell} s_1'$ then there is a transition $s_2 \xrightarrow{\ell} s_2'$ such that $s_1' R s_2'$. R is a *ready simulation* if it is a simulation and, for each pair $s_1 R s_2$, if $s_1 \not\xrightarrow{\ell}$ then $s_2 \not\xrightarrow{\ell}$.

Recall that a preorder is a reflexive and transitive relation, and an equivalence is a symmetric preorder. The largest equivalence contained in a preorder is called the kernel of the preorder. The kernel of a ready simulation coinciding with the kernel of a simulation is a *bisimulation*, denoted by $\approx$.

The idea of a restriction in Definition 2.2 allows us to determine the neuron labels of an *sns* that are *bound* using the restriction operation; a neuron label not in the scope of a restriction operation is said to be *free*; and a label l is *pending* if l is not used to label any neuron in the system, and there are some neurons in the system willing to receive spikes from a neuron labeled with l.

Definition 2.5 (Bound, free, and pending labels). *The set of bound labels, free labels, and pending labels of a spiking neural system sns, denoted* *by* $BL(sns)$, $FL(sns)$, $PL(sns) \subseteq \mathcal{L}$ *respectively, are recursively defined as follows:*

$$BL(sns) = \begin{cases} \emptyset, \text{ if } sns = [c]_l^L, \\ BL(sns_1) \cup BL(sns_2), \text{ if } sns = sns_1|sns_2, \\ \{l\} \cup BL(sns'), \text{ if } sns = (l)sns'. \end{cases}$$

$$FL(sns) = \begin{cases} \{l\}, \text{ if } sns = [c]_l^L, \\ FL(sns_1) \cup FL(sns_2), \text{ if } sns = sns_1|sns_2, \\ FL(sns') \setminus \{l\}, \text{ if } sns = (l)sns'. \end{cases}$$

$$PL(sns) = \begin{cases} L, \text{ if } sns = [c]_l^L, \\ PL(sns_1) \setminus FL(sns_2) \cup PL(sns_2) \setminus FL(sns_1), \text{ if } sns = sns_1|sns_2, \\ PL(sns'), \text{ if } sns = (l)sns'. \end{cases}$$

An sns is said to be *complete* if and only if $PL(sns) = \emptyset$. Only complete sns have corresponding SNP systems, because noncomplete sns have synapses that are not properly specified.

3. Results

We recall that we denote by Π a simple semi-homogenous SNP system with delay, and by $\overline{\Pi}$ a simple semi-homogeneous SNP system without delay. Unless we mention otherwise, we assume for every Π and $\overline{\Pi}$ module considered in this work, only their initial neurons have a spike in their initial configurations. We show using SNP algebra and the notion of LTS, that given a module Π_α where $\alpha \in \{seq, split, join, iter\}$, we can construct a $\overline{\Pi}_\alpha$ such that $\Pi_\alpha \approx \overline{\Pi}_\alpha$.

3.1. *Sequential Routing*

Proposition 3.1. *Given a module* Π_{seq} *performing sequential routing, we can construct a module* $\overline{\Pi}_{seq}$ *performing sequential routing such that* $\Pi_{seq} \approx \overline{\Pi}_{seq}$.

Proof. We refer to Fig. 2 for illustrations. For any d as the rule delay, we have the following definitions for Π_{seq} and $\overline{\Pi}_{seq}$:

$$\Pi_{seq} ::= (i)\left([a^+/a \rightarrow a, a, 0]_i^\emptyset \mid [a^+/a \rightarrow a; d, \emptyset, 0]_o^{\{i\}}\right)$$

$$\overline{\Pi}_{seq} ::= (i)(1)\dots(d)\left([a^+/a \rightarrow a, a, 0]_i^\emptyset \mid [a^+/a \rightarrow a, \emptyset, 0]_1^{\{i\}} \mid \dots\right.$$

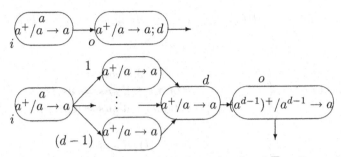

Fig. 2. Sequential routing: Π_{seq} (top) with delay d, and $\overline{\Pi}_{seq}$ (bottom).

$$\left| [a^+/a \to a, \emptyset, 0]_{(d-1)}^{\{i\}} \right| [a^+/a \to a, \emptyset, 0]_d^{\{1,\ldots,(d-1)\}}$$
$$\left| [(a^{d-1})^+/a^{d-1} \to a, \emptyset, 0]_o^{\{d\}} \right)$$

From SNP algebra semantic rules, we infer the following transitions and let $\Pi_{seq} = \Pi_{seq}^{A_1,A_2,t}$ such that A_1, A_2 represent the multiset of spikes for σ_i, σ_o respectively, and t is the timer for σ_o:

$$\Pi_{seq}^{a,\emptyset,0} \xrightarrow{\emptyset,\{(o,\emptyset)\}} \Pi_{seq}^{\emptyset,a,0}$$

$$\Pi_{seq}^{\emptyset,a,0} \xrightarrow{\emptyset,\{(o,\emptyset)\}} \Pi_{seq}^{\emptyset,a,t}$$

$$\Pi_{seq}^{\emptyset,a,t} \xrightarrow{\emptyset,\{(o,\emptyset)\}} \Pi_{seq}^{\emptyset,a,t-1}$$

$$\Pi_{seq}^{\emptyset,a,1} \xrightarrow{\emptyset,\{(o,a)\}} \Pi_{seq}^{\emptyset,\emptyset,0}$$

The first inferred rule starts with the initial configuration, where the initial neuron σ_i has a spike. Once a computation step (i.e. a labeled transition) occurs, σ_o starts its timer countdown. It is understood as mentioned earlier, that by SNP system and algebra semantics, the timer starts with a value d (the delay) and counts down to one (second and third inferred rules). Once the timer is equal to one, the fourth and final inferred rule is applied and Π halts, setting its timer back to zero. We also infer the following transitions and let $\overline{\Pi}_{seq} = \overline{\Pi}_{seq}^{A_i,A_1,\ldots,A_d,A_o}$ so that $A_i, A_1, \ldots, A_d, A_o$ represent the multiset of spikes for $\sigma_i, \sigma_1, \ldots, \sigma_d, \sigma_o$ respectively:

$$\overline{\Pi}_{seq}^{a,A_1,\ldots,A_d,\emptyset} \xrightarrow{\emptyset,\{(o,\emptyset)\}} \overline{\Pi}_{seq}^{\emptyset,A_1,\ldots,A_{d-1},\emptyset,\emptyset}$$

$$\overline{\Pi}_{seq}^{\emptyset,A_1,\ldots,A_{d-1},\emptyset,\emptyset} \xrightarrow{\emptyset,\{(o,\emptyset)\}} \overline{\Pi}_{seq}^{\emptyset,A_1,\ldots,A_{d-1},a^x,a^y}$$

$$\overline{\Pi}_{seq}^{\emptyset,A_1,\ldots,A_{d-1},a^x,a^y} \xrightarrow{\emptyset,\{(o,\emptyset)\}} \overline{\Pi}_{seq}^{\emptyset,A_1,\ldots,A_{d-1},a^{x-1},a^{y+1}}$$

$$\overline{\Pi}_{seq}^{\emptyset,A_1,\ldots,A_d,a^{d-1}} \xrightarrow{\emptyset,\{(o,a)\}} \overline{\Pi}_{seq}^{\emptyset,A_1,\ldots,A_d,\emptyset}$$

Where $A_j \in \{\emptyset, a\}$, $x \in [1, d-1]$, $y \in [0, d-2]$, $j \in \{1, \ldots, d\}$. The first inferred rule is the initial configuration of Π_{seq} transitioning to a configuration where the $d-1$ parallel neurons have one spike each, i.e. σ_i

sends one spike each to $\sigma_1, \ldots, \sigma_{d-1}$ in parallel. For the sake of brevity, we refer to these $d-1$ parallel neurons as *multiplier neurons*. On one hand, it is understood that once σ_d starts receiving spikes it starts with a^{d-1} spikes. These $d-1$ spikes are sent in parallel from the multiplier neurons to σ_d (second inferred rule). The a^{d-1} spikes in σ_d then decrease by one every transition (third inferred rule) down to a^0, i.e. the empty multiset. It is also understood in the second till the third inferred rule that $A_d = a^x$ where x counts down from $d-1$ to 1 while $A_o = a^y$ counts up from 0 to $d-2$. On the other hand, once σ_o starts receiving spikes, it starts with a and the spikes increase up to a^{d-1} before spiking to the environment (also in the third inferred rule). The last inferred rule is a transition to a halting configuration where σ_o accumulates a^{d-1} spikes and finally sends one spike to the environment.

We have the following bisimulation relation R_{seq} between Π_{seq} and $\overline{\Pi}_{seq}$ to be

$$R_{seq} = \{(\Pi_{seq}^{a,\emptyset,0}, \overline{\Pi}_{seq}^{a,A_1,\ldots,A_d,\emptyset}), (\Pi_{seq}^{\emptyset,a,0}, \overline{\Pi}_{seq}^{\emptyset,A_1,\ldots,A_{d-1},\emptyset,\emptyset})\} \cup$$
$$\{(\Pi_{seq}^{\emptyset,a,t}, \overline{\Pi}_{seq}^{\emptyset,A_1,\ldots,A_{d-1},a^x,a^y}), (\Pi_{seq}^{\emptyset,a,1}, \overline{\Pi}_{seq}^{\emptyset,A_1,\ldots,A_d,a^{d-1}})\} \cup$$
$$\{(\Pi_{seq}^{\emptyset,\emptyset,0}, \overline{\Pi}_{seq}^{\emptyset,A_1,\ldots,A_d,\emptyset})\}. \qquad \square$$

3.2. Iteration Routing

Proposition 3.2. *Given a module Π_{iter} performing iteration routing, we can construct a module $\overline{\Pi}_{iter}$ performing iteration routing such that $\Pi_{iter} \approx \overline{\Pi}_{iter}$.*

Proof. For iteration routing, we have Fig. 3 for illustrations. We also have the following definitions:

$$\Pi_{iter} ::= (i)\Big([a^+/a \to a, a, 0]_i^{\{o\}} \;\Big|\; [a^+/a \to a; d, \emptyset, 0]_o^{\{i\}}\Big)$$

$$\overline{\Pi}_{iter} ::= (i)(1)\ldots(d-1)(d)\Big([a^+/a \to a, a, 0]_i^{\{o\}} \;\Big|$$
$$[a^+/a \to a, \emptyset, 0]_1^{\{i\}} \;\Big|\; \ldots \;\Big|\; [a^+/a \to a, \emptyset, 0]_{(d-1)}^{\{i\}} \;\Big|$$
$$[a^+/a \to a, \emptyset, 0]_d^{\{1,\ldots,(d-1)\}} \;\Big|\; [(a^{d-1})^+/a^{d-1} \to a, \emptyset, 0]_o^{\{d\}}\Big)$$

We let $\Pi_{iter} = \Pi_{iter}^{A_1,A_2,t}$ where A_1, A_2 represent the multiset of spikes for σ_i, σ_o respectively and t is the timer, and we let $\overline{\Pi}_{iter} = \overline{\Pi}_{iter}^{A_i,A_1,\ldots,A_d,A_o}$, where $A_i, A_1, \ldots, A_d, A_o$ represent the multiset of spikes for $\sigma_i, \sigma_1, \ldots, \sigma_o$ respecitvely. We infer the following transitions for Π_{iter}:

$$\Pi_{iter}^{a,\emptyset,0} \xrightarrow{\emptyset,\{(o,\emptyset)\}} \Pi_{iter}^{\emptyset,a,0}$$
$$\Pi_{iter}^{\emptyset,a,0} \xrightarrow{\emptyset,\{(o,\emptyset)\}} \Pi_{iter}^{\emptyset,a,t}$$

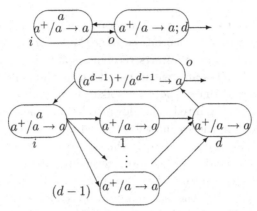

Fig. 3.   Iteration routing: Π_{iter} (top) has a delay d and $\overline{\Pi}_{iter}$ (bottom).

$$\Pi_{iter}^{\emptyset,a,t} \xrightarrow{\emptyset,\{(o,\emptyset)\}} \Pi_{iter}^{\emptyset,a,t-1}$$
$$\Pi_{iter}^{\emptyset,a,1} \xrightarrow{\emptyset,\{(o,a)\}} \Pi_{iter}^{a,\emptyset,0}$$

The first inferred rule is the initial configuration for Π_{iter}. As with sequential routing, once σ_o receives a spike, the timer t counts down from d to one (second and third inferred rules). At transition where $t = 1$, the final inferred rule is performed and the state of Π_{iter} returns to the state of the first inferred rule. For $\overline{\Pi}_{iter}$ we infer the following transitions:

$$\overline{\Pi}_{iter}^{a,A_1,\ldots,A_d,\emptyset} \xrightarrow{\emptyset,\{(o,\emptyset)\}} \overline{\Pi}_{iter}^{\emptyset,A_1,\ldots,A_{d-1},\emptyset,\emptyset}$$
$$\overline{\Pi}_{iter}^{\emptyset,A_1,\ldots,A_{d-1},\emptyset,\emptyset} \xrightarrow{\emptyset,\{(o,\emptyset)\}} \overline{\Pi}_{iter}^{\emptyset,A_1,\ldots,A_{d-1},a^x,a^y}$$
$$\overline{\Pi}_{iter}^{\emptyset,A_1,\ldots,A_{d-1},a^x,a^y} \xrightarrow{\emptyset,\{(o,\emptyset)\}} \overline{\Pi}_{iter}^{\emptyset,A_1,\ldots,A_{d-1},a^{x-1},a^{y+1}}$$
$$\overline{\Pi}_{iter}^{\emptyset,A_1,\ldots,A_d,a^{d-1}} \xrightarrow{\emptyset,\{(o,a)\}} \overline{\Pi}_{iter}^{a,A_1,\ldots,A_d,\emptyset}$$

Where $A_j \in \{\emptyset, a\}$, $x \in [1, d-1]$, $y \in [0, d-2]$, $j \in \{1,\ldots,d\}$. As with sequential routing, the first inferred rule involves a transition from the initial configuration, where the single spike from σ_i is sent to the multiplier neurons. The second inferred rule moves the spikes from the multiplier neurons to σ_d, while the third inferred rule moves the $d-1$ spikes in σ_d one by one to σ_o. Again, it is understood in the second till the third inferred rule that $A_d = a^x$ where x counts down from $d-1$ to 1 while $A_o = a^y$ counts up from 0 to $d-2$. The final inferred rule, starting with σ_o having accumulated $d-1$ spikes, transitions to the initial configuration in the first inferred rule of $\overline{\Pi}_{iter}$. We have the following bisimulation between Π_{iter} and $\overline{\Pi}_{iter}$ to be

$$R_{iter} = \{(\Pi_{iter}^{a,\emptyset,0}, \overline{\Pi}_{iter}^{a,A_1,\ldots,A_d,\emptyset}), (\Pi_{iter}^{\emptyset,a,0}, \overline{\Pi}_{iter}^{\emptyset,A_1,\ldots,A_{d-1},\emptyset,\emptyset})\}, \cup$$
$$\{(\Pi_{iter}^{\emptyset,a,t}, \overline{\Pi}_{iter}^{a,A_1,\ldots,A_{d-1},a^x,a^y}), (\Pi_{iter}^{\emptyset,a,1}, \overline{\Pi}_{iter}^{\emptyset,A_1,\ldots,A_d,a^{d-1}})\}. \qquad \square$$

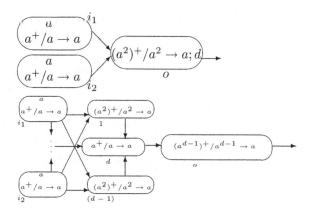

Fig. 4. Join routing : Π_{join} (top) has delay d and $\overline{\Pi}_{join}$ (bottom).

3.3. Join Routing

Proposition 3.3. *Given a module Π_{join} performing join routing, we can construct a module $\overline{\Pi}_{join}$ performing join routing such that $\Pi_{join} \approx \overline{\Pi}_{join}$.*

Proof. For join routing, illustrations are given in Fig. 4. We define Π_{join} and $\overline{\Pi}_{join}$ as follows:

$$\Pi_{join} ::= (i_1)(i_2)\Big([a^+/a \to a, a, 0]_{i_1}^{\emptyset} \;\Big|\; [a^+/a \to a, a, 0]_{i_2}^{\emptyset} \;\Big|$$
$$[(a^2)^+/a^2 \to a; d, \emptyset, 0]_o^{\{i_1,i_2\}}\Big)$$

$$\overline{\Pi}_{join} ::= (i_1)(i_2)(1)...(d)\Big([a^+/a \to a, a, 0]_{i_1}^{\emptyset} \;\Big|\; [a^+/a \to a, a, 0]_{i_2}^{\emptyset} \;\Big|$$
$$[(a^2)^+/a^2 \to a, \emptyset, 0]_1^{\{i_1,i_2\}} \;\Big|\; \cdots \;\Big|\; [(a^2)^+/a^2 \to a, \emptyset, 0]_{d-1}^{\{i_1,i_2\}} \;\Big|$$
$$[a^+/a \to a, \emptyset, 0]_d^{\{1,...,(d-1)\}} \;\Big|\; [(a^{d-1})^+|a^{d-1} \to a, \emptyset, 0]_o^{\{d\}} \Big).$$

We infer the following transition rules for Π_{join} and let $\Pi_{join} = \Pi_{join}^{A_{i_1}, A_{i_2}, A_o, t}$ where A_{i_1}, A_{i_2}, A_o represent the multiset of spikes for $\sigma_{i_1}, \sigma_{i_2}, \sigma_o$ respectively and t is the timer,

$$\Pi_{join}^{X,Y,\emptyset,0} \xrightarrow{\emptyset,\{(o,\emptyset)\}} \Pi_{join}^{\emptyset,\emptyset,XY,0}$$

$$\Pi_{join}^{\emptyset,\emptyset,a^2,0} \xrightarrow{\emptyset,\{(o,\emptyset)\}} \Pi_{join}^{\emptyset,\emptyset,a^2,t}$$

$$\Pi_{join}^{\emptyset,\emptyset,a^2,t} \xrightarrow{\emptyset,\{(o,\emptyset)\}} \Pi_{join}^{\emptyset,\emptyset,a^2,t-1}$$

$$\Pi_{join}^{\emptyset,\emptyset,a^2,1} \xrightarrow{\emptyset,\{(o,a)\}} \Pi_{join}^{\emptyset,\emptyset,\emptyset,0}$$

Note that $X, Y \in \{\emptyset, a\}$. The first inferred rule is where the two initial neurons, in this case σ_{i_1} and σ_{i_2}, have one spike each.[a] The two initial neurons then send one spike each to σ_o. The second rule is where the σ_o applies its spiking rule, starting the counter at timer value $t = d$. The third rule is where the timer of σ_o counts down to $t = 1$ while the fourth and final rule is where σ_o consumes the a^2 spikes. Consuming the a^2 spikes means σ_o sends a spike to the environment and the system halts. For $\overline{\Pi}_{join}$, let $\overline{\Pi}_{join} = \overline{\Pi}_{join}^{A_{i_1}, A_{i_2}, A_1, \ldots, A_d, A_o}$ where $A_{i_1}, A_{i_2}, A_1, \ldots, A_d, A_o$ represent the multiset of spikes for $\sigma_{i_1}, \sigma_{i_2}, \sigma_1, \ldots, \sigma_d, \sigma_o$ respectively, we have:

$$\overline{\Pi}_{join}^{a,a,A_1,\ldots,A_{d-1},\emptyset,\emptyset} \xrightarrow{\emptyset, \{(o,\emptyset)\}} \overline{\Pi}_{join}^{\emptyset,\emptyset,A_1,\ldots,A_{d-1},\emptyset,\emptyset}$$

$$\overline{\Pi}_{join}^{\emptyset,\emptyset,A_1,\ldots,A_{d-1},\emptyset,\emptyset} \xrightarrow{\emptyset, \{(o,\emptyset)\}} \overline{\Pi}_{join}^{\emptyset,\emptyset,A_1,\ldots,A_{d-1},a^x,a^y}$$

$$\overline{\Pi}_{join}^{\emptyset,\emptyset,A_1,\ldots,A_{d-1},a^x,a^y} \xrightarrow{\emptyset, \{(o,\emptyset)\}} \overline{\Pi}_{join}^{\emptyset,\emptyset,A_1,\ldots,A_{d-1},a^{x-1},a^{y+1}}$$

$$\overline{\Pi}_{join}^{\emptyset,\emptyset,A_1,\ldots,A_{d-1},\emptyset,a^{(d-1)}} \xrightarrow{\emptyset, \{(o,a)\}} \overline{\Pi}_{join}^{\emptyset,\emptyset,A_1,\ldots,A_{d-1},\emptyset,\emptyset}$$

with $A_i \in \{\emptyset, a^2\}$, $x \in [1, d-1]$, $y \in [0, d-2]$, $j \in \{1, \ldots, d\}$. The first inferred rule is where the two initial neurons σ_{i_1} and σ_{i_2} send one spike each to all the multiplier neurons. The second inferred rule is where these multiplier neurons send one spike each to σ_d so that σ_d collects a^{d-1} spikes. The third inferred rule is where σ_d sends one spike to σ_o every time step. Again, it is understood in the second till the third inferred rule that $A_d = a^x$ where x counts down from $d-1$ to 1 while $A_o = a^y$ counts up from 0 to $d-2$. The final inferred rule is where σ_o collects a^{d-1} spikes and sends a spike to the environment, halting the system.

We have the following bisimulation relation R_{join} for join routing:

$$R_{join} = \{(\Pi_{join}^{a,a,\emptyset,0}, \overline{\Pi}_{join}^{a,a,[\emptyset,\ldots,\emptyset],\emptyset,\emptyset}), (\Pi_{join}^{\emptyset,\emptyset,a^2,0}, \overline{\Pi}_{join}^{\emptyset,\emptyset,A_1,\ldots,A_{d-1},\emptyset,\emptyset})\} \cup$$

$$\{(\Pi_{join}^{\emptyset,\emptyset,a^2,t}, \overline{\Pi}_{join}^{\emptyset,\emptyset,A_1,\ldots,A_{d-1},a^x,a^y}), (\Pi_{join}^{\emptyset,\emptyset,a^2,1}, \overline{\Pi}_{join}^{\emptyset,\emptyset,A_1,\ldots,A_{d-1},\emptyset,a^{(d-1)}})\} \cup$$

$$\{(\Pi_{join}^{\emptyset,\emptyset,\emptyset,0}, \overline{\Pi}_{join}^{\emptyset,\emptyset,A_1,\ldots,A_{d-1},\emptyset,\emptyset})\} \qquad \square$$

3.4. *Split Routing*

Proposition 3.4. *Given a module Π_{split} performing split routing, we can construct a module $\overline{\Pi}_{split}$ performing split routing such that $\Pi_{split} \approx \overline{\Pi}_{split}$.*

Proof. Recall the split routing module from Fig. 1. Notice that a Π_{seq} is a special case of a split where there is only one sibling neuron. For Π_{split}

---

[a]Later in this section, when juxtaposing modules, we will use the first inferred rule to also mean the case where the two neurons do not receive a spike at the same time.

we can have delays in some or all of the sibling neurons. Regardless of how many sibling neurons have delays however, the inferred rules for Π_{split} (respectively, $\overline{\Pi}_{split}$) follow from the inferred rules in Π_{seq} (respectively, $\overline{\Pi}_{seq}$), where instead of having only one sibling neuron we can have k sibling neurons. The first inferred rule for both Π_{split} and $\overline{\Pi}_{split}$ has their respective parent neurons sending a spike in parallel to their respective k siblings.

Notice that split routing is implicitly included in iteration routing, where the output neuron performs a split, i.e. sends its spike to more than one distinct neuron. For both Π_{split} and $\overline{\Pi}_{split}$ we again have $\mathcal{I} = \emptyset$. For Π_{split} the $\sigma_1, \sigma_2, \ldots, \sigma_{k-1}, \sigma_k$ sibling neurons can have $d_1, d_2, \ldots, d_{k-1}, d_k$ distinct delays respectively. For the second till the final inferred rule, $\mathcal{O}$ will have pairs $(o_i, a), 1 \leq i \leq k$, where the nth inferred rule containing a pair (o_i, a) means sibling neuron i has already counted down its timer from d_i to zero and has produced a spike. Each sibling neuron with delay d_i in Π_{seq} is replaced by a $\overline{\Pi}_{seq}$ module in $\overline{\Pi}_{split}$. In particular, the spiking rules in these $\overline{\Pi}_{seq}$ modules have spiking rules of the form $(a^m)^+/a^m \rightarrow a$ where $m \in \{1, d_i - 1\}$. The bisimulation relation R_{split} can be derived from R_{seq} and R_{iter}. $\square$

Now that we have provided the LTS definitions of the Π and $\overline{\Pi}$ modules for the four routing constructs, we will use these modules, i.e. to juxtapose them, in order to build larger Π and $\overline{\Pi}$ systems. For the succeeding juxtapositions, we emphasize the following restrictions and assumptions

(1) There is only one input and one output neuron. The module containing the input neuron is referred to as the input module and the module containing the output neuron is the output module.

(2) The input module can only be one of the two modules: sequential, or split; the output module can only be one of the two modules: sequential, or join.

(3) The SNP system has a directed acyclic graph (DAG) structure, where each node of the DAG is one Π_α.

(4) Each Π_α module of the DAG structured SNP system have no overlaps, i.e. distinct modules do not share a common neurons or neuron labels.

(5) Spike loss does not occur, aside from the fact that forgetting rules are not included in the routing modules. Since spikes can be considered as markers or tokens representing a system or work state, we do not want to lose them. Another way that spike loss occurs is when a spike is sent to a closed neuron. Therefore, for any two neurons σ_i and σ_j, if a path exists from σ_i with delay d_i to σ_j with delay d_j then $d_i \geq d_j$.

We now define a spiking neural system with delay Π_{jux}, which is a juxtaposition of any of the four routing modules and any multiplicities of these, as follows:

$$\Pi_{jux} ::= (l_1, \ldots, l_k)(\Pi_1 \mid \cdots \mid \Pi_r)$$

where $\Pi_i \in \{\Pi_{seq}, \Pi_{iter}, \Pi_{join}, \Pi_{split}\}, 1 \le i \le r$ for some $r, k \in \mathbb{N}$. We can also define a spiking neural system without delay, $\overline{\Pi}_{jux}$, as

$$\overline{\Pi}_{jux} ::= (l_1, \ldots, l_k)(\overline{\Pi}_1 \mid \cdots \mid \overline{\Pi}_r)$$

where $\overline{\Pi}_i \in \{\overline{\Pi}_{seq}, \overline{\Pi}_{iter}, \overline{\Pi}_{join}, \overline{\Pi}_{split}\}, 1 \le i \le r$ for some $r, k \in \mathbb{N}$. Note that every Π_i ($\overline{\Pi}_i$, resp.) as well as Π_{jux} ($\overline{\Pi}_{jux}$, resp.) are complete. For all $1 \le j \le k$,

$$l_j \in FL(\Pi_1) \cup \cdots \cup FL(\Pi_r) \setminus FL(\Pi_r)$$

However, other than the designated output neuron of Π_{jux}, each $l_j \in BL(\Pi_{jux})$. Π_r is designated as the output module of Π_{jux}. The input modules of Π_{jux} are those that do not have incoming synpase from any other modules. Only the input modules of Π_{jux} will contain a single spike in their respective initial neurons. When connecting any two modules together, the following notes and minor changes must be observed with regards to propositions 3.1 up to 3.4:

(1) Any spike in the initial configuration of the two modules are removed.
(2) Let Π_i and Π_j be module, with $i \ne j$ and $i, j \in \{1, ..., r\}$. If Π_i is to be connected to Π_j (meaning the receiver of spike of the output neuron of Π_i are the initial neurons of Π_j), then the set of incoming labels of the initial neurons of Π_j will include the label of the output neuron of Π_i.
(3) For each routing module Π_α, where $\alpha \in \{seq, iter, join, split\}$, the following transition rules are added, where l is the label of the output neuron of the module with an outgoing synapse to the input neuron of module Π_α:

    (a) For Π_{seq}, add transition $\Pi_{seq}^{\emptyset,\emptyset,0} \xrightarrow{\{(l,a)\},\{(o,\emptyset)\}} \Pi_{seq}^{a,\emptyset,0}$,

    (b) For Π_{iter}, add transition $\Pi_{iter}^{\emptyset,\emptyset,0} \xrightarrow{\{(l,a)\},\{(o,\emptyset)\}} \Pi_{iter}^{a,\emptyset,0}$,

    (c) For Π_{join}, add transitions

        i. $\Pi_{join}^{\emptyset,\emptyset,\emptyset,0} \xrightarrow{\{(l_1,a),(l_2,a)\},\{(o,\emptyset)\}} \Pi_{join}^{a,a,\emptyset,0}$,

        ii. $\Pi_{join}^{\emptyset,\emptyset,\emptyset,0} \xrightarrow{\{(l_2,a)\},\{(o,\emptyset)\}} \Pi_{join}^{\emptyset,a,\emptyset,0}$,

        iii. $\Pi_{join}^{\emptyset,\emptyset,\emptyset,0} \xrightarrow{\{(l_1,a)\},\{(o,\emptyset)\}} \Pi_{join}^{a,\emptyset,\emptyset,0}$

iv, where l_1 and l_2 are the output neuron labels with a synapse towards neuron i_1 and i_2, respectively.

(d) For Π_{split}, add transition $\Pi_{split}^{\emptyset,\emptyset,0} \xrightarrow{\{(l,a)\},\{(o,\emptyset)\}} \Pi_{split}^{a,\emptyset,\emptyset,0}$.

We collectively call these *initialization* transitions for Π_{jux} and their corresponding initialization transitions in $\overline{\Pi}_{jux}$ as R_{init}. Note that for Π_{split} and $\overline{\Pi}_{split}$, the spikes from their output neurons may be recieved by two distinct modules. In that case, only one of the labels of the two output neurons will be included in the set of incoming labels of the initial neuron for each of the receiving module. The following theorem summarizes the results of propositions 3.1 up to 3.4.

Theorem 3.1. *Given a complete spiking neural system Π_{jux}, we can construct a complete spiking neural system $\overline{\Pi}_{jux}$ such that $\Pi_{jux} \approx \overline{\Pi}_{jux}$.*

Proof. (Sketch)

Suppose Π_{jux} is the given complete spiking neural system containing n modules, for n a positive integer. By definition of Π_{jux}, it is composed of modules Π_i, for all $1 \leq i \leq n$, such that $\Pi_i \in \{\Pi_{seq}, \Pi_{iter}, \Pi_{join}, \Pi_{split}\}$. $\overline{\Pi}_{jux}$ also contains n modules. We construct $\overline{\Pi}_{jux}$ in the following manner:

For every module Π_i of Π_{jux}, a module $\overline{\Pi}_i$ is constructed for $\overline{\Pi}_{jux}$ as follows: Π_i may contain neurons that do not have delays (i.e. a delay d associated with a rule of a neuron is equal to zero). We can have two cases:

(1) Case without delay: $\overline{\Pi}_i$ is constructed the same as Π_i.
(2) Case with delay: let Π_α be equal to Π_i, with $\alpha \in \{seq, iter, join, split\}$ since Π_i performs one of those four routings. Then $\overline{\Pi}_i$ is constructed as $\overline{\Pi}_\alpha$.

In order to show the bisimulation of Π_{jux} and $\overline{\Pi}_{jux}$, the relation R_{jux} is defined as follows:

$$R_{jux} \subseteq \bigcup_{\alpha \in \{seq, iter, split, join\}} R_\alpha \cup R_{init}$$

where R_{init} is the set of additional initialization relations, completing the proof.

4. Final Remarks

Based on the given examples in,[14] we would like to extend our work to include neurons that contain more than one rule. Removing the constraint of not losing spikes by adding forgetting rules or allowing closed neurons to receive spikes, is also interesting. In allowing spike loss, in terms of modeling or verification this could mean we lose some information of a process or work state. Additionally, the current constructions of the routings can only handle multiple incoming spikes as long as the arrival of these spikes have long intervals (as a function of the delay within the routing) in between them. We strongly think that the integration of forgetting rules can enable constructions of routings that can handle spike flows with little to no intervals between the incoming spikes to a routing. We could device a construction method for these routings that varies only by the occurring delays within a routing. These investigations could eventually suggest ways how we can use Π and $\overline{\Pi}$ modules (and their juxtapositions) to perform routings, perhaps for verification of systems such as workflows, for example.

Relaxing other constraints and restrictions for the construction of Π_{jux} is also worth pursuing. For example, can we still use the four modules (or some modification of them) so that their juxtapositions (with or without overlaps) can include cycles? More complex routings such as a Π with routing consisting of synapses $(\sigma_a, \sigma_b), (\sigma_b, \sigma_c), (\sigma_c, \sigma_d), (\sigma_c, \sigma_a), (\sigma_d, \sigma_b)$ are also interesting to explore. Furthermore, we intend to simplify the four routings presented in this work into a base routing framework. Notice for example that the iteration routing can be thought of as a combination of an iteration and join routing. The base framework can simply contain a module Π_0 consisting of exactly one neuron with delay only, i.e. the sns has only one neuron, and synapses are covered in the abstraction. The corresponding $\overline{\Pi}_0$ will also be simpler than the current four routings. The current four routings for Π and $\overline{\Pi}$ can then be constructed using Π_0 and $\overline{\Pi}_0$, respectively.

Acknowledgments

F. G. C. Cabarle is supported by the ERDT program of the Department of Science and Technology (DOST). H.N. Adorna is funded by a DOST-ERDT research grant and the Semirara Mining Corporation Professorial Chair of the UP Diliman College of Engineering. The authors also thank the unknown reviewers for their comments that helped improve this work.

References

1. Păun, Gh.: Computing with membranes. Journal of Computer and System Science 61(1):108–143 (1999).

2. Păun, Gh.: Membrane Computing: An Introduction. Springer (2002).
3. Ionescu, M., Păun, Gh., Yokomori, T.: Spiking Neural P Systems. Fundamenta Informaticae, Vol. 71, issue 2,3 279–308, Feb. (2006).
4. Ibarra, O.H., Păun A., Păun Gh., Rodríguez-Patón A., Sosik P., Woodworth S.: Normal forms for spiking neural P systems. Theor Comput Sci 372(2–3):196217 (2007).
5. Milner, R.: Communicating and Mobile Systems: the Pi-Calculus. Cambridge University Press (1999).
6. Aceto, L., Fokkink, W.J., Verhoef, C.: Handbook of Process Algebra, Ch. Structural Operational Semantics, Elsevier, 197–292 (2001).
7. Zeng, X., Zhang, X., Pan, L.: Homogeneous Spiking Neural P. Systems. Fundamenta Informaticae vol 97(1–2):275–294 (2009).
8. Cabarle, F. G. C, Adorna, H. N.: On Structures and Behaviors of Spiking Neural P Systems and Petri Nets. E. Csuhaj-Varjú et al. (Eds.): CMC 2012, LNCS 7762, pp. 145-160, Springer-Verlag, (2013).
9. Kleijn, J. H. C. M., Koutny, M., Rozenberg, G.: Towards a Petri Net Semantics for Membrane Systems. R. Freund et al. (Eds.): WMC 2005, LNCS 3850, pp. 292–309, Springer-Verlag (2006).
10. Metta, V. P., Krithivasan, K., Garg, G.: Spiking Neural P systems and Petri nets. Proc. of the Int'l Workshop on Machine Intelligence Res. (2009) [Online]. http://www.mirlabs.org/nagpur/paper02.pdf.
11. Qi, Z., You, J., Mao, H.: P Systems and Petri Nets. Martín-Vide et al. (eds.), WMC 2003, LNCS 2933, (2004) 286–303.
12. Andreai, O., Ciobanu, G., Lucanu, D.: Structural operational semantics of P Systems. Proc. 6th Workshop on Membrane Computing. LNCS Vol. 3850:31–28, Springer (2006).
13. Barbuti, R., Maggiolo-Schettini, A., Milazzo, P., Tini, S.: Compositional semantics and behavioral equivalences for P systems. Theor Comput Sci 395:77–100 (2008).
14. Barbuti, R., Maggiolo-Schettini, A., Milazzo, P. Tini S.: Compositional semantics of spiking neural P systems. The Journal of Logic and Algebraic Programming 79(10):304–316 (2010).
15. van der Aalst, W. M. P.: Verification of Workflow Nets. Azéma, P., Balbo, G. (Eds), Application and Theory of Petri Nets, LNCS 1248, pp. 407–426, Springer-Verlag (1997).
16. van der Aalst, W. M. P., Hauschildt, D., Verbeek, H. M. W.: A Petri-net-based Tool to Analyze Workflows. Farwer, B., Moldt, D., Stehr, M.O. (Eds), Proc. Petri Nets in Sys. Eng. '97, pp. 78–90, Hamburg, Germany, September (1997).
17. Păun, Gh., Rozenberg, G., Salomaa A. The Oxford Handbook of Membrane Computing, Oxford University Press (2010).
18. Păun, Gh., Pérez-Jiménez, M. J.: Spiking Neural P Systems. Recent Results, Research Topics. A. Condon et al. (eds.), Algorithmic Bioprocesses, Springer (2009).

19. Cabarle, F. G. C., Buño, K. C., Adorna, H. N.: On The Delays In Spiking Neural P Systems. Philippine Computing Journal vol. 7(2):12-17, (2013) preprint online: http://arxiv.org/abs/1212.2529.
20. Cabarle, F. G. C., Buño, K. C., Adorna, H. N.: Time after Time: Notes on Delays in Spiking Neural P Systems. Workshop on Computation: Theory and Practice. Proc. in ICT Vol. 7, pp. 82–92, Springer Japan (2013).

PROBING THE HARDNESS OF THE APPROXIMATE GENE CLUSTER DISCOVERY PROBLEM (AGCDP)

G. S. CABUNDUCAN*, J. B. CLEMENTE, H. N. ADORNA

Algorithms and Complexity Laboratory
Department of Computer Science
University of the Philippines
Diliman 1101, Quezon City, Philippines
http://aclab.dcs.upd.edu.ph/

R. T. RELATOR

Institute of Mathematics
University of the Philippines
Diliman 1101, Quezon City, Philippines

We present a polynomial-time transformation of the input for a variant of Median String Problem (MSP) that employs Hamming distance into the input for Approximate Gene Cluster Discovery Problem (AGCDP). Since MSP is NP-complete, the transformation forms the integral part of the reduction of MSP into AGCDP, for all input instances, such that AGCDP is confirmed to be NP-hard.

Keywords: Approximate Gene Cluster Discovery Problem; Median String Problem; Reduction; NP-hard.

1. Introduction

Approximate gene cluster discovery problem (AGCDP) aims to find a set of genes that are kept more or less together in a set of sequences. Genes belonging to a cluster are believed to perform similar functions or are involved in the same cellular process. AGCDP shows strong similarity to an NP-complete problem called median string problem (MSP),[1] which gives a possibility that it is NP-hard. Certain variants of MSP has been shown to be NP-complete,[2] and this includes the case of unbounded alphabet.[3] In some research articles, MSP is also known as the consensus patterns problem in

---

*corresponding author email: gscabunducan@up.edu.ph

which Hamming distance is used as the distance measure. This is a more studied variant of MSP, and it is NP-complete as discussed in Fellows et al., 2006[4] and shown in Li *et al.*, 2002.[5] Moreover, it also admits a polynomial time approximation scheme (PTAS).[5] Given the different possibilities in the parameters for MSP, certain parameterized variants, e.g. a version parameterized to the number of strings and length of the median string, have been shown to be fixed-parameter tractable (FPT) under bounded alphabet and $W[1]$-hard under unbounded alphabet[4].[6] We have explored the possibility that AGCDP is NP-hard through our initial results in a previously presented paper;[7] and in this article, we present a different and more precise perspective of the reduction of MSP into AGCDP in order to provide a proof that AGCDP is indeed NP-hard.

The formal definition of AGCDP and MSP are defined in Section 2. It is then followed by our proof in Section 3, which includes the discussion of the proof idea, polynomial-time transformation, and the correctness of the reduction.

2. Basic Definitions and Notations

2.1. *Median String Problem (MSP)*

Given a set of sequences, a *median string* is a pattern in which the distance to all other strings in the sequence is minimized. This distance can be obtained using different measures, such as *Levenshtein distance* and *Hamming distance*.[8] The Hamming distance requires less computing power than the Levenshtein distance, but in both measures, MSP is NP-complete. This article will focus on MSP that employs the Hamming distance similar to the MSP variant tackled in Li *et al.*, 2002.[5] For the notations, we will use Σ as the alphabet, Σ^* as the set of strings from Σ, and $length(s)$, $length : \Sigma^* \to \mathbb{N}$, for any string $s \in \Sigma^*$, as the number of symbols in s. We will be dealing with the substrings of s in the transformation so that any substring from s of length l is called an l-mer. Moreover, given any set X, we will use $|X|$ to denote its cardinality.

Definition 2.1 (Hamming Distance). *Given two strings w and w' in Σ^*, where $length(w) = length(w')$, the Hamming distance between the two, denoted by $d_H(w, w')$ is equal to the total number of mismatched characters.*

For example, the Hamming distance as defined in Definition 2.1 between the strings '0113200', and '0133210' is equal to 2. Throughout the article, we will be using the following notations in addition to those previously defined. Given an ordered set of t sequences say $\mathcal{S} = \{s^1, s^2, s^3, \ldots, s^t\}$, where s^i is a sequence of length n defined over some alphabet Σ. Let $s^i(x)$ (or alternatively s^i_x) denote the character in position x at i^{th} sequence. Let $r = \{r^1, r^2, r^3, \ldots, r^t\}$ be a vector containing t starting positions in $\mathcal{S}$, and $\bar{r}^i = s^i(r^i) \ldots s^i(r^i + l - 1)$ be the l-mer corresponding to the starting position r^i in the ith sequence. From r, we can define a set of l-mers $\bar{r}^i$s which forms a $(t \times l)$ alignment $\mathcal{A}(r)$. For instance, if we have $\mathcal{S} = \{12312, 23113, 12132\}$, $r = \{2, 3, 1\}$, and $l = 3$, the alignment obtained is $\mathcal{A}(r) = \{231, 113, 121\}$.

Given a string v, we can compute the distance of v from a set of strings or an alignment $\mathcal{A}(r)$. We call it the *Total Hamming Distance*, which is equal to

$$\text{Total Hamming Distance}(v, r) = \sum_{i=0}^{t} d_H(v, \bar{r}^i), \tag{1}$$

where $d_H(v, \bar{r}^i)$ is the *Hamming distance* of v to string $\bar{r}^i$. Moreover, we define the *Total Distance* function to be the minimum *Total Hamming Distance* over all r in $\mathcal{S}$ such that

$$\text{Total Distance}(v, \mathcal{S}) = min \text{ (Total Hamming Distance}(v, r)), \ \forall \ r \tag{2}$$

The MSP uses the *Total Distance* function to get the median string of $\mathcal{S}$.

Definition 2.2 (Median String Problem[8]). *Given a set of sequences $\mathcal{S}$, find a median string v^*.*

Input: *Set of t n-length sequences $\mathcal{S} = \{s^1, s^2, \ldots s^t\}$ and median string length l, where $1 \leq l \leq n$*
Output: *A string v^* of length l that minimizes the Total Distance$(v, \mathcal{S})$ over all l-length string v in $\mathcal{S}$*

In the naive MSP, the *Total Hamming Distance*(v, r) given an l-mer v over all possible starting positions r in $\mathcal{S}$ is minimized first. Then the next task will be finding a string v such that it minimizes the *Total Distance* for all possible v's in Σ^*. Take note, that the above computation requires the traversal of all possible l-mers, that is Σ^l. The computation of the *Total Distance* will no longer require to check all possible starting positions, but a single pass over $\mathcal{S}$ in $O(n \cdot t)$ steps.[8] Therefore, the running time complexity of the naive MSP is $O(|\Sigma|^l \cdot n \cdot t)$.

2.2. *Approximate Gene Cluster Discovery Problem (AGCDP)*

Gene cluster is a set of genes that has been kept in the same segment in different genomes mainly for biological reasons. Some of these reasons are functional pressure, being part of biochemical network, evolutionary proximity, not enough time for enough speciation, or co-expression. In *Phylogenomics*, which involves comparative genomics, identification of gene clusters are useful.

The paper by Bergeron *et al.*, 2008[9] presents combinatorial models for gene clusters: common interval (the exact gene cluster) and max-gap (gene cluster that allows gap) as applied to either permutations or sequences (allows gene duplications and deletions). In this paper, we will tackle common interval for permutations and sequences. We first define *occurrence*.

Definition 2.3 (Occurrence[9]). *Given a set of genes $\mathcal{X}$ and a genome g represented by a string $a_1 a_2 \ldots a_k$, $k \in \mathbb{N}^+$, an occurrence of the set $\mathcal{X}$ is a substring $a_i \ldots a_j$, $i \leq j$ such that,*

(1) Both a_i and a_j belong to the set of genes $\mathcal{X}$.

(2) The set of genes $\mathcal{X}$ is contained in the multiset $\{a_i \ldots a_j\}$.

(3) If a substring of $a_i \ldots a_j$ contains no gene in $\mathcal{X}$, then its length must be less than or equal to δ, a fixed integer that represents the maximal allowed gap size.

(4) The flanking substring $a_{i-1-\delta} \ldots a_{i-1}$ and $a_{i+1} \ldots a_{j+1+\delta}$ contain no gene in $\mathcal{X}$.

To illustrate the definition of an *occurrence*, Let $\mathcal{X} = \{n, g, e\}$ and γ be the the sentence *'rearrangements of genomes involve genes and chromosomes'*, the occurrences of the set $\mathcal{X}$ with $\delta = 0$, on γ are "nge", "gene", and "gen". If we let $\delta = 1$, the occurrences are "ngemen", "gene", and "gen". Below are the gene cluster models related to the notion of common interval.

(1) **Common interval in permutations**: In this model, the genomes are assumed to be permutations of each other, and the gene cluster is composed of *common intervals* of the given set of genomes.

Definition 2.4 (Common Interval[9]). *Let P be a set of permutations on the set of genes $\mathcal{U}$. A subset of $\mathcal{U}$ is a common interval if it has an occurrence in each permutation of P without gaps.*

Consider two permutations in $P = \{g^1, g^2\}$ of the set $\mathcal{U} = \{1, 2, \ldots, 11\}$

$$g^1: \quad 1 \quad 2 \quad 3 \quad 4 \quad 5 \quad 6 \quad 7 \quad 8 \quad 9 \quad 10 \quad 11$$
$$g^2: \quad 4 \quad 2 \quad 1 \quad 3 \quad 7 \quad 8 \quad 6 \quad 5 \quad 11 \quad 9 \quad 10$$

If the cardinality of the common interval $\mathcal{X}_\mathcal{U} \subseteq \mathcal{U}$ is equal to 3, then the common intervals of g^1 and g^2 are $\{2,1,3\}$, $\{7,8,6\}$, and $\{11,9,10\}$.

(2) **Common interval in sequences**: Previous models assume that genes appear only once, which is not good because repetition and deletion of genes are expected. This is true especially in the task of comparing a set of genomes from different species. Instead of finding an exact common interval on the permutation of $\mathcal{S}$, the common interval in sequences model extends the representation of genomes to strings. We will use the same *common interval* in Definition 4, but instead of looking on permutations, we will now consider strings.

Definition 2.5 (Approximate Gene Cluster Discovery Problem[1]).
Given a multiset of genomes, more specifically ordered multiset since each element in the multiset is indexed based on order of the elements, we find a set of genes called gene clusters, where genes belonging to the set are "more or less" together in the set of genomes.

Input:

- *gene pool $\mathcal{U} = \{0,1,\ldots,N\}$, where 0 denotes non-significant genes*
- *ordered multiset of genomes $\mathcal{G} = \{ g^1, g^2, g^3, \ldots, g^t \}$, where g^i is a sequence of length n_i defined over the alphabet $\mathcal{U}$*
- *either a size range of gene cluster $[D^-, D^+]$, $D^-, D^+ \in \mathbb{N}^+$ or a constant D, $D \in \mathbb{N}^+$, such that using D^- and D^+ to define D, it is the case when $D^- = D^+$*
- *integer weights w^-, $w^+ \geq 0$, respective penalty of each missed and additional gene in an interval*

Output:

- *$\mathcal{X}^* \subset \mathcal{U}$ with $0 \notin \mathcal{X}^*$ and $D^- \leq |\mathcal{X}^*| \leq D^+$ or $|\mathcal{X}^*| = D$ such that $\mathcal{X}^*$ is the gene cluster $\mathcal{X} \subset \mathcal{U}$ that has cost function value of $min\{cost^*(\mathcal{X}, \mathcal{G}) \mid \forall \mathcal{X} \subset \mathcal{U}\}$ where $cost^*(\mathcal{X}, \mathcal{G}), cost^* : \mathcal{P}(\mathcal{U}) \times \mathcal{G} \to \mathbb{N}$ with $\mathcal{P}(\mathcal{U})$ as the power set of $\mathcal{U}$, is defined as*

$$cost^*(\mathcal{X}, \mathcal{G}) = \sum_{i=1}^{t} cost_{J_i^*}(\mathcal{X}, g^i); \tag{3}$$

and cost function $cost_{J_i^*}(\mathcal{X}, g^i)$, $cost_{J_i^*} : \mathcal{P}(\mathcal{U}) \times \mathcal{G} \to \mathbb{N}$, is given by

$$cost_{J_i^*}(\mathcal{X}, g^i) = min\{cost(\mathcal{X}, J_i) \mid \forall J_i \in \mathcal{J}_i \text{ of } g^i \in \mathcal{G}\} \tag{4}$$

where function $cost(\mathcal{X}, J_i)$, $cost : \mathcal{P}(\mathcal{U}) \times \mathcal{J}_i \to \mathbb{N}$, is stated as

$$cost(\mathcal{X}, J_i) = (w^- \times |\mathcal{X} \setminus \mathcal{G}^i_{J_i}|) + (w^+ \times |\mathcal{G}^i_{J_i} \setminus \mathcal{X}|), \tag{5}$$

$\mathcal{G}^i_{J_i}$ is the gene content of any interval J_i in g^i, $\mathcal{X} \setminus \mathcal{G}^i_{J_i}$ is the set of missing genes, $\mathcal{G}^i_{J_i} \setminus \mathcal{X}$ is the set of additional genes, and $\mathcal{J}_i$ is the set of valid intervals in g^i such that

$$\mathcal{J}_i = \{[j:k] \mid \forall\, j, k \leq n_i \,\wedge\, j \leq k \text{ given } n_i \text{ of } g^i \in \mathcal{G}\}. \tag{6}$$

- linear interval $J^*_i \in \mathcal{J}_i$ for each genome g^i, which is the J_i with cost function value of $\text{cost}_{J^*_i}(\mathcal{X}, g^i)$ associated with the $\mathcal{X}^*$ output

Algorithm 2.1. *ILP solution for the basic AGCDP.*

Input: Genomes $\mathcal{G}$, gene set cardinality range $[D^-, D^+]$, weights w^-, and w^+

Output: Gene set $\mathcal{X}$, linear interval J^*_i

(1) Tentatively set $\mathcal{X}$ to the gene set for each interval in each genome.

(2) For each genome g^i, except the one where $\mathcal{X}$ is taken from,

  (a) Compare $\mathcal{X}$ to the character set of each interval J_i in g^i,

  (b) Compute the $\text{cost}(\mathcal{X}, J_i)$ according to the number of missing and additional genes of $\mathcal{X}$ from the gene set $\mathcal{G}^i_{J_i}$ corresponding to J_i,

  (c) Pick the interval J_i in g^i, which becomes J^*_i, with $\text{cost}_{J^*_i}(\mathcal{X}, g^i)$.

(3) Return $\mathcal{X}$, that is $\mathcal{X}^*$, and J^*_i, such that $\text{cost}^*(\mathcal{X}, \mathcal{G})$ is minimum over all $\mathcal{X}$ in $\mathcal{G}$.

There are two possible output cases in AGCDP, either report the best set $\mathcal{X}$, or report each $\mathcal{X}$ for each genome g^i, where $\text{cost}^*(\mathcal{X}, \mathcal{G})$ remains below a given threshold. The detailed discussion of ILP solver as outlined in Algorithm 2.1 is discussed in Rahman and Klau, 2008.[1] If AGCDP is proven to be NP-hard, then the existence of the ILP solver shows the possibility that AGCDP may admit a PTAS.

3. Main Results

3.1. *Proof Idea*

To prove that AGCDP is NP-hard, we must show that all problems in NP are reducible to it in polynomial time, regardless whether AGCDP is in NP. Showing a polynomial-time reduction of MSP to AGCDP, is equivalent to showing that all problems in NP are polynomial-time reducible to AGCDP, because all problems in NP are polynomial-time reducible to NP-complete problems.[10]

In this reduction, we consider the unbounded alphabet case so that the transformation of the input depends on an alphabet size that grows along with the length of every sequence involved. In this case, we will show that the transformation is done in polynomial time without the fixed alphabet size term in the complexity of the transformation.

3.2. *Reduction of MSP to AGCDP*

The main component of the reduction is the transformation of input sequences $\mathcal{S}$ to a multiset of genomes $\mathcal{G}$ as discussed below.

3.2.1. *MSP Input Transformation*

The input $\mathcal{S}$ of the Median String Problem consists of t sequences, each of which is of the form $s^k = (s^k_p)_{p=1\ldots n} = s^k_1 \ldots s^k_n$ where s^k is the kth sequence, $k = 1\ldots t$, $s^k_p \in \Sigma$, and $length(s^k) = n$, for all k. Given Σ^l with l as the input parameter in MSP, let $\bar{\Sigma}$ be the alphabet used in representing each l-mer in Σ^l such that $\bar{\Sigma} = \{\lambda_1, \lambda_2, \ldots, \lambda_{|\Sigma|^l}\}$ and $\lambda_i = \alpha_1\alpha_2\ldots\alpha_l$ where $\alpha_1, \alpha_2, \ldots, \alpha_l \in \Sigma$, and $i \in \mathbb{N}^+$ is the lexicographic order of the sequence $\alpha_1\alpha_2\ldots\alpha_l$ among all possible elements of Σ^l. We will use the following notations:

- $lmers(s^k)$ denotes a set of distinct l-mers of s^k in which each l-mer has its first symbol located at every index i of s^k, $1 \leq i \leq length(s^k) - l + 1$. Through the set notation, this set is given by:

$$\{\lambda^k_i \mid \forall \text{ distinct } \lambda^k_i = \prod_{u=i}^{i+l-1} s^k_u, 1 \leq i \leq length(s^k) - l + 1, \lambda^k_i \in \Sigma^l\} \quad (7)$$

- $lmers_{\mathcal{S}}(\mathcal{S})$ denotes a set of distinct l-mers found in all sequences s^k, $\forall\, k$, $1 \leq k \leq t$, such that

$$lmers_{\mathcal{S}}(\mathcal{S}) = \bigcup_{k=1}^{t} lmers(s^k) \quad (8)$$

- $lmers_H(s^k, \Delta)$ denotes a set of distinct l-mers in $lmers(s^k)$ with minimum Hamming distance Δ, $0 \leq \Delta < l$, with respect to all elements of $lmers(s^k)$, and are not elements of sets $lmers(s^k)$ and $lmers_H(s^k, \Delta')$, $\forall\, \Delta' \neq \Delta$. The set is given by:

$$\{\lambda^{k,\Delta} \mid \forall \text{ distinct } \lambda^{k,\Delta} \in lmers_{\mathcal{S}}(\mathcal{S}) - lmers(s^k), \text{ and}$$
$$\Delta = min\{d_H(\lambda^{k,\Delta}, \lambda^k) \mid \forall\, \lambda^k \in lmers(s^k)\}\} \quad (9)$$

- $\delta(\lambda)$, $\delta : \Sigma^l \to \bar{\Sigma}$, which is a function that maps an l-mer in Σ^l to a symbol in $\bar{\Sigma}$.

Remark 3.1. Given the s^k input and the sets $lmers(s^k)$ and $lmers_H(s^k, \Delta)$, the following properties hold:

(1) $lmers(s^k) \cap (lmers_H(s^k, \Delta)$, for any $\Delta) = \phi$
(2) $\bigcap_{\Delta=1}^{l-1} lmers_H(s^k, \Delta) = \phi$
(3) $lmers(s^k) \cap \bigcap_{\Delta=1}^{l-1} lmers_H(s^k, \Delta) = \phi$
(4) $lmers(s^k) = lmers_H(s^k, 0)$ such that $\bigcap_{\Delta=0}^{l-1} lmers_H(s^k, \Delta) = \phi$

The MSP input s^k, $k \geq 1$, is transformed into ordered multiset $\bar{s}^k$ such that through the multiset sum operation:

$$\bar{s}^k = \biguplus_{m=1}^{l} \bar{s}^{k,m} \uplus \left(\biguplus_{\Delta=1}^{l-1} \biguplus_{p=1}^{l-\Delta} \bar{s}^{k,\Delta,p} \right), \tag{10}$$

where

$$\bar{s}^{k,m} = \prod_{\lambda^k \in lmers(s^k)} \delta(\lambda^k), \text{ for any } m = 1, 2, \ldots, l \tag{11}$$

and

$$\bar{s}^{k,\Delta,p} = \prod_{\lambda^{k,\Delta} \in lmers_H(s^k, \Delta)} \delta(\lambda^{k,\Delta}), \text{ for any } p = 1, 2, \ldots, l - \Delta \tag{12}$$

Alternatively, with $\Delta = 0$,

$$\bar{s}^{k,m} = \bar{s}^{k,0,p} = \prod_{\lambda^{k,0} \in lmers_H(s^k, 0)} \delta(\lambda^{k,0}), \text{ for any } p = 1, 2, \ldots, l \tag{13}$$

given $lmers(s^k) = lmers_H(s^k, 0)$ in Remark 3.1 such that

$$\bar{s}^k = \biguplus_{\Delta=0}^{l-1} \biguplus_{p=1}^{l-\Delta} \bar{s}^{k,\Delta,p} \tag{14}$$

with $\bar{s}^{k,\Delta,p}$ defined in Eq. 12.

Remark 3.2. In the $\bar{s}^k$ transformation of the MSP input s^k, there are l copies of sequence $\prod_{\lambda^k \in lmers(s^k)} \delta(\lambda^k)$ based on Eq. 11 and $l - \Delta$ copies of sequence $\prod_{\lambda^{k,\Delta} \in lmers_H(s^k, \Delta)} \delta(\lambda^{k,\Delta})$, $1 \leq \Delta \leq l - 1$, based on Eq. 12. This means that there are $l - \Delta$ copies of sequence $\prod_{\lambda^{k,\Delta} \in lmers_H(s^k, \Delta)} \delta(\lambda^{k,\Delta})$, $0 \leq \Delta \leq l - 1$, based on Eqs. 12 and 14 given any Δ.

Remark 3.3. Since sequence $\prod_{\lambda^{k,\Delta} \in lmers_H(s^k, \Delta)} \delta(\lambda^{k,\Delta})$ for a specific Δ is unique given that $\bigcap_{\Delta=0}^{l-1} lmers_H(s^k, \Delta) = \phi$ from Remark 3.1, the number of distinct sequences in $\bar{s}^k$ is l, while the total number of sequences in $\bar{s}^k$ is

$$\sum_{\Delta=0}^{l-1} \sum_{p=1}^{l-\Delta} 1 = l + l - 1 + l - 2 + \ldots + 1 = l \times (l+1)/2.$$

3.2.2. Transformation of MSP into Approximate Gene Cluster Discovery Problem (AGCDP)

Recall that the input of the Median String Problem forms a $t \times n$ matrix given t sequences of length n, denoted by $\mathcal{S}$, and the length l, $1 \leq l \leq n$, of the pattern to find; while its output is a string v^* of l nucleotides that minimizes $TotalDistance(v,\mathcal{S})$ for all $v \in \Sigma^l$. The AGCDP input and output will be modified as follows with the summary of the reduction shown in Table 1.

Input: The gene pool $\mathcal{U} = \{\lambda_1, \lambda_2 \ldots \lambda_{|\Sigma|^l}\}$ is the set of symbols in $\bar{\Sigma}$. Given that the multiset of sequences $\bar{s}^k$ is derived from s^k, $k = 1, 2, \ldots, t$, based on input $\mathcal{S}$ and l, the multiset of genomes $\mathcal{G}$ is given by:

$$\mathcal{G} = \biguplus_{k=1}^{t} \bar{s}^k = \biguplus_{k=1}^{t} (\biguplus_{m=1}^{l} \bar{s}^{k,m} \uplus (\biguplus_{\Delta=1}^{l-1} \biguplus_{p=1}^{l-\Delta} \bar{s}^{k,\Delta,p}))$$

$$= \biguplus_{k=1}^{t} (\biguplus_{\Delta=0}^{l-1} \biguplus_{p=1}^{l-\Delta} \bar{s}^{k,\Delta,p}) \tag{15}$$

based on Eqs. 10, 11, 12 and 14. Set $\mathcal{G}$ now corresponds to the transformation of $\mathcal{S}$, which will be denoted as $\bar{\mathcal{S}}$; this means $\mathcal{G} = \bar{\mathcal{S}}$. Each sequence in $\mathcal{G}$ is given by:

$$g^i = \bar{s}^{k,\Delta,p}, \tag{16}$$

where $i = (k - 1) \times (l(l + 1))/2 + \Delta(l - (\Delta - 1)) + p$, $p = 1, 2, \ldots, l - \Delta$, $\Delta = 0, 1, \ldots, l - 1$, and $k = 1, 2, \ldots, t$ using the total number of sequences in $\bar{s}^k$ from Remark 3.3.

Let J_k^* be a set of linear intervals in $\bar{s}^k$ and $J_{k,\Delta,p}^*$ be a linear interval in $\bar{s}^{k,\Delta,p}$ such that $J_{k,\Delta,p}^* \in J_k^*$, for every Δ and p. Moreover, let $cost_{J_{k,m}^*}$ be a linear interval in $\bar{s}^{k,m}$. Then the AGCDP cost of pattern $\psi \in \bar{\Sigma}$ on the set of sequences $\bar{s}^k$ is given by:

$$cost_{J_k^*}(\psi, \bar{s}^k) = \sum_{m=1}^{l} cost_{J_{k,m}^*}(\psi, \bar{s}^{k,m}) + \sum_{\Delta=1}^{l-1} \sum_{p=1}^{l-\Delta} cost_{J_{k,\Delta,p}^*}(\psi, \bar{s}^{k,\Delta,p}) \tag{17}$$

or, alternatively,

$$cost_{J_k^*}(\psi, \bar{s}^k) = \sum_{\Delta=0}^{l-1} \sum_{p=1}^{l-\Delta} cost_{J_{k,\Delta,p}^*}(\psi, \bar{s}^{k,\Delta,p}) \tag{18}$$

with $\bar{s}^{k,m}, \bar{s}^{k,\Delta,p} \in \bar{s}^k$ defined in Eqs. 11 and 12, respectively. From Eq. 4 with $g^i \in \bar{s}^k$ defined in Eq. 16,

$$cost_{J_i^*}(\psi, g^i) = min\{cost(\psi, J_i) \mid \forall J_i \in \mathcal{J}_i \text{ of } g^i \in \bar{s}^k \text{ and } g^i \in \mathcal{G} \text{ such that}$$
$$g^i = \bar{s}^{k,\Delta,p}, i = (k-1) \times (l(l+1))/2 + \Delta(l - (\Delta - 1)) + p,$$
$$p = 1, 2, \ldots, l - \Delta, \Delta = 0, 1, \ldots, l - 1, k = 1, 2, \ldots, t\}. \quad (19)$$

Equation 17 holds since $\bar{s}^{k,m}$, for every m, and $\bar{s}^{k,\Delta,p}$, for every Δ and p, are separate sequences so that through Eq. 3:

$$cost^*(\psi, \mathcal{G}) = \sum_{k=1}^{t} cost_{J_k^*}(\psi, \bar{s}^k) = \sum_{k=1}^{t} \sum_{\Delta=0}^{l-1} \sum_{p=1}^{l-\Delta} cost_{J_{k,\Delta,p}^*}(\psi, \bar{s}^{k,\Delta,p}) \quad (20)$$

Based on Remark 3.3 and considering t sequences in MSP, there will be $tl \times (l+1)/2$ genomes in AGCDP. Note the length of every genome in AGCDP varies unlike the uniform sequence lengths in MSP. The size range for the reference gene $\mathcal{X}$ is $[1,1]$ such that $|\mathcal{X}| = 1$ (or $D = 1$), and the integer weights w^- and w^+, respective cost of each missed and additional gene in an interval, will all be set to 1.

Output: Find $\mathcal{X}^* \subset \mathcal{U}$ with $0 \notin \mathcal{X}^*$ and $|\mathcal{X}^*| = 1$, and linear interval J_i^* for each genome associated with $\mathcal{X}$ that has $min\{cost^*(\mathcal{X}, \mathcal{G}) \mid \forall \mathcal{X} \subset \mathcal{U}\}$, where $cost^*(\mathcal{X}, \mathcal{G})$ is defined in Eq. 3. The reference gene set $\mathcal{X}$ will correspond to the string v^* of l nucleotides in MSP.

3.2.3. *Correctness of the Reduction*

Lemma 3.1. *If $\psi \in \bar{\Sigma}$ has a match in $\bar{s}^k$, then it only occurs in sequence $\bar{s}^{k,\Delta,p}$, for a particular value Δ, $0 \leq \Delta \leq l-1$ and for all $p = 1, 2, \ldots, l - \Delta$.*

Proof. Given the equation for $\bar{s}^{k,\Delta,p}$ in Eq. 12, $\lambda^{k,\Delta} \in lmers_H(s^k, \Delta)$ such that $\delta(\lambda^{k,\Delta}) \in \bar{\Sigma}$. Since the elements of $lmers_H(s^k, \Delta)$, for every Δ, $0 \leq \Delta \leq l - 1$, are unique given Remark 3.1, ψ will have a match among the elements of the set $lmers_H(s^k, \Delta)$ for a unique Δ value. $\square$

Lemma 3.2. *If $\psi \in \bar{\Sigma}$ does not exist in $\bar{s}^k$, then*

$$cost_{J_k^*}(\psi, \bar{s}^k) = (w^- + w^+) \sum_{\Delta=0}^{l-1} (l - \Delta).$$

MSP	AGCDP
$\mathcal{S} = s^k, k = 1 \ldots t$	$\bar{\mathcal{S}} = \mathcal{G} = \biguplus_{k=1}^{t}(\biguplus_{\Delta=0}^{l-1}\biguplus_{p=1}^{l-\Delta} \bar{s}^{k,\Delta,p})$ (see Eq. 15)
s^k	$\bar{s}^k = \biguplus_{\Delta=0}^{l-1}\biguplus_{p=1}^{l-\Delta} \bar{s}^{k,\Delta,p}$
l	$\bar{l} = |\mathcal{X}| = 1$
t	$\bar{t} = tl \times (l+1)/2$
Σ	$\bar{\Sigma} = \{\delta(\lambda) \mid \forall\, \lambda \in \Sigma^l\},\, \delta : \Sigma^l \to \bar{\Sigma}$

Proof. If ψ does not exist in $\bar{s}^k$, then it does not have a match in sequence $\bar{s}^{k,\Delta,p}$, for all Δ. Note that $|\mathcal{X}|$ in the transformation is restricted to one. Since comparing every symbol in $\bar{s}^{k,\Delta,p}$ (in this case $|J_{k,\Delta,p}| = 1$) with ψ results to a mismatch, the number of missing genes in the linear interval is one; and the number of additional genes is also one. If $|J_{k,\Delta,p}| > 1$, the number of additional genes with respect to $\mathcal{X} = \psi$ is always greater than one, and the number of missing genes is always equal to one given that $|\mathcal{X}| = 1$. This results to an increase in AGCDP cost. Thus, the minimum is found at $|J_{k,\Delta,p}| = 1$, and $cost_{J^*_{k,\Delta,p}}(\psi, \bar{s}^{k,\Delta,p}) = w^- + w^+$. From Remark 3.2, there are $l - \Delta$ copies of $\bar{s}^{k,\Delta,p}$ so that, for all p in $\bar{s}^{k,\Delta,p}$, the cost is $(w^- + w^+)(l - \Delta)$. Considering all Δ, $0 \leq \Delta \leq l - 1$, the total AGCDP cost of ψ in $\bar{s}^k$ is $(w^- + w^+)\sum_{\Delta=0}^{l-1}(l - \Delta)$. $\qquad\square$

Lemma 3.3. *If $\psi \in \bar{\Sigma}$ has a match in $\bar{s}^k$, then $cost_{J^*_{k,\Delta,p}}(\psi, \bar{s}^{k,\Delta,p}) = 0$, for a particular Δ, $0 \leq \Delta \leq l - 1$, and for all $p = 1, 2, \ldots, l - \Delta$ with $|J_{k,\Delta,p}| = 1$.*

Proof. A match in sequence $\bar{s}^k$ for ψ means that there is a symbol in sequence $\bar{s}^{k,\Delta,p}$, for all p, that matches ψ, in this case $|J_{k,\Delta,p}| = 1$, such that the number of missing and additional genes is equal to zero. Since all symbols in sequence $\bar{s}^{k,\Delta,p}$ is unique given the definition of $lmers_H(s^k, \Delta)$, if $|J_{k,\Delta,p}| > 1$, the number of additional genes is greater than or equal to one. Given Lemma 3.1, this means that $cost_{J^*_{k,\Delta,p}}(\psi, \bar{s}^{k,\Delta,p}) = 0$ for a particular Δ, $0 \leq \Delta \leq l - 1$, and for all $p = 1, 2, \ldots, l - \Delta$. $\qquad\square$

Lemma 3.4. *If $\psi \in \bar{\Sigma}$ has a match in $\bar{s}^k$, then*

$$cost_{J^*_k}(\psi, \bar{s}^k) = (w^- + w^+)\sum_{\Delta=0}^{l-1}(l - \Delta) - (w^- + w^+)(l - \Delta')$$

where $\Delta' = min\{d_H(\delta^{-1}(\psi), \lambda) \mid \forall\, \lambda \in lmers(s^k)\}$.

Proof. From Lemma 3.2, AGCDP cost is $(w^- + w^+)\sum_{\Delta=0}^{l-1}(l-\Delta)$ if ψ has no match in $\bar{s}^k$. If ψ has a match in $\bar{s}^k$, then it has a match in sequence $\bar{s}^{k,\Delta',p}$, for a particular value Δ', $0 \le \Delta' \le l-1$. Based on Lemma 3.3, AGCDP cost is zero if ψ has a match in $\bar{s}^{k,\Delta',p}$, for a particular Δ' and for all p; thus, the cost is zero for $l - \Delta'$ sequences given Remark 3.2. Exclusion of these sequences from the sequences where ψ has no match gives an AGCDP cost of $(w^- + w^+)\sum_{\Delta=0}^{l-1}(l-\Delta) - (w^- + w^+)(l-\Delta')$. $\square$

Lemma 3.5. *Regardless of whether $\psi \in \bar{\Sigma}$ has a match in $\bar{s}^k$,*

$$cost_{J_k^*}(\psi, \bar{s}^k) = (w^- + w^+)\sum_{\Delta=0}^{l-1}(l-\Delta) - (w^- + w^+)(l-\Delta'), 0 \le \Delta' \le l,$$

where $\Delta' = min\{d_H(\delta^{-1}(\psi), \lambda) \mid$ for all $\lambda \in lmers(s^k)\}$.

Proof. If ψ has no match in $\bar{s}^k$, $\Delta' = l$ since ψ has no match among the elements in $lmers(\bar{s}^k, \Delta)$, for all Δ, $0 \le \Delta < l$, in which sequence $\bar{s}^{k,\Delta,p}$ is derived. If ψ has a match, then Lemma 3.4 applies. In the case when ψ has no match in $\bar{s}^k$, same formula from Lemma 3.4 applies since the $(w^- + w^+)(l - \Delta')$ component becomes zero when $\Delta' = l$ such that the formula in Lemma 3.2 is obtained. $\square$

Lemma 3.6. *Given the MSP input S and l, then for any $\psi \in \bar{\Sigma}$ with $w^- + w^+ > 0$, $\mathcal{X}^* = \psi$ in AGCDP if and only if $v^* = \delta^{-1}(\psi)$ in MSP, $\delta^{-1}(\psi) \in \Sigma^l$.*

Proof. ($\Rightarrow$) The AGCDP cost for ψ is generalized in Lemma 3.5. Since $\delta^{-1}(\psi) \in lmers_H(s^k, \Delta')$, $s^k \in S$, $1 \le k \le t$, it follows that $\Delta' = min\{d_H(\delta^{-1}(\psi), \lambda), \forall \lambda \in lmers(s^k)\}$, $0 \le \Delta' \le l$. If $w^- + w^+ > 0$, the magnitude of the $(w^- + w^+)(l - \Delta')$ term in Lemma 3.4 cost equation decreases as Δ' increases such that $cost_{J_k^*}(\psi, \bar{s}^k)$ increases as Δ' increases. In this case, if $\mathcal{X}^* = \psi$, then

$$\sum_{k=1}^{t} cost^*(\psi, \bar{s}^k) = min\left\{ \sum_{k=1}^{t} cost_{J_k^*}(\mathcal{X}, \bar{s}^k) \mid \text{ for all } \mathcal{X} \subset \mathcal{U} \right\}$$

$$= \sum_{k=1}^{t}\{ (w^- + w^+)\sum_{\Delta=0}^{l-1}(l-\Delta) - (w^- + w^+)(l-\Delta'),$$

$$\Delta' = min\{d_H(\delta^{-1}(\psi), \lambda) \mid \forall\lambda \in lmers(s^k)\}, 0 \le \Delta' < l\}$$

based on Lemma 3.5 when applied to the transformed sequences in $\bar{S}$. Therefore, regardless of whether ψ has a match in $\bar{s}^k$, $k = 1, 2, \ldots, t$,

$cost_{J_k^*}(\psi, \bar{s}^k)$ is dependent on Δ' given that ψ occurs only in $\bar{s}^{k,\Delta',p} \in \bar{s}^k$, for all p, which are all identical sequences. Given the equation for Δ' in Lemma 3.4 and 3.5, if the Hamming distance of $\delta^{-1}(\psi)$ is minimized with respect to every sequence s^k, then the Total Hamming Distance$(\delta^{-1}(\psi), r)$ from Eq. 1, for a particular alignment $\mathcal{A}(r)$, is minimum with respect to all possible values for r. This is true with Δ' in which the minimum Hamming distance of $\delta^{-1}(\psi)$ with respect to all l-mers of s^k is obtained given that $\bar{r}^k$ of Eq. 1 is an l-mer that corresponds to a particular starting position r^k in sequence s^k. Thus, Total Distance$(\delta^{-1}(\psi), \mathcal{S})$ based on Eq. 2 is obtained so that $v^* = \delta^{-1}(\psi)$.

($\Leftarrow$) Given that $v^* = \delta^{-1}(\psi)$, $min\{$Total Hamming Distance$(\delta^{-1}(\psi), r) \mid \forall r \}$ is therefore obtained. This means that for every sequence s^k, $1 \leq k \leq t$, $d_H(\delta^{-1}(\psi), \bar{r}^k)$ is the minimum Hamming distance with respect to all possibilities for $\bar{r}^k$, which is an l-mer in s^k. The corresponding transformation of s^k in AGCDP is an ordered multiset of sequences $\bar{s}^k$ and the corresponding transformation for $\delta^{-1}(\psi)$ is ψ. Since $cost_{J_k^*}(\psi, \bar{s}^k)$ given in Lemma 3.5 is dependent on and directly proportional to Δ', where Δ' is the minimum Hamming distance of ψ with respect to all l-mers in $lmers(s^k)$, Total Distance$(\delta^{-1}(\psi), \mathcal{S})$ in MSP therefore corresponds to $cost^*(\psi, \mathcal{G})$ in AGCDP, which is the sum of $cost_{J_k^*}(\psi, \bar{s}^k)$, for all k, given in Eq. 20. □

Lemma 3.7. *Given MSP input $\mathcal{S}$ and l, the transformation of $\mathcal{S}$ into $\bar{\mathcal{S}}$ can be obtained in polynomial time.*

Proof. Given each sequence $s^k \in \mathcal{S}$ of length n, $|lmers(s^k)| \leq n - l + 1$ and $|lmers_{\mathcal{S}}(\mathcal{S})| \leq t(n - l + 1)$. Determining the membership in $lmers_H(s^k, \Delta)$ involves computation of the Hamming distance of every element in $lmers_{\mathcal{S}}(\mathcal{S}) - lmers(s^k)$ with respect to every element in $lmers(s^k)$. It is known that $|lmers_{\mathcal{S}}(\mathcal{S}) - lmers(s^k)| \leq (t - 1)(n - l + 1)$ such that obtaining $lmers_H(s^k, \Delta)$ takes $(t - 1)(n - l + 1)^2$ operations. For all Δ, $1 \leq \Delta \leq l - 1$, the total number of operations is $(t - 1)(n - l + 1)^2(l - 1)$ and combined with the number of operations to obtain $lmers(s^k)$ gives $(t - 1)(n - l + 1)^2(l - 1) + n - l + 1$. Generating copies of the sequences, given the total number of sequences in $\bar{s}^k$ from Remark 3.3, takes at most $nl \times (l+1)/2$ operations. Let N be the combined length of all sequences in $\mathcal{S}$ such that $N = t \times n$. Considering the key operations in s^k transformation, $\forall k$, the total number of operations is $t \times ((t - 1)(n - l + 1)^2(l - 1) + n - l + 1) + (tnl \times (l + 1)/2)$, which is $O(N^{O(1)})$ given that $1 \leq l \leq n$. □

Theorem 3.1. *AGCDP with unbounded alphabet is NP-hard.*

Proof. Given the MSP input transformation to AGCDP input in Eq. 15, the proof follows from the correctness of the reduction in Lemma 3.6 and the polynomial-time transformation of the input shown in Lemma 3.7. □

4. Conclusion

We have presented a reduction of MSP to AGCDP, and then we have shown that the transformation made runs in polynomial time under the unbounded alphabet. We have also proven the correctness of the reduction by proving the correspondence between MSP total distance and AGCDP cost for all input instances. Given the polynomial-time reduction of MSP to AGCDP, AGCDP with unbounded alphabet is therefore NP-hard.

References

1. S. Rahmann and G. Klau, *Integer Linear Programming Techniques for Discovering Approximate Gene Clusters*, in *Bioinformatics Algorithm: Techniques and Applications*, 2008.
2. C. de la Higuera and F. Casacuberta, Topology of strings: Median string is np-complete, *Theor. Comput. Sci.* **230**, 39 (1999).
3. F. Nicolas and E. Rivals, Complexities of the centre and median string problems, in *Proc. 14th Annual Symposium on Combinatorial Pattern Matching*, 2003.
4. M. Fellows, J. Gramm and R. Niedermeier, On the parameterized intractability of motif search problems, *Combinatorica* **26**, 141 (2006).
5. M. Li, B. Ma and L. Wang, *Journal of Computer and System Sciences* **65**, 73 (2002).
6. D. Marx, Closest substring problems with small distances, *SIAM J. Comput.* **38**, 1382 (2008).
7. G. Cabunducan, J. Clemente, R. Relator and H. Adorna, Approximate gene cluster discovery problem is np-hard, in *Proc. National Conference on Information Technology Education*, 2011.
8. *An Introduction to Bioinformatics Algorithms* (Massachusetts Institute of Techology, 2004).
9. A. Bergeron, C. Chauve and Y. Gingras, *Formal Models of Gene Clusters*, in *Bioinformatics Algorithm: Techniques and Applications*, 2008.
10. *Introduction to the Theory of Computation*, 2nd edn. (Massachusetts Institute of Techology, 2007).

WEAK BISIMULATION BETWEEN TWO
BIOGEOCHEMICAL CYCLES

J. B. CLEMENTE* and H. A. ADORNA†

Algorithms and Complexity Laboratory,
Department of Computer Science,
University of the Philippines Diliman
* E-mail: jbclemente@up.edu.ph
†hnadorna@up.edu.ph

J. J. S. VILLAR

Scientific Computing Laboratory, Department of Computer Science,
University of the Philippines Diliman
E-mail: justine.villar@up.edu.ph

In this paper, we show that the two biogeochemical processes, carbon and nitrogen cycles are weakly bisimilar or weakly equivalent. We model each process as labeled transition system (LTS), where transitions between Carbon and Nitrogen states are movements from different compartment of Earth. We showed that there exist a binary relation S over the states of the two systems, such that one weakly simulates the other with respect to their changes in location.

Keywords: Bisimulation; Biogeochemical Cycles; Carbon Cycle; Nitrogen Cycle.

1. Introduction

Bisimulation, a binary relation between two communicating systems, is considered as one of the most important concepts in concurrency theory, which studies a family of simultaneously evolving components that interacts (i.e., communicates) synchronously. Roughly defined, a bisimulation is a binary relation between labeled transition systems (LTS), with an associated system which behave (i.e., simulates) the other system.[4] Moreover, the bisimulation equality, called bisimilarity, is the most studied form of behavioral equality for processes as it is used to abstract from certain details of the systems of interest.[4]

Bisimulation is widely applied to various fields of computer science, but not limited to, functional and object-oriented languages, data structures, domains, databases, compiler optimization, program analysis, verification, and others. In this paper, the authors attempt to apply the concepts in concurrency theory to two biogeochemical processes to provide preliminary analyses, as well as predictions on the biological systems of interest.

A biogeochemical cycle is defined as a pathway by which a chemical element or molecule moves through both biotic (biosphere) and abiotic (lithosphere, atmosphere, and hydrosphere) compartments of Earth. This interests the scientists as these cycles significantly affect the biotic components (plants and animals) as they draw carbon dioxide and nitrogen (in plants) to perform bodily processes. The exchange of chemical nutrients impact some of the Earth's compartments as some of these release more of the nutrient or absorbed by a compartment faster, which may harm several interacting components involved in the cycle. Most studies intend to show how changing climate alter the carbon and nitrogen cycles, and vice-versa. Another interesting fact is that the starting state of the cycle is the gaseous state of the elements (carbon and nitrogen), and is absorbed by the plants and animals as a first chemical process. This may provide some lead on how different forms of carbon and nitrogen transfer between Earth's compartment.

The main goal of this paper is to draw several theoretical hypotheses about the behavior of the carbon and nitrogen cycles, given the location of the chemical forms of carbon and nitrogen.

2. Carbon Cycle

Carbon, the fourth most abundant element in the Universe, is both the foundation of all life on Earth and the source of the majority of energy consumed by human civilization.[7] Most of Earth's carbon – about 65,500 billion metric tons – is stored in rocks, and the rest is in the ocean, atmosphere, plants, soil, and fossil fuels.

Its flow, called the carbon cycle,[5] between each Earth's reservoirs has been heavily studied by ecologists, climatologists and marine scientists, among others, as it directly affects global temperature, climate ecological change. The imbalance of carbon between the biotic and abiotic compartments primarily harm the different living things because excess carbon in the atmosphere warms the planet and helps plants on land grow more. Moreover, excess carbon in the ocean makes the water more acidic, putting marine life in danger.

Note that carbon takes different chemical forms all through out the carbon cycle, in which the important forms considered in this paper are the following:

- *pure carbon* (C) – present commonly in the Earth's lithosphere
- *carbon monoxide* (CO) – present in the Earth's atmosphere
- *carbon dioxide* (CO_2) – present in the Earth's atmosphere
- *methane* (CH_4) – present in the Earth's atmosphere
- *glucose* $((CH_2O)_6)$ – present in the Earth's biosphere

Also, the processes involved in the carbon cycle are summarized below:

- Photosynthesis
- Respiration
- Decomposition
- Volcanic activity
- Erosion
- Deposition
- Diffusion
- Industrial Activities

Furthermore, Fig. 1 illustrates the flow of carbon in the different biogeochemical spheres.

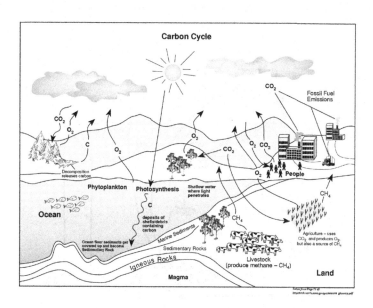

Fig. 1.   The Carbon Cycle

3. Nitrogen Cycle

Nitrogen is a colorless, odorless, tasteless, and mostly inert gas at standard conditions. It constitutes 78.09% by volume of the Earth's atmosphere. Nitrogen is a required nutrient for all living organisms to produce a number of complex organic molecules like amino acids, the building blocks of proteins, and nucleic acids, including DNA and RNA. In ecology, the abundance of nitrogen is measured to identify the amount of food that can be grown in a piece of land.[1]

Nitrogen can take different forms all through out the nitrogen cycle. Aside from the organic nitrogen (N) which is present inside living organisms, nitrogen can take the following molecular forms, alongside with the location where they are present.

- *Inorganic nitrogen (N_2)* - present in the Earth's atmosphere
- *Ammonium (NH_4^+)* - present in the Earth's lithosphere
- *Ammonia (NH_3)* - present in the Earth's atmosphere
- *Nitrite (NO_2^-)* - present in the Earth's lithosphere
- *Nitrate (NO_3^-)*- present in the Earth's lithosphere
- *Nitrous oxide (N_2O)* - present in the Earth's atmosphere
- *Nitric oxide (NO)* - present in the Earth's atmosphere

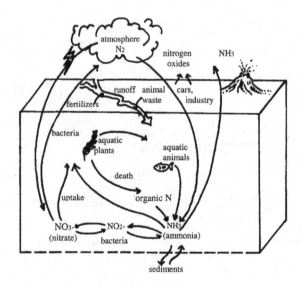

Fig. 2. Nitrogen Cycle

Inorganic nitrogen (N_2) is abundant in the Earth's atmosphere. However, it is unusable in its current form. The inorganic nitrogen undergoes nitrogen fixation through lightning and nitrogen fixing bacteria to become usable. In the atmosphere, lightning converts N_2 to NO, and when it precipitates the NO in the atmosphere reach the ground as nitrates NO_3. Nitrogen fixing bacteria that are present in roots of leguminous plants absorbs N_2 in the atmosphere and releases ammonium (NH_4), which is then converted to ammonia (NH_3). Industrial processes can also convert N_2 to either nitrate or nitrite through combustion.

Nitrogen from the soil is absorbed by plants through the process of assimilation. The nitrogen from living organisms such as plants and animals are released to the Earth's lithosphere during decomposition and egestion, nitrogen molecules are converted into ammonium and ammonia. The process is called ammonification. The complete illustration of processes involved in Nitrogen cycle is shown in Fig. 2. A detailed list of transition from one nitrogen state to another is presented in Section 4.2.

4. Labeled Transition System Construction

4.1. *Preliminaries*

The relevant terms used in the following sections are provided below:

Definition 4.1 (Labeled Transition System (LTS)). *A labeled transition system (LTS) over Act is a pair $(\mathcal{Q}, \mathcal{T})$ consisting of*

- *a set $\mathcal{Q}$ of states*
- *a ternary relation $\mathcal{T} \subseteq \mathcal{Q} \times Act \times \mathcal{Q}$, known as the transition function.*

If $(q, \alpha, q') \in \mathcal{T}$ we write $q \xrightarrow{\alpha} q'$, and we call q the source and q' the target of the transition.

Definition 4.2 (Strong Simulation). *Let $(\mathcal{Q}, \mathcal{T})$ be an LTS, and let $\mathcal{S}$ be a binary relation over $\mathcal{Q}$. Then $\mathcal{S}$ is a strong simulation over $(\mathcal{Q}, \mathcal{T})$ if, whenever $p\mathcal{S}q$,*

if $p \xrightarrow{\alpha} p'$ then there exists $q' \in \mathcal{Q}$ such that $q \xrightarrow{\alpha} q'$ and $p'\mathcal{S}q'$.

Definition 4.3 (Converse of a Binary Relation). *The converse $\mathcal{R}^{-1}$ of any binary relation $\mathcal{R}$ is the set of pairs (y, x) such that $(x, y) \in \mathcal{R}$.*

Definition 4.4 (Strong Bisimulation, Strong Equivalence). *A binary relation $\mathcal{S}$ over $\mathcal{Q}$ is said to be a strong bisimulation over the LTS $(\mathcal{Q}, \mathcal{T})$ if both $\mathcal{S}$ and its converse are simulations. We say that p and q are* *strongly bisimilar or strongly equivalent, written $p \sim q$, if there exists a strong bisimulation S such that pSq.*

Definition 4.5 (Experiment Relations). *The relations $\Rightarrow$ and $\stackrel{s}{\Rightarrow}$, for any $s \in Act^*$, are defined as follows:*

(1) $P \Rightarrow Q$ means that there is a sequence of zero or more reactions $P \rightarrow \ldots \rightarrow Q$. Formally, $\Rightarrow \stackrel{def}{=} \rightarrow^*$, the transitive closure of $\rightarrow$.

(2) Let $s = \alpha_1 \ldots \alpha_n$. Then $P \stackrel{s}{\Rightarrow} Q$ means $P \Rightarrow \stackrel{\alpha_1}{\rightarrow} P_1 \ldots \Rightarrow \stackrel{\alpha_n}{\rightarrow} P_n \Rightarrow Q$. Formally, $\stackrel{s}{\Rightarrow} \stackrel{def}{=} \Rightarrow \stackrel{\alpha_1}{\rightarrow} \Rightarrow \ldots \Rightarrow \stackrel{\alpha_n}{\rightarrow} \Rightarrow$.

Definition 4.6 (Weak Bisimulation). *Let S be a binary relation over $\mathcal{P}$. Then S is said to be a weak simulation if, whenever PSQ,*

if $P \stackrel{e}{\Rightarrow} P'$ then there exists $Q' \in \mathcal{P}$ such that $Q \stackrel{e}{\Rightarrow} Q'$ and $P'SQ'$.

We say that Q weakly simulates P if there exists a weak simulation S such that PSQ.

4.2. The Nitrogen and Carbon Cycle LTSs

4.2.1. *Assumptions.*

In this paper, we assume the following

- We only considered presence of carbon and nitrogen (with its chemical by-products) in the **atmosphere, lithosphere, hydrosphere** and **biosphere**, as well as man-made industrial influences.
- We only considered major chemical compounds that mainly participate in the carbon and nitrogen cycles.
- We also assume that other chemical compounds (without carbon/nitrogen) involved in the reaction (LHS and RHS of the equation) are disregarded in the construction of the LTS. For example, in the chemical process of photosynthesis, given by $CO_2 + H_2O + $ (Nutrients) $\rightarrow (CH_2O)_6 + O_2$, we only considered CO_2 and $(CH_2O)_6$ to participate in the transition.

4.2.2. *Carbon Cycle LTS.*

The LTS for carbon cycle is $(\mathcal{Q}_c, \mathcal{T}_c)$, where the set $\mathcal{Q}_c$ includes the different forms of carbon, i.e. $\mathcal{Q}_c = \{$C, CO, CO_2, CH_4, $(CH_2O)_6\}$ and $\mathcal{T}_c = \mathcal{Q} \times x \times \mathcal{Q}$ with $x \in Act_c \subseteq L_c \times L_c$, $L_c = \{a, l, h, b, i\}$. Here a, l, h, b and i corresponds to the atmosphere, lithosphere, hydrosphere, biosphere, and the industrial domain. In the construction of transitions, x is stated without the parentheses (instead of the ordered pair notation) for simplicity, i.e., x is written as yz instead of (y, z).

The transitions of the LTS are derived from the chemical processes involved in conversion of one form carbon to the other. Since we are interested in the location of the chemical nutrient as it changes its form, the label of the actions are represented as the change of locations. The following enumerates the transitions of the LTS involved in each process of the carbon cycle.

- photosynthesis:
  $CO_2 \xrightarrow{ab} (CH_2O)_6$
- respiration, decomposition:
  $(CH_2O)_6 \xrightarrow{ba} CO_2$
- photosynthesis:
  $CO_2 \xrightarrow{hb} (CH_2O)_6$
- respiration, decomposition:
  $(CH_2O)_6 \xrightarrow{ba} CH_4$
- decomposition: $(CH_2O)_6 \xrightarrow{bl} C$
- decomposition:
  $(CH_2O)_6 \xrightarrow{bl} CO_2$
- disintegration: $CO_2 \xrightarrow{ll} C$
- volcanic activity: $C \xrightarrow{la} CO$
- volcanic activity: $C \xrightarrow{la} CO_2$
- combustion: $C \xrightarrow{la} CH_4$

- combustion: $(CH_2O)_6 \xrightarrow{ba} CH_4$
- erosion: $C \xrightarrow{lh} C$
- deposition: $C \xrightarrow{hl} C$
- diffusion: $CO_2 \xrightarrow{ah} CO_2$
- diffusion: $CO_2 \xrightarrow{ha} CO_2$
- diffusion: $CO_2 \xrightarrow{la} CO_2$
- industrial emission: $C \xrightarrow{ia} CO$
- industrial emission: $C \xrightarrow{ia} CO_2$
- industrial emission: $C \xrightarrow{ia} CH_4$

In total, we have 19 transitions. Using the set of states and the list of transitions derived from the processes in the carbon cycle, as stated above, Fig. 3 shows the complete labeled transition system diagram.

4.2.3. Nitrogen Cycle LTS.

The LTS for nitrogen cycle is $(\mathcal{Q}_n, \mathcal{T}_n)$, where the set $\mathcal{Q}_n$ includes the different forms of nitrogen, i.e.

$$\mathcal{Q}_n = \{N, N_2, NO, N_2O, NO_x, NO_2^-, NO_3^-, NH_3, NH_4^+\}$$

and $\mathcal{T}_n = \mathcal{Q} \times x \times \mathcal{Q}$ with $x \in Act_n \subseteq L_n \times L_n$, $L_n = \{a, l, b\}$. Note that, $L_n \subset L_c$, because several locations such as h, b, and $i \in L_c$ are not considered in the nitrogen cycle. Biological processes for three different location, i.e. atmosphere, biosphere, and lithosphere were only considered in

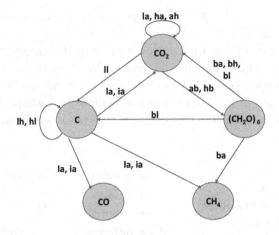

Fig. 3.   Carbon Cycle LTS

the LTS. The transitions of the LTS are derived from the chemical processes involved in conversion of one nitrogen form to the other.

The transition labels of the actions follows our convention presented in the previous subsection. The following enumerates the transitions of the LTS involved in each process of the nitrogen cycle.

- Nitrogen Fixation
  - lightning: $N_2 \xrightarrow{aa} NO$
  - precipitation: $NO \xrightarrow{al} NO_3^-$
  - nitrogen fixing bacteria:
    $N_2 \xrightarrow{ab} N$
  - nitrogen fixing bacteria:
    $N \xrightarrow{ba} NH_3$
  - combustion: $N_2 \xrightarrow{aa} NH_3$
  - combustion: $N_2 \xrightarrow{aa} NO_x$
- Assimilation
  - $NH_3 \xrightarrow{ab} N$
  - $NO_3 \xrightarrow{lb} N$
  - $NH_4^+ \xrightarrow{lb} N$

- Ammonification
  - $N \xrightarrow{bl} NH_4^+$
  - $NH_4^+ \xrightarrow{la} NH_3$
- Nitrification
  - $NH_4^+ \xrightarrow{ll} NO_2^-$
  - $NO_2^- \xrightarrow{ll} NO_3^-$
- Denitrification
  - $NO_3^- \xrightarrow{la} N_2$
- Ammonium Oxidation
  - $NO_2^- \xrightarrow{la} N_2$
  - $NH_4^+ \xrightarrow{la} N_2$

Using the set of states we previously defined and the list of transitions derived from the processes of nitrogen cycle. Figure 4 shows the complete labeled transition system diagram.

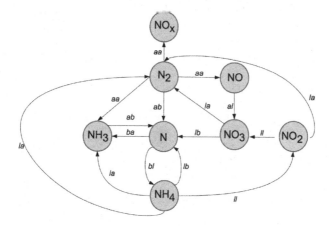

Fig. 4.   Nitrogen Cycle LTS

4.2.4. *LTS with Merged State and Transition Spaces.*

In order to use the definition of bisimulations presented in Section 2, we define a new LTS $(\mathcal{Q}, \mathcal{T})$, with $\mathcal{Q} = \mathcal{Q}_c \cup \mathcal{Q}_n$ and $\mathcal{T} = \mathcal{T}_c \cup \mathcal{T}_n$. The relation $\mathcal{S}$ will be defined over the set $\mathcal{Q}$. Since we would like to assess the equivalence of nitrogen and carbon cycle, we will not consider a pair of molecules obtained from the same subsystem.

5. Reduction of Derived LTS

Note that we have two different set of actions Act_c and Act_n involved in both LTS. This is primarily because molecules of carbon and nitrogen thrive in different locations all through out the cycle. For instance, majority of carbon molecules are produced in hydrosphere while usable nitrogen molecules are produced mainly in the atmosphere and biosphere. In order to compare two different systems, we obtained a reduced versions of each LTS such that we can ignore several transitions involving actions that are not common to both. We can look at the reduced LTSs as restricted versions of the two LTSs with respect to common locations of nitrogen and carbon molecules.

In order to do so, we derived the dual of the LTS as shown in Fig. 5. The states in the corresponding LTS are the different locations of carbon and nitrogen molecules. The transition labels between two locations are represented by an ordered pair of molecules where there exists a process that converts one to the another in the corresponding biogeochemical process. It is shown from Fig. 5 that not all states in the LTS is present to the other. From this two LTS, we obtained a reduced LTS where they contain

58

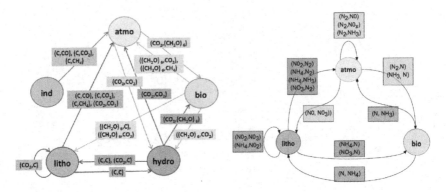

Fig. 5.   Carbon Cycle and Nitrogen Cycle LTS with location as states

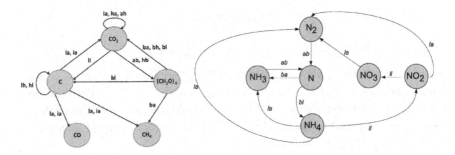

Fig. 6.   Reduced Carbon Cycle and Nitrogen Cycle LTS

the same transitions. The resulting carbon and nitrogen cycle LTS, with transitions common to both cycles are shown in Fig. 6.

Note that the reduction involved removing processes or transitions involved in each of the system, instead of collapsing several processes into one to eliminate actions not common to both. This latter type of reduction is not considered in the study because we would like to treat each transition as an independent process, i.e. we do not impose ordering in the processes involved. We also intend to preserve the integrity (i.e., natural occurrence) of the processes involved in both biogeochemical processes so that the subsequent analyses will be as sound as possible.

6. Discussion

6.1. *Construction of $\mathcal{S}$*

Now that we have the both LTS constructed in such a way that they share the same actions, we try to find a set $\mathcal{S} = \{(p,q)|p \in \mathcal{Q}_c, q \in \mathcal{Q}_n\}$ that

Table 1. List of all transition pairs derived from the reduced Nitrogen and Carbon cycle LTSs with the same action labels.

$(\mathbf{p}, \mathbf{q}) \rightarrow (\mathbf{p}', \mathbf{q}')$		$(\mathbf{p}, \mathbf{q}) \rightarrow (\mathbf{p}', \mathbf{q}')$	
$(CO_2, NO_2) \rightarrow (C, NO_3)$	(1)	$(C, NO_3) \rightarrow (CH_4, N_2)$	(14)
$(CO_2, NH_4) \rightarrow (C, NO_2)$	(2)	$(CO_2, NH_4) \rightarrow (CO_2, N_2)$	(15)
$(C, NH_4) \rightarrow (CO, N_2)$	(3)	$(CO_2, NO_2) \rightarrow (CO_2, N_2)$	(16)
$(C, NO_2) \rightarrow (CO, N_2)$	(4)	$(CO_2, NH_4) \rightarrow (CO_2, NH_3)$	(17)
$(C, NH_4) \rightarrow (CO, NH_3)$	(5)	$(CO_2, NO_3) \rightarrow (CO_2, N_2)$	(18)
$(C, NO_3) \rightarrow (CO, N_2)$	(6)	$(CO_2, N_2) \rightarrow ((CH_2O)_6, N)$	(19)
$(C, NH_4) \rightarrow (CO_2, N_2)$	(7)	$(CO_2, NO_3) \rightarrow ((CH_2O)_6, N)$	(20)
$(C, NO_2) \rightarrow (CO_2, N_2)$	(8)	$(CO_2, NH_3) \rightarrow ((CH_2O)_6, N)$	(21)
$(C, NH_4) \rightarrow (CO_2, NH_3)$	(9)	$((CH_2O)_6, N) \rightarrow (CO_2, NH_3)$	(22)
$(C, NO_3) \rightarrow (CO_2, N_2)$	(10)	$((CH_2O)_6, N) \rightarrow (CH_4, NH_3)$	(23)
$(C, NH_4) \rightarrow (CH_4, N_2)$	(11)	$((CH_2O)_6, N) \rightarrow (C, NH_4)$	(24)
$(C, NO_2) \rightarrow (CH_4, N_2)$	(12)	$((CH_2O)_6, N) \rightarrow (CO_2, NH_4)$	(25)
$(C, NH_4) \rightarrow (CH_4, NH_3)$	(13)		

the resulting LTS derived from $\mathcal{S}$ gives us a bisimulation. The list shown in Table 1 provides a transition $(p, q) \rightarrow (p', q')$ which means that the transitions $p \rightarrow p'$ and $q \rightarrow q'$ have the same actions. Equations (1)-(2) have the actions ll, (3)-(18) have the actions la, (19)-(20) have the actions ab, (21)-(22) have the actions ba, and (23)-(25) have the actions bl.

In order to obtain the set $\mathcal{S}$, we construct a transition graph $\mathcal{G}$, where we can start on any arbitrary node (p, q). A directed edge e from (p, q) to (p', q') exists, if transition is found in Table 1. Based from Definition 4.6, we can obtain $\mathcal{S}$ by getting a set of vertices $V(\mathcal{G}_\mathcal{S}) \subseteq V(\mathcal{G})$ such that for all vertices $v \in V(\mathcal{G}_\mathcal{S})$, there exists an edge between v and w where $w \in V(\mathcal{G}_\mathcal{S})$. The vertices in $V(\mathcal{G}_\mathcal{S})$ are the pair of states in $\mathcal{S}$.

From the transition graph $\mathcal{G}$ in Fig. 7, we can infer that $\mathcal{S} = \{(CO_2, NO_2), (C, NO_3), (CO_2, N_2), ((CH_2O)_6, N), (CO_2, NH_3), (CO_2, NH_4), (C, NO_2)\}$, which has 7 ordered pairs. The ordered pairs in a lighter shade are not included in $\mathcal{S}$ as they does not induce a cycle. Note also that the entries of the ordered pair (p, q) belong to the same compartment, i.e., $p, q \in L$.

6.2. Further Analysis

We constructed two pairs of LTS in which the states come from the entries of the ordered pairs in $\mathcal{S}$. Note that in $\mathcal{S}$, we have two ordered pairs which

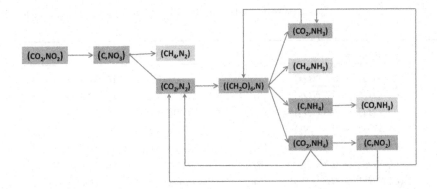

Fig. 7. Transition Graph $\mathcal{G}$ obtained from the list of transitions in Table 1. The pair included in set $\mathcal{S}$ are the nodes with darker shade.

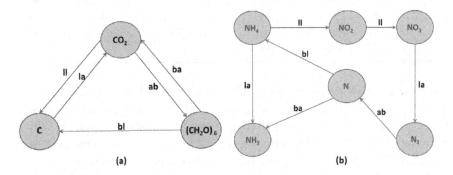

Fig. 8. Derived Carbon Cycle (a) and Nitrogen (b) LTS

have the same second entry, i.e. (CO_2, NO_2) and (C, NO_2), which results to two comparisons. Figures 8 (a) and (b) shows the resulting LTS derived from $\mathcal{S}$ for the carbon and nitrogen cycles, respectively.

In the two cases, we considered the ordered pairs (CO_2, NO_2) and (C, NO_2) respectively as starting points. Both cases in Fig. 9, infer that LTS from Nitrogen cycle and Carbon cycle are bisimilar.

7. Conclusion and Future Works

In this paper, we have shown a weak bisimulation between Carbon and Nitrogen cycle. We constructed a general and restricted versions of the LTS to be able to provide a valid comparison. In showing the bisimulation between the two systems, we defined a larger LTS, $(\mathcal{Q}, \mathcal{T})$ containing both LTS from Carbon and Nitrogen cycle. We then obtain a relation $\mathcal{S} =$

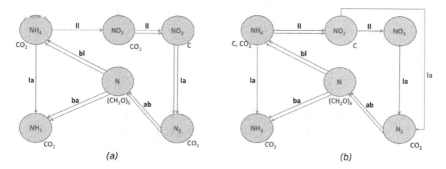

Fig. 9. (a) Case 1: Used (CO_2, NO_2) as a starting point (b) Case 2: Used (C, NO_2) as a starting point

$\{(CO_2, NO_2),\ (C, NO_3),\ (CO_2, N_2),\ ((CH_2O)_6, N),\ (CO_2, NH_3),\ (CO_2, NH_4),\ (C, NO_2)\}$ defined over the set of states in $\mathcal{Q}$. The pair of molecules from carbon and nitrogen respectively may help in inferring relationships between molecules involved in analyzing complex systems in environmental science. One possible extension of this study is to incorporate environmental data in transition systems in order to measure quantitative effects of perturbation in the environment. For larger systems, identifying if a bisimulation exists is much harder. Therefore, another possible extension is to develop an efficient algorithm for obtaining a relation $\mathcal{S}$ given two large LTS.

References

1. A. Bernhard, The Nitrogen Cycle: Processes, Players, and Human Impact. Nature Education Knowledge 3(10):25, 2012
2. P. Falkowski, R. J. Scholes, E. Boyle, J. Canadell, D. Canfield, J. Elser, N. Gruber, K. Hibbard, P. Högberg, S. Linder, F. T. Mackenzie, B. Moore III, T. Pedersen, Y. Rosenthal, S. Seitzinger, V. Smetacek, W. Steffen. "The Global Carbon Cycle: A Test of Our Knowledge of Earth as a System". Science 290 (5490): 291296., 2000.
3. D. Bodkin and E. Keller, Environmental Science (5th ed). John Wiley and Sons, 2004.
4. R. Milner, Communicating and Mobile Systems: The Pi-Calculus. Computer Laboratory, University of Cambridge, 1999.
5. I. C. Prentice, Climate change 2001: The carbon cycle and atmospheric carbon dioxide. Cambridge University Press, p. 183-237, 2001
6. V. F. Krapivin and C. Varotsos, Biogeochemical Cycles in Globalization and Sustainable Development. Springer, 2008
7. NASA. *The Carbon Cycle.* http://earthobservatory.nasa.gov/Features/ CarbonCycle/page1.php. Retrieved March 1, 2013.

A SIMULATION OF TRANSITION P SYSTEMS IN WEIGHTED SPIKING NEURAL P SYSTEMS

Richelle Ann B. Juayong, Nestine Hope S. Hernandez,

Francis George C. Cabarle, Henry N. Adorna

Algorithms & Complexity Lab
Department of Computer Science
University of the Philippines Diliman
Diliman 1101 Quezon City, Philippines
E-mail: rbjuayong@up.edu.ph, nshernandez@up.edu.ph, fccabarle@up.edu.ph,
hnadorna@up.edu.ph

Two of the general families of membrane systems in Membrane computing are cell-like and neural-like systems. Transition P systems or TP systems and Spiking Neural P systems or SNP systems are part of the cell-like and neural-like families, respectively. In this work we provide a relation between TP systems with noncooperative rules or nTP systems and SNP systems with weighted synapses or wSNP systems (both are synchronous and nondeterministic). In particular we define a reasonable operating mode of nTP systems we refer to as k-restricted object-minimal region-maximal parallelism or k-O_{min}, R_{max} mode. We show that there exists a simulation of nTP systems operating in 1-O_{min}, R_{max} mode with wSNP systems. Remarks for further study of cell-like and neural-like relations are also provided.

Keywords: Membrane computing, weighted Spiking Neural P systems, Transition P systems, simulation, operation mode.

1. Introduction

In Membrane computing, two of the general families of membrane systems are cell-like and neural-like systems.[1,2] On the one hand, cell-like P systems involve computations that capitalize on the hierarchical and compartmentalized membrane structure of the cell. On the other hand, neural-like P systems capitalize mono-membranar cells as nodes in a directed graph. In this work we focus on Transition P systems with noncooperative rules (from the cell-like family) or nTP systems, and Spiking Neural P systems with weighted synapses (from the neural-like family) or wSNP systems. TP systems were one of the earliest systems investigated in Membrane computing (appearing in a seminal paper in Ref. 3) while SNP systems were more recently introduced in Ref. 4.

Aside from the structural differences of cell- and neural-like systems, the two often have different operating modes i.e. the application number and order of rules. TP systems often operate in a maximally parallel mode whereas SNP systems are maximal at the system level but sequential at the neuron level. More information about P system mode of operations and about nTP systems can be found in Refs. 1,2,5, about SNP systems in Refs. 1,6–8 and the references therein.

A common result in the research on models of computations is the study of the relations among various models, e.g. languages accepted or generated in deterministic and nondeterministic models,[9] as well as on simulations and congruence of labeled transition systems.[10] Relations of P systems with other P systems and computing models abound in literature.[11–15] In this work we provide a relation similar to Refs. 10,11. A motivation of this work is to contribute towards the goal of realizing further relations of cell-like and neural-like systems. The relation in particular for this work is that of simulation (we clarify this in the next section), and we provide such between nTP systems and wSNP systems. A more specific contribution is as follows: suppose we are given a P system Π composed of modules of various families of P systems such as cell-like P systems A and neural like P systems N. If however a given module A becomes nonoperational or unusable[a], how can we replace A with a module N such that N interacts with Π or its environment the same way A does?

Additionally, the notion of maximal parallelism is not always practically (whether biologically or otherwise) desirable or even plausible. Therefore, to make TP or SNP systems closer to reality (whether implemented biologically or by some other media), it is desirable to allow parallelism, but only to some extent. Before presenting the simulation of an nTP system in wSNP systems, we first define a reasonable mode of operation for nTP systems such that parallelism is still prevalent, but in a more limited (hence more realistic) sense. In this paper A is an nTP system, and N is a wSNP system. We then construct a wSNP system simulating a given nTP system that operates in the mode of operation we introduce in the next section.

This paper is organized as follows: Sec. 2 provides preliminaries for our results, such as definitions of nTP and wSNP systems, the mode of

---

[a]Possibly due to certain operations or other environment stimuli, which for the moment, are not important in this work.

operation we introduce in this work, and the notion of simulation. Section 3 provides our main result, which is the simulation of nTP systems in wSNP systems, using the mode from Sec. 2. An example of the simulation is also provided. Lastly, we provide final remarks and directions for further work in Sec. 4.

2. Preliminaries

It is assumed that the readers are familiar with the basics of Membrane Computing[b] and formal language theory as in Ref. 9. We only briefly mention notions and notations which will be useful throughout the paper.

We denote the set of all natural numbers as $\mathbb{N} = \{1, 2, 3 \ldots\}$. Let V be an alphabet, V^* is the free monoid over V with respect to concatenation and the identity element λ (the empty string). The set of all non-empty strings over V is denoted as V^+ so $V^+ = V^* - \{\lambda\}$. V is a *singleton* if $V = \{a\}$ and we simply write a^* and a^+ instead of $\{a^*\}$ and $\{a^+\}$. The length of a string $w \in V^*$ is denoted by $|w|$. If a is a symbol in V, $a^0 = \lambda$. A language $L \subseteq V^*$ is regular if there is a regular expression E over V such that $L(E) = L$. A regular expression over V is constructed starting from λ and the symbols of V using the operations union, concatenation, and $+$, using parentheses when necessary to specify the order of operations. Specifically, (i) λ and each $a \in V$ are regular expressions, (ii) if E_1 and E_2 are regular expressions over V then $(E_1 \cup E_2)$, $E_1 E_2$, and E_1^+ are regular expressions over V, and (iii) nothing else is a regular expression over V. With each expression E we associate a language $L(E)$ defined in the following way: (i) $L(\lambda) = \{\lambda\}$ and $L(a) = \{a\}$ for all $a \in V$, (ii) $L(E_1 \cup E_2) = L(E_1) \cup L(E_2)$, $L(E_1 E_2) = L(E_1)L(E_2)$, and $L(E_1^+) = L(E_1)^+$, for all regular expressions E_1, E_2 over V, and $E^+ \cup \{\lambda\}$ is written as E^*.

We define a noncooperative transition P (nTP) system without dissolution, similar to Ref. 16 as follows:

Definition 2.1. A noncooperative transition P (nTP) system without dissolution is a construct of the form

$$\Pi_{\mathrm{nTP}} = (O, \mu, w_1, \ldots, w_m, R_1, \ldots, R_m, i_{out})$$

where:

(1) m is the total number of membranes;

---

[b]A good introduction is Ref. 1 with recent results and information in the P systems webpage at http://ppage.psystems.eu/ and a recent handbook in Ref. 2.

(2) O is the alphabet of objects;

(3) μ is the membrane structure which can be denoted by a set of paired square brackets with labels. We say that membrane i is the *parent membrane* of a membrane j, denoted $parent(j)$, if the paired square brackets representing membrane j is located inside the paired square brackets representing membrane i, i.e. $[_i \ldots [_j \,]_j]_i$. Reversely, we say that membrane j is a *child membrane* of membrane i, denoted $j \in children(i)$ where $children(i)$ refers to the set of membranes contained in membrane i. The relation of parent and child membrane becomes more apparent when we represent the membrane structure as a tree. Since order does not matter in our model, there can be multiple trees (isomorphic with respect to children of a node), each corresponding to the same membrane structure representation.

(4) $w_1, \ldots, w_m$ are strings over O^* where w_i, $1 \leq i \leq m$, denotes the initial multiset of objects present in the region bounded by membrane i.

(5) $R_1, \ldots, R_m$ are sets of evolution rules, each associated with a region delimited by a membrane in μ;

- An evolution rule $r \in R_i$, $1 \leq i \leq m$, is of the form $\alpha \rightarrow v$, $\alpha \in O$ and $v \in (O \times Tar_i)^*$ where $Tar_i = \{here, out\} \cup \{in_j | j \in children(i)\}$. If a copy of object α is present in region i, we say that rule r can be applied to evolve (a copy of) object α.

  Upon application of rule r, the object α is consumed, i.e. removed from region i (region bounded by membrane i) and a multiset of objects given in v are produced in the next time step. The symbols *here*, *out* and *in_j* are target commands indicating the destination of the objects produced. This means

  - if v contains $(\beta, here)$, the object β will be placed in region i. This also means the same when the target of β is omitted, i.e. $(\beta, here)$ means the same as β.
  - if v contains (β, out), the object β will be placed in region $parent(i)$
  - if v contains (β, in_j), the object β will be placed in region $j \in children(i)$

  As a short-hand notation to simplify our examples and illustrations, we use strings in place of objects for the right-hand side of a rule r. Thus, if v contains (v', tar) where $v' \in O^+$, $tar \in Tar_i$, this means that the string v' is placed in the region corresponding to tar. If e^k is contained in v', this means, there are k copies or multiplicity of object e produced.

(6) $i_{out} \in \{0, 1, \ldots, m\}$ is the output membrane. If $i_{out} = 0$, this means that the environment is the placeholder of the output.

In most P system models, rules are applied in a nondeterministic and maximally parallel manner. Nondeterminism implies that whenever at least two rules can possibly be applied to a (copy of an) object in a certain time step, the system only chooses a single rule for each copy of the object. Maximal parallelism requires that all copies of objects that can evolve must evolve. In this paper, we impose a restriction on this manner of applying rules in which we require that maximal parallelism only applies to regions while objects per region are k-restricted minimally parallel (similar to its description in Ref. 5) in the objects per region. This mode of operation is readily applicable in nTP systems. The next definition describes how this mode is applied.

Definition 2.2. An nTP system without dissolution Π_{nTP} that runs in k-restricted, object-minimal, region-maximally parallel mode (denoted by k-O_{min}, R_{max} mode) requires that per region, all objects that can evolve must evolve (region-maximally parallel). If an object can evolve in a region, at most k copies of an object should evolve in a time step (k-restricted minimally parallel).

Throughout this paper, rules for nTP systems run in a nondeterministic and 1-O_{min}, R_{max} mode, i.e. maximally parallel with respect to the regions but sequential with respect to distinct objects in a region.

To illustrate application of this 1-O_{min}, R_{max} mode, we refer to Fig. 1 for a graphical illustration of an example nTP system. Since in region 1, both objects c and d can evolve, both objects must evolve as required by region-maximally parallel application. Similarly, object d in region 2 must evolve since rule r_{21} can be applied to d. For region 1, object c will be evolved using rule r_{13} following 1-restricted object-minimally parallel application.

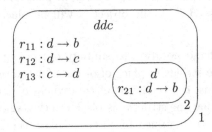

Fig. 1.   A noncooperative transition P system.

However, only one copy of object d will be evolved through nondeterministically choosing one of rules r_{11} and r_{12}. The next configuration will be one of the following:

- In region 1, there are two copies of object d and one copy of object b while region 2 has one copy of object b.
- In region 1, there are two copies of object d and one copy of object c while region 2 has one copy of object b.

Next we define a weighted Spiking Neural P (wSNP) system, based on Refs. 6,8, of a finite degree $n \geq 1$ as follows:

Definition 2.3. A wSNP system is a construct of the form

$$\Pi_{\text{wSNP}} = (O, \sigma_1, \ldots, \sigma_n, syn, out),$$

where:

1. $O = \{a\}$ is the singleton alphabet (a is called *spike*).
2. $\sigma_1, \ldots, \sigma_n$ are neurons of the form $\sigma_i = (x_i, R_i), 1 \leq i \leq n$, where:

    (a) $x_i \geq 0$ represents the initial number of spikes in σ_i, $x_i \in \mathbb{N} \cup \{0\}$.
    (b) R_i is a finite set of rules of the general form

    $$E/a^c \rightarrow a^b$$

    where E is a regular expression over O, $c \geq 1$, $b \geq 0$, with $c \geq b$.
3. $syn \subseteq \{1, 2, \ldots, n\} \times \{1, 2, \ldots, n\} \times \mathbb{N}$, $(i, i, k) \notin syn$ for $1 \leq i \leq m$ are weighted synapses between neurons.
4. $out \in \{1, 2, \ldots, m\}$ is the index of the *output* neuron.

A wSNP system is a directed graph, where nodes are neurons and weighted edges between neurons are synapses. A *spiking rule* is where $b \geq 1$. A *forgetting rule* is where $b = 0$ such that $L(E) = \{a^c\}$ written as $a^c \rightarrow \lambda$. If $L(E) = \{a^c\}$ then spiking rules are simply written as $a^c \rightarrow a^b$. Applications of rules are as follows: if neuron σ_i contains k spikes, $a^k \in L(E)$ and $k \geq c$, then the rule $E/a^c \rightarrow a^b \in R_i$ is enabled and the rule can be fired or applied. If $b \geq 1$, the application of this rule removes c spikes from σ_i, so that only $k - c$ spikes remain in σ_i. Neuron σ_i fires b number of spikes, so that every σ_j receives br number of spikes where $(i, j, r) \in syn$, i.e. the b spikes are multiplied to the synapse weight r before arriving at every σ_j. If $b = 0$ then no spikes are produced. SNP systems assume a global clock, so the application of rules and the sending of spikes by neurons are all synchronized.

At most one rule can be applied in a neuron at a given time. If in a neuron σ_i there are two rules each having regular expressions E_1 and E_2 such that $L(E_1) \cap L(E_2) \neq \emptyset$, then σ_i nondeterministically chooses which rule to apply. In SNP systems therefore, parallelism is at the level of the system (since neurons apply rules sequentially). Note the restriction that if a spiking rule can be applied, then there is no forgetting rule that can be applied, and vice versa i.e. if a spiking and forgetting rule have regular expressions E_{spik} and E_{forg} respectively in a neuron, then $L(E_{spik}) \cap L(E_{forg}) = \emptyset$. In SNP system literature, there are several ways to obtain an output of the system. Two common ways to obtain an output is to: (1) consider the time difference between only the first two time steps the output neuron spikes, and (2) consider a spike train, i.e. a series of spikes or no spikes, so a binary output can be encoded in the output.

We now describe the notion of configuration, transition and computation for both P system models defined previously. We let $sys \in \{nTP, wSNP\}$, and configuration C_{sys} refers to a state of the system sys. For nTP systems, this corresponds to the multiset of objects within each membrane written in the form $[_i \ldots [_j \ldots]_j]_i$. Similarly, this configuration consists of the number of spikes per neuron for wSNP systems. The notation C_{sys}^i corresponds to a configuration of the system at time i. For example, given Π_{wSNP} of degree n, at a certain time step i we have the configuration $C_{wSNP}^i = \langle \alpha_1, \alpha_2, \ldots, \alpha_{n-1}, \alpha_n \rangle$ where $1 \leq i \leq n$ and $\alpha_i \in \mathbb{N} \cup \{0\}$ is the number of spikes in neuron σ_i. The initial configuration of Π_{wSNP} is therefore represented as $C_{wSNP}^0 = \langle x_1, x_2, \ldots, x_{n-1}, x_n \rangle$.

A *transition* from a configuration C_{sys}^i to configuration C_{sys}^{i+1}, denoted by $C_{sys}^i \Rightarrow C_{sys}^{i+1}$, is a change from C_{sys}^i to C_{sys}^{i+1} through application of a set of rules. For wSNP system, a *valid transition* is a transition where the manner of application is given in Definition 2.3. For nTP systems, the manner of rule application to validate a transition will be dependent on the operating mode the system uses. As mentioned earlier and throughout this entire paper, every nTP system we define runs in a nondeterministic and 1-O_{min}, R_{max} mode. A *computation*, denoted by $C_{sys}^i \overset{*}{\Rightarrow} C_{sys}^j$, where $i < j$, is a sequence of valid transitions wherein the combination of rule application satisfies the condition of nondeterminism and parallelism in a predetermined mode. Computation succeeds when the system halts; this occurs when the system reaches a configuration wherein none of the rules can be applied. This configuration is called a *halting configuration*. If the system does not reach a halting configuration, computation fails because the system did not produce any output.

Before we proceed to the next section, we define a notion of simulation in the context of P systems, as adapted from Ref. 10. We note that a binary relation S over configurations in Π and Π' is a set of ordered pairs (c_1, c_2) where c_1 is a configuration in Π and c_2 is a configuration in Π'. The notation $c_1 S c_2$ implies that element $(c_1, c_2) \in S$.

Definition 2.4. Let Π and Π' be two P systems and let S be a binary relation over configurations in Π and Π'. S is a simulation over Π and Π' if whenever $C_\Pi S C_{\Pi'}$

if $C_\Pi \Rightarrow C'_\Pi$, there exists $C'_{\Pi'}$ such that $C_{\Pi'} \overset{*}{\Rightarrow} C'_{\Pi'}$ and $C'_\Pi S C'_{\Pi'}$. We say $C_{\Pi'}$ simulates C_Π and Π' simulates Π.

In the succeeding section, we explore the relation of nTP systems without dissolution and wSNP systems with respect to this notion of simulation. Note that the simulation relation S is over configurations of two P systems, which in this paper will be nTP and wSNP systems. The output of both systems are obviously different, so it is important to mention that their outputs are not the main considerations in this work. Instead, and similar to Ref. 17, the systems we consider here are taken to be portions or modules of larger systems, hence the simulation relation over their configurations. We will consider a simulation not only over their configurations but as well as their outputs in a future work.

3. Main Results

In this section, we show how we can construct a wSNP system that simulates a given nTP system operating in $1\text{-}O_{min}, R_{max}$ mode. Before we formalize our simulation result, we first provide a brief description of such construction:

- For each object β in each membrane k in a given nTP system:

  - **Adding Neurons**:
    (a) Add a neuron with initial spikes equal to the number of initial copies of β in k.
    (b) If there exists at least one rule triggered by β (i.e. a rule consuming β), add an auxiliary neuron.
    (c) For each rule triggered by β, we add one neuron.

– **Adding Rules in Neurons:**

(d) For neuron in (a), we add a rule $a^+/a \to a$ if and only if there exists a rule triggered by β.

(e) Let q be the number of rules triggered by β. For neuron in (b), we add the rules, $a^n \to a^i$, $1 \le i \le q$.

(f) For neuron in (c) associated with the ith rule for β, $1 \le i \le q$, we add the rule $a^i \to a$ and rules, $a^j \to \lambda$ for $1 \le j \le q, i \ne j$.

– **Adding Weighted Synapses:**

(g) Add a synapse from neuron in (a) to neuron in (b) with weight equal to q.

(h) Add a synapse from neuron in (b) to all neurons in (c) with weight equal to 1.

(i) Add a synapse from a neuron in (c) to all neurons corresponding to objects β' produced by its associated rule. Each synapse has weight equal to the number of produced copies of the object β'.

From this procedure, we can observe that a single rule application in an nTP system can be simulated in three time steps for its corresponding wSNP systems. A firing from neuron in (a) to neuron in (b) signals that a copy of an object β is being consumed, whereas the number of spikes being fired from neuron in (b) to neuron in (c) determines the rule that consumes β, thus handling nondeterminism. A firing from a neuron in (c) signals the production of necessary objects, signaling the effect of applying a rule associated with a neuron in (c). Since wSNP systems is parallel at system level, evolving a single copy of an object (that can evolve) in all membranes is simulated in our constructed wSNP systems, providing an idea of how the 1-O_{min}, R_{max} mode is preserved.

Figures 2 and 3 provide an illustration showing an nTP system and its corresponding wSNP system, respectively. Neurons labelled d_1, b_1 and c_1 in Fig. 3 are representative of neurons in (a) for region 1 of the nTP system in Fig. 2, whereas the neuron labelled d_2 represents object d in region 2. Neurons labelled R_{d_1} and R_{c_1} are auxiliary neurons (for neurons d_1 and c_1), while no auxiliary neurons are added for neurons b_1 and d_2 due to the lack of rules triggered by their corresponding objects. Finally, all remaining neurons are representative of rules in the given nTP system, added as indicated in (c). A detailed description of how both system computes follows after we state our theorem and proof.

Theorem 3.1. *For every nTP system Π_{nTP} without dissolution that runs in a nondeterministic and $1\text{-}O_{min}, R_{max}$ mode, there exists a wSNP system Π_{wSNP} that simulates Π_{nTP}.*

Proof. To prove the above theorem, we shall divide our proof into two parts.

- The first part constructs a wSNP system Π_{wSNP} from a given nTP system Π_{nTP}. Afterwards, we discuss how Π_{wSNP} computes.
- Following Definition 2.4, the second part shows that there is a simulation from Π_{nTP} to Π_{wSNP}. Specifically, we show that there exists a binary relation S over configurations in Π_{nTP} and Π_{wSNP} such that whenever $C_{\Pi_{nTP}} S C_{\Pi_{wSNP}}$ if $C_{\Pi_{nTP}} \Rightarrow C'_{\Pi_{nTP}}$, there exists $C'_{\Pi_{wSNP}}$ such that $C_{\Pi_{wSNP}} \overset{*}{\Rightarrow} C'_{\Pi_{wSNP}}$ and $C'_{\Pi_{nTP}} S C'_{\Pi_{wSNP}}$.

Before we proceed with the technical details of the proof, we introduce notations we shall use in this section. Given an nTP system Π_{nTP} (from Definition 2.1):

- $TO(k)$ is the set of trigger objects in region k, i.e. $TO(k) = \{\beta \mid \exists r : \beta \to v \in R_k\}$.
- $TR(\beta, k)$ is the set of all rules in R_k triggered by β, i.e. $TR(\beta, k) = \{r : \beta \to v \mid \beta \in TO(k)\}$.
- $PO(k)$ is the set of possible objects in O that can occur in region k. Formally, $PO(k) = TO(k) \cup \{\beta \mid \exists r : b \to v \in R_k, v \text{ contains } (\beta, here)\}$ $\cup \{\beta \mid \exists r : b \to v \in R_{k'}, v \text{ contains } (\beta, out), k = parent(k')\}$ $\cup \{\beta \mid \exists r : b \to v \in R_{k'}, v \text{ contains } (\beta, in_j), k = j \in children(k')\}$.

We also define a total mapping for $\overline{m} : TR(\beta, k) \to \{1, \ldots, |TR(\beta, k)|\}$.

We now proceed with the first part of our proof which is the construction of Π_{wSNP}. Given Π_{nTP} without dissolution,

$$\Pi_{wSNP} = (O, \sigma_1, \ldots, \sigma_n, syn)$$

where $n = \sum_{k=1}^{m} |PO(k)| + \sum_{k=1, \forall \beta \in TO(k)}^{m} |TR(\beta, k)| + \sum_{k=1}^{m} |TO(k)|$ and

- For every k, $1 \le k \le m$:
  - $\beta \in PO(k)$, we add a neuron $\sigma_{\beta_k} = (\alpha_{\beta_k}, R_{\beta_k})$ where α_{β_k} is equal to the multiplicity of β in w_k and $a \to a \in R_{\beta_k}$ iff $\beta \in TO(k)$,
  - For every $r \in TR(\beta, k)$, $\beta \in TO(k)$, we add a neuron $\sigma_{R_{\beta_{kp}}} = (0, R_{R_{\beta_{kp}}})$ where $p = \overline{m}(r)$, $\{a^p \to a, a^{p'} \to \lambda\} \in R_{R_{\beta_{kp}}}$, $1 \le p' \le |TR(\beta, k)|$, $p' \ne p$,

- We let N be the set of all neurons added in Π_{wSNP} and a total mapping $\overline{m}' : N \rightarrow \{1, \ldots, n\}$ so all neurons are uniquely identified as some σ_i, $1 \leq i \leq n$,
- The triple $(\overline{m}'(\sigma_{\beta_k}), \overline{m}'(\sigma_{R_{\beta_k}}), |TR(\beta, k)|) \in syn$,
- For every k, $1 \leq k \leq m$, the triple $(\overline{m}'(\sigma_{\beta_k}), \overline{m}'(\sigma_{\beta'_{k'}}), p) \in syn$ iff there exists $r : \beta \rightarrow v \in R_k$ and v contains (β', Tar_k), where
  - either $Tar_k = here$ and $k' = k$,
    $Tar_k = out$ and $k' = parent(k)$, or
    $Tar_k = in_j$ and $k' = j$,
  - and p is the number of (β', Tar_k) contained in v.
- For every k, $1 \leq k \leq m$ and for every $\beta \in TO(k)$, we add a neuron $\sigma_{R_{\beta_k}} = (0, R_{R_{\beta_k}})$ where $a^q \rightarrow a^p \in R_{R_{\beta_k}}$, $1 \leq p \leq |TR(\beta, k)|$, $(\overline{m}'(\sigma_{\beta_k}), \overline{m}'(\sigma_{R_{\beta_k}}), q) \in syn$

The system computes as follows:

Initially, all neurons are empty except for neurons σ_{β_k} whose initial spikes are equal to the number of copies of β in w_k. From this configuration, every σ_{β_k} $(\beta_k \in TO(k))$ containing at least one spike fires the rule $a \rightarrow a$. This implies that a copy of object β in region k will be evolved through a single application of any rule in $TR(\beta, k)$.

The spike released from σ_{β_k} will be sent to $\sigma_{R_{\beta_k}}$ indicating that the system can already choose which rule will be used to evolve a copy of β. If the weight of the synapse connecting these neurons is p, the spike given to $\sigma_{R_{\beta_k}}$ will become p spikes. Since $p = |TR(\beta, k)|$, this assures us that none of the rules in $\sigma_{R_{\beta_k}}$ will violate the condition for a spiking rule in which the spikes it consumes (left-hand side of the rule) is always greater than or equal to the spikes it produces (right-hand side). The number of spikes in the left-hand side of every spiking rule in $\sigma_{R_{\beta_k}}$ has the same value. Thus, the system nondeterministically chooses a rule to be applied. This rule will be uniquely identified using the mapping $\overline{m}$. If a rule $r \in TR(\beta, k)$ is chosen, q spikes will be replicated to each neuron $\sigma_{R_{\beta_{kq'}}}$, $1 \leq q' \leq |TR(\beta, k)|$, $q = \overline{m}(r)$. In this step, only $\sigma_{R_{\beta_{kq}}}$ will release a spike through the rule $a^q \rightarrow a$. Other neurons $\sigma_{R_{\beta_{kq'}}}$ will forget the spikes they received via rules of the form $a^{q'} \rightarrow \lambda$, $q' \neq q$. This shows that nondeterminism in Π_{nTP} is preserved in the constructed Π_{wSNP}.

Spiking of a rule in $\sigma_{R_{\beta_{kq}}}$ signals the application of the chosen rule corresponding to q. The spike from $\sigma_{R_{\beta_{kq}}}$ will be sent to all $\sigma_{\beta'_{k'}}$ where β' is in the right-hand side of the rule associated with q, and k' is the destination as identified by its corresponding target indication. Since only a single spike io relcased from $\sigma_{R_{\beta_{kq}}}$, the weight of the synapse connecting $\sigma_{R_{\beta_{kq}}}$ and $\sigma_{\beta'_{k'}}$ determines the number spikes to be received by $\sigma_{\beta'_{k'}}$. This guarantees that the correct number of copies of β' is produced in region k'.

We now move on to the second part of our proof which constructs a binary relation S over configurations in Π_{nTP} and Π_{wSNP}. Our description of how the system computes assures us that a single application of a rule in Π_{nTP} is performed in exactly three time steps in Π_{wSNP}. Due to parallelism, it is possible that every neuron contains some number of spikes. The parallelism at the system-level guarantees that all neurons σ_{β_k} having at least one spike (where β_k is in any $TO(k)$) will process each spike at the same time. This processing implies that per region, all objects that can evolve will evolve. This implication assures us that maximal parallelism in the region level is also preserved in the constructed Π_{wSNP}. Due to the design of rules, we are assured that at any single time, every neuron $\sigma_{R_{\beta_k}}$ is either empty or has p spikes where $p = |TR(\beta, k)|$. This implies that each neuron $\sigma_{R_{\beta_{kq}}}$ has at most $|TR(\beta, k)|$ number of spikes. This means that only one copy is applied per object β in each region, that is, 1-*restricted* minimal parallelism is preserved in Π_{wSNP}.

We end our proof by providing the simulation relation S over configurations in Π_{wSNP} and Π_{nTP} required by Definition 2.4 as follows: a pair $(C_{nTP}, C_{wSNP}) \in S$ if and only if, for every $\beta \in PO(k)$, if r is the total copy of β in region k for the configuration C_{nTP}, then, in C_{wSNP}, exactly one of the following cases holds:

- Neuron σ_{β_k} has r spikes.
- if $\beta \in TO(k)$, neuron σ_{β_k} has $r-1$ spikes and neuron $\sigma_{R_{\beta_k}}$ has $|TR(\beta, k)|$ spikes.
- if $\beta \in TO(k)$, neuron σ_{β_k} has $r - 2$ spikes, neuron $\sigma_{R_{\beta_k}}$ has $|TR(\beta, k)|$ spikes, and for every q', $1 \le q' \le |TR(\beta, k)|$ neuron $\sigma_{R_{\beta_{kq'}}}$ has s spikes, for some s, $1 \le s \le |TR(\beta, k)|$.

It can be observed that for every pair $(C_{nTP}, C_{wSNP}) \in S$, if there is a transition $C_{nTP} \Rightarrow C'_{nTP}$, there exists a computation $C_{wSNP} \overset{*}{\Rightarrow} C'_{wSNP}$ where $(C'_{nTP}, C'_{wSNP}) \in S$. The configuration C'_{wSNP} is any one of the three cases mentioned above for configuration C'_{nTP}. □

Example 3.1. Figure 2 shows an nTP system without dissolution rule formally defined as

$\Pi_{nTP_1} = (\{b, c, d\}, [_1[_2]_2]_1, dbc, \lambda, R_1, R_2, 2)$ where $R_1 = \{d \to d^2, d \to (b, in), d \to b^2c, c \to b, c \to d^2b^2c^2\}$ and $R_2 = \{b \to d\}$.

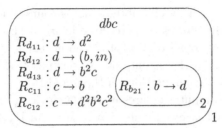

Fig. 2. A noncooperative transition P system Π_{nTP_1}.

Given the initial multiset configuration $C^0_{\mathrm{nTP}_1} = [_1dbc[_2]_2]_1$ of Π_{nTP_1} and taking into consideration that rule application follows $1\text{-}O_{min}, R_{max}$ mode, a sample computation is as follows:

Step 1: Initially, both objects c and d can be used for the given evolution rules in region 1. If we let rule $R_{d_{11}}$ be used to consume a copy of object d and use $R_{c_{11}}$ to consume object c, then a possible next configuration will be $C^1_{\mathrm{nTP}_1} = [_1d^2b^2[_2]_2]_1$. In this step (and the succeeding steps), the object b in region 1 is carried over to the next configuration since no rule is triggered by its existence.

Step 2: In the next step, we can consume a copy of d in region 1 by using rule $R_{d_{13}}$, resulting to a configuration $C^2_{\mathrm{nTP}_1} = [_1db^4c[_2]_2]_1$.

Step 3: The copy of object d and c in region 1 can be used for rules $R_{d_{12}}$ and $R_{c_{12}}$, respectively, resulting to a configuration $C^3_{\mathrm{nTP}_1} = [_1d^2b^6c^2[_2b]_2]_1$.

Step 4: In region 1, we can apply rules $R_{d_{12}}$ and $R_{c_{11}}$ for a single copy of objects d and c, respectively. The copy of object b in region 2 may also be evolved using rule $R_{b_{21}}$. These will lead to a configuration $C^4_{\mathrm{nTP}_1} = [_1db^7c[_2db]_2]_1$.

Step 5: The single copy of object d in region 1 can trigger rule $R_{d_{12}}$. Similarly, object c may trigger rule $R_{c_{11}}$. Applying both rules in parallel with rule $R_{b_{21}}$ to consume object b in region 2, a possible next configuration will be $C^5_{\mathrm{nTP}_1} = [_1b^8[_2d^2b]_2]_1$.

Step 6: Lastly, when object b in region 2 is consumed through rule $R_{b_{21}}$, a final configuration will be $C^6_{\mathrm{nTP}_1} = [_1b^8[_2d^3]_2]_1$. The nTP system Π_{nTP_1} then halts.

A wSNP system simulating Π_{nTP_1} is shown in Fig. 3. We do not formally define Π_{wSNP_1} here, so we refer to Fig. 3 instead. The initial configuration is $C^0_{\mathrm{wSNP}_1}$ where $x_i = 1$ and $x_j = 0, i \in \{d_1, b_1, c_1\}$ and $j = N_{\mathrm{wSNP}_1} \setminus i$, i.e. only neurons $\sigma_{d_1}, \sigma_{b_1}, \sigma_{c_1}$ have one spike each (corresponding to the initial

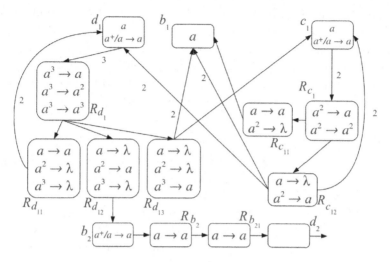

Fig. 3. A wSNP system Π_{wSNP_1}.

multiset configuration $C^0_{nTP_1}$ of Π_{nTP_1}) while the remaining neurons have no initial spikes. Π_{wSNP_1} works as follows:

Neuron σ_{d_1} sends three spikes to $\sigma_{R_{d_1}}$ due to the weight three of synapse $(d_1, R_{d_1}, 3)$, and σ_{c_1} sends two spikes to $\sigma_{R_{c_1}}$ due to the weight two of synapse $(c_1, R_{c_1}, 2)$. R_{d_1} nondeterministically chooses which among its three rules it will apply now, since $\alpha_{R_{d_1}} = 3$. Due to the construction outlined in Theorem 3.1, the behavior of $\sigma_{R_{d_1}}$ is such that if it applies rule $a^3 \to a$ then only $\sigma_{R_{d_{11}}}$ will spike at the next time step, since both $\sigma_{R_{d_{12}}}$ and $\sigma_{R_{d_{13}}}$ will forget the a spike sent to them. Likewise, if $\sigma_{R_{d_1}}$ applies $a^3 \to a^2$ (rule $a^3 \to a^3$), only $\sigma_{R_{d_{12}}}$ (only $\sigma_{R_{d_{13}}}$) will spike at the next time step. This behavior can be seen similarly with the spiking of $\sigma_{R_{c_1}}$ (since $\alpha_{R_{c_1}} = 2$ now) to $\sigma_{R_{c_{11}}}$ and $\sigma_{R_{c_{12}}}$. If $\sigma_{R_{d_{11}}}$ spikes, σ_{d_1} receives two spikes, meaning two copies of the object d in region 1 of Π_{nTP_1}. If $\sigma_{R_{d_{12}}}$ spikes, then σ_{b_2} receives one spike (one copy of b in region 2 of Π_{nTP_1}).

The spike from σ_{b_2} is then sent (via $\sigma_{R_{b_2}}$ and $R_{b_{21}}$) to σ_{d_2} (one copy of d in region 2 of Π_{nTP_1}). If $\sigma_{R_{d_{13}}}$ spikes, then one and two spikes are sent to σ_{b_1} and σ_{c_1} respectively, corresponding to two copies of b and one copy of c in region 1 of Π_{nTP_1}. If $\sigma_{R_{c_{12}}}$ spikes then two spikes are sent to σ_{d_1}, σ_{b_1} and σ_{c_1} corresponding to two copies of objects d, b, c in region 1 of Π_{nTP_1}. Once Π_{wSNP_1} halts, its final configuration is such that only σ_{b_1} (with eight spikes) and σ_{d_2} (with three spikes) have spikes, corresponding to the final multiset configuration $C^6_{nTP_1}$ of Π_{nTP_1}.

The halting configuration consists of three copies of d in output membrane 2 and three spikes in output neuron σ_{d_2} for Π_{nTP_1} and Π_{wSNP_1}, respectively. Neuron σ_{d_2} can have a rule $a^+/a \to a$, for example, which will send three spikes to the environment or to another wSNP system. Again, the simulation relation S is over configurations of two P system families, and that outputs will be considered in a future work.

4. Final Remarks

In this work we have shown a relation between nTP systems operating in $1\text{-}O_{min}, R_{max}$ mode and wSNP systems. The relation is such that the latter simulates the former. We note that the $k\text{-}O_{min}, R_{max}$ is a reasonable operating mode for nTP systems, maintaining the usual parallelism in P systems while restricting up to some k the number of objects to evolve per region. Maintaining parallelism while working with a restricted number of objects makes this mode more suitable for implementation, whether for software or hardware.

In the proof and example in Sec. 3, an object m in a region n corresponds to a neuron σ_{m_n}. As a future work and in order to better make sense of the computations in both nTP and wSNP systems, the outputs should be considered in greater detail. However, nTP and other cell-like systems often have multiple objects in their alphabets while wSNP systems and other SNP system variants only have a singleton alphabet. In order to extend the idea and construction presented in this work, wSNP systems simulating nTP systems should either have the following output mechanisms: (1) a special neuron (or set of neurons) that will output, in some encoding, the multiplicity of objects in the output membrane of the simulated nTP system, or (2) consider a modification of the wSNP system definition so that there is a specific output neuron per object, as in Ref. 18.

Other questions that we can ask based on this work are the following: How can nTP systems (among other cell-like systems) with cooperative (including antiport rules) rules be simulated with SNP systems? How are such cooperative rules (or even noncooperative rules) performed in a maximally parallel mode in SNP systems? It seems that SNP systems with dynamic structures are necessary to perform such cooperation and maximal parallelism so that "space" i.e. neurons, are created or "budded" as in Ref. 19. What other "ingredients" are necessary for SNP systems in order to simulate other modes of operations (e.g. asynchronous, minimal parallelism, etc.) of cell-like systems? This dynamic structure could perhaps be used to simulate cell-like systems with dissolution rules as well. It is also interesting to further explore the resources, e.g. time and space complexities, required in order for neural-like systems to simulate cell-like systems (and vice versa). Finally, another line of research towards the goal of further realizing how closely related cell- and neural-like systems are can be done by using process algebra as was done in Refs. 20, 21, 17.

Acknowledgments

R.A.B. Juayong and F.G.C. Cabarle are supported by the DOST-ERDT program. N.H. S. Hernandez would like to thank the UP Diliman College of Engineering (UPD CoE) through the Jose P. Dans Jr. professorial chair for the financial support. H.N. Adorna is funded by a DOST-ERDT research grant and the Semirara Mining Corporation professorial chair of the UPD CoE. The authors would like to thank the UP Information Technology Development Center. Lastly, the unknown reviewers for their comments that helped improve this work.

References

1. Ciobanu, G., Păun, Gh., Pérez-Jiménez, M. J.: Chapter 1 Introduction to Membrane Computing. Applications of Membrane Computing, Springer-Verlag (2006).
2. Păun, Gh., Rozenberg, G., Salomaa A. The Oxford Handbook of Membrane Computing, Oxford University Press (2010).
3. Păun, Gh.: Computing with Membranes. Journal of Computer and System Sciences Vol. 61, pp. 108–143 (2000).
4. Ionescu, M., Păun, Gh., Yokomori, T.: Spiking Neural P Systems. Fundamenta Informaticae, Vol. 71(2,3) 279–308, Feb. (2006).
5. Freund, R., Verlan, S.: (Tissue) P systems working in the k-restricted minimally or maximally parallel transition mode. Natural Computing. Vol. 10 pp. 821–833 (2011).
6. Păun, Gh., Pérez-Jiménez, M. J.: Spiking Neural P Systems. Recent Results, Research Topics. A. Condon et al. (eds.), Algorithmic Bioprocesses, Springer (2009).
7. Wang, J., Hoogeboom, H. J., Pan, L., Păun, Gh., Pérez-Jiménez, M. J.: Spiking Neural P Systems with Weights. Neural Computation 22, pp. 2615–2646, MIT press (2010).
8. Pan, L., Zeng, X., Zhang, X., Jiang, Y.: Spiking Neural P Systems with Weighted Synapses. Neural Process Lett 35, pp. 13–27, Springer (2012).
9. Hopcroft, J. E., Ullman, J. D.: Introduction to Automata Theory, Languages, and Computation. Addison-Wesley (1979).
10. Milner, R.: Communicating and Mobile Systems: The Pi-Calculus. Cambridge University Press (1999).

11. Frisco, P.: P Systems, Petri Nets, and Program Machines. WMC 2005, LNCS 3850, pp. 209–223, (2006).
12. Metta, V. P., Krithivasan, K., Garg, D.: Modelling and analysis of spiking neural P systems with anti-spikes using Pnet lab. Nano Communication Networks Vol. 2, pp. 141–149 (2011).
13. Cabarle, F. G. C., Adorna, H. N.: On Structures and Behaviors of Spiking Neural P Systems and Petri Nets. E. Csuhaj-Varjú *et al.* (Eds.): CMC 2012, LNCS 7762, pp. 145–160, Springer-Verlag (2013).
14. Ibarra, O., Pérez-Jiménez, M. J., Yokomori, T.: On spiking neural P systems. Natural Computing, Vol. 9, pp. 475–491 (2010).
15. Cabarle, F. G. C., Buño, K. C., Adorna, H. N.: On The Delays In Spiking Neural P Systems. Philippine Computing Journal Vol. 7(2), preprint available online: http://arxiv.org/abs/1212.2529.
16. Gutiérrez-Naranjo, M. A., Pérez-Jiménez, M. J.: Computing Backwards with P systems, WMC10, Curtea de Argeş, Romania, pp. 282–295, (2009).
17. Barbuti, R., Maggiolo-Schettini, A., Milazzo, P. Tini S.: Compositional semantics of spiking neural P systems. The Journal of Logic and Algebraic Programming 79(10):304–316 (2010).
18. Alhazov, A., Freund, R., Oswald, M., Slavkovik, M.: Extended Spiking Neural P Systems. Păun, Gh., Rozenberg, G., Salomaa, A. (eds) WMC7, LNCS, Vol. 4361. pp. 123–134, Springer-Verlag (2006).
19. Pan, L., Păun, Gh., Pérez-Jiménez, M. J.: Spiking neural P systems with neuron division and budding. Science China Information Sciences. Vol. 54(8) pp. 1596–1607 (2011).
20. Andreai, O., Ciobanu, G., Lucanu, D.: Structural operational semantics of P Systems. Proc. 6th Workshop on Membrane Computing. LNCS Vol. 3850:31–28, Springer (2006).
21. Barbuti, R., Maggiolo-Schettini, A., Milazzo, P., Tini, S.: Compositional semantics and behavioral equivalences for P systems. Theor Comput Sci 395:77–100 (2008).

ROBUSTNESS ANALYSIS ON HUMAN-MADE FAULTS IN PROCEDURAL MANUALS

Naoyuki Nagatou

PRESYSTEMS Inc.,
Kamimuzata 1461, Togane, Chiba, 283-0011, Japan
E-mail: nagatou@acm.org

Takuo Watanabe

Department of Computer Science,
Graduate School of Information Science and Engineering,
Tokyo Institute of Technology,
2-12-1 Oookayama, Meguro-ku, Tokyo, 152-8552, Japan
E-mail: takuo@acm.org

In this study, we propose a formal approach for the analysis of robustness with regard to human-made faults in procedural manuals. In many cases, fault detection and recovery tasks are embedded in procedural manuals that allow us to detect human-made faults. This investigation is important in preserving the trust of workflows in safety critical domains. We define the formal semantics of human-made faults according to Discrete Action Classification, which classifies fault actions of experts in a domain —the formal definition of the faults is based on a transition system. Using these semantics, we inject faults into a fault-free model of a procedural manual. After that, we verify that the model embedded with faulty tasks satisfies a property as the goal of a procedural manual by model checking. A model checking tool is given the opposite of the formula as a goal, and if this tool reports counter examples, we say that the procedural manual is not robust. We apply our framework to a procedural manual that a nurse executes for taking blood samples. In the case, we conclude that the procedural manual is not robust because that tool reports counter examples.

Keywords: Linear temporal logic; process algebra; procedural manual; workflow; human-made fault; dependability; robustness.

1. Introduction

We design procedural manuals for many cases such as factories, plants, planes, and hospitals. Procedural manuals in safety-critical domains typically require high levels of dependability, where dependability is preserved by not only the skills and knowledge of domain experts but also the inherent clarity of procedural manuals. Such procedural manuals require robustness from human-made faults which experts may commit.

Human-made faults are essentially human actions exceeding limits of acceptability that are defined by a situation in which a person performs an action. Human performance can be affected by many factors, such as insufficient skills, the level of motivation regarding correct performance, expectations that the performer senses, and a work situation that may not be in accord with an individual's abilities. The effects of these factors involve some faulty actions. It is difficult to identify all faulty actions; however, such actions have certain features of fault, and in this study, we identify these features.

We focus on unintentional faults committed by experts. On the basis of attention(performance) level [1, pp. 53–96], such unconscious faults are classified into the following three categories: skill-based faults, rule-based faults and knowledge-based faults. This classification is useful for psychological research but not for robustness analysis because these refer to human variables. We are interested in human outputs as a result to be yielded, while the classifications in [1, pp. 53–96] mention internal processes of the mind. A person perceives external inputs, processes such inputs, and then produces outputs, which influence the success of given tasks and procedures.

Discrete Action Classification(DAC)[2] is a classification of human-made faults based on incorrect human outputs. The classification is organized as follows:

- Faults of Omission:
  - omits entire task
  - omits a step in a task
- Faults of Commission:
  - Selection fault: selects wrong control, mispositions control or issues the wrong command and/or information.
  - Sequence fault: out of order.
  - Timing fault: too early or too late.
  - Qualitative fault: too much or too little.

An omission fault is a fault in which one forgets the entire task or a step of the task for some reason. In this study, we assume that all tasks are atomic. On account of this assumption(simplification), we ignore "omit a step of a task" classification. A commission fault is a fault in which one performs an incorrect action. Commission faults are classified into the four abovementioned categories. However, in this paper, we focus only on selection and sequence faults, because our modeling language[3] does not have notion of time or quality.

Pertinent to our research is the research area of computer systems dependability. Numerous researchers have concerned themselves with formal expressions of fault-tolerance and fault analysis.[4–8] Their formalizations require a fault model for modeling incorrect behavior that systems manifest. We propose a mechanism by which the analysis of fault-tolerance of procedural manuals can be systematically performed. We use the above fault model based on DAC for human-made faults.

First, we formalize the semantics of faults in DAC using the notion of transition systems, e.g., Calculus of Communicating Systems(CCS).[9] Then, faulty tasks are injected into a model of a procedural manual. After such injection, we verify a property with a model-checking tool.[3] The property, which we call recoverability, represents the process in which one reaches a goal via a recovery task after an error occurs. As an example, a test of a procedural manual in a hospital is presented. We construct two distinct scenarios: single patient and two patients, and then investigate the recoverability of the manual.

In addition to this introductory section, we organize this study as follows. Section 2 describes a motivating example for this study. Section 3 presents the formal frameworks (i.e., process algebra and linear temporal logic, which are used in[3]). Section 4 provides a formalism of workflows in process algebra. Section 5 provides a fault model for human errors. Section 6 provides a notion of robustness and recovery, and describes how we investigate the robustness of workflows by model checking. In the last section, we summarize the contributions of our study and present avenues of future work.

2. A Motivating Example

Figure 1 shows an example procedural manual that describes the steps required for obtaining blood samples from a patient in a hospital. The manual starts with a patient presenting his/her ID-card, after he or she arrives in a room for blood sample extraction. A clerk makes a receipt system read the ID-card. The system checks the patient's ID-number in a data-base; if it corresponds to the ID-number of the extraction request, the system prints two receipt sheets and labels. The clerk receives the sheets and gives one of the sheets to the patient; the other sheet and the labels are given

(1) A patient gives a clerk in the room his/her ID-card.
(2) The clerk has the receipt system read the ID card.
(3) The system gives the clerk two receipt sheets and gives a nurse labels.
(4) The clerk gives the patient one of the two receipt sheets; the clerk gives a nurse the other.
(5) The nurse prepares tubes.
(6) The nurse has the system read the labels.
(7) The nurse puts the labels on the tubes.
(8) The system calls a receipt ID.
(9) The nurse confirms the name on the labels with a name on the receipt sheet.
(10) The nurse receives a receipt sheet from the patient after the patient sits down.
(11) The nurse compares the names on the receipt sheets.
(12) The nurse extracts blood samples from the patient.
(13) The nurse sends the blood samples to a lab.

Fig. 1.   An example scenario for taking blood samples in a hospital

to a nurse. The nurse then prepares tubes and applies labels to the tubes. The nurse also confirms the labels and makes the system read the labels. If an ID-number on the labels is different from that on the sheet, then the nurse corrects the labels. The system displays the ID-number on an electrical board to call the patient. The called patient then takes his/her seat and hands the sheet to the nurse. The nurse asks the patient his/her name, compares his/her name with the name on a terminal. If these names are identical, then the nurse extracts blood into tubes. The nurse takes both the blood samples and the sheets to a laboratory as the final step.

The designer (typically, a supervisor) of the procedural manual for nurse will adjust it whenever an incident happens. The designer believes that the manual prevents nurses from mistaking one patient for another because of the redundant checks at steps 9 and 11; in other words, confirming ID-numbers and comparing names become mistake-detection tasks however, each task is performed by a human, and the manual does not guarantee that they are correctly performed. A nurse may forget a particular task and may perform other tasks on the basis of his/her mistaken knowledge, wrong rules or insufficient skills(see Chapter 3 in[1]). The trust in procedural manuals depends on his/her experience and skill. To avoid human-made faults, we must design procedural manuals to be robust against his/her faults.

In business process management, we produce a model of a process. This model helps us to understand a process.[10] Moreover, we can use formal verification techniques to check soundness properties of the model.[11–14] This leads us to apply formal techniques to robustness analysis of process models in addition to soundness checks and flexibility and conformance checking[a].

3. Preliminaries

In this section, we present a subset of CCS to express workflows,[9] and a subset of linear temporal logic to express properties required by the workflows.[15]

3.1. *Process Algebra*

CCS is a framework in process algebra. The framework is based on communication between agents. Communication causes two types of actions: input and output actions. An input action is labeled by a name and has a corresponding output action. An output port is identified by a bijective function with a name. We call $\bar{a}$ of name a a co-name. We assume that a set of co-names is disjointed from the set of names.

The syntax of the subset is given as follows: if E and F are agents and a is a name,

- output prefix $(\bar{a}(e_1, \cdots, e_n) : E)$ is an agent,
- input prefix $(a(x_1, \cdots, x_n) : E)$ is an agent,
- summation of E and F, $E+F$ is an agent,
- composition of E and F, $E\,|\,F$ is an agent,
- constant $P(x_1, \cdots, x_n)$ is an agent given by $P(x_1, \cdots, x_n) \stackrel{\text{def}}{=} E$,
- conditional if (b) (E) (F) is also an agent.

where $x_1, \cdots$ are variables over a fixed set of values V, $e_1, \cdots$ are expressions over V and b is a boolean expression over V. We use $STOP^{\text{b}}$ as a significant agent that does nothing. We will describe the behavior of each agent via value passing. Consider $(a(x_1, \cdots, x_n) : E)$, wherein if $i \neq j$, then x_i is a symbol different from x_j. This contains offering values at a,

---

[a] Our adaptation focus on a model, not BPEL program
[b] Although CCS writes such an agent as $ZERO$, we use $STOP$ in this paper.

and a transforms $(a(x_1, \cdots, x_n) : E)$ into E, whose behavior depends on $x_1, \cdots, x_n$, where $x_1, \cdots, x_n$ are free variables in E. We next introduce the scope of variables before the explanation of free variables. We say that a binds $x_1, \cdots, x_n$ to $v_1, \cdots, v_n$, respectively, and their scopes are in E. If variables are not bound, then they become free variables. We write the substitution of variables $x_1, \cdots, x_n$ to $[v_1/x_1, \cdots, v_n/x_n]$. For example, $(a(x_1, \cdots, x_n) : E)$ becomes $E[v_1/x_1, \cdots, v_n/x_n]$. We can then write the inference rule for input prefix as

$$\langle a(x_1, \cdots, x_n) : E, k, env \rangle \overset{a(v_1, \cdots, v_n)}{\rightarrow} \langle E, k, env[v_1/x_1, \cdots, v_n/x_n] \rangle,$$

where k and env are a continuation and an environment, respectively.

We next consider $\bar{a}(e_1, \cdots, e_n) : E$. $\bar{a}$ demands values of expressions. $\bar{a}$ always enables an experiment. Let v_i be a value to evaluate e_i for $1 \leq i \leq n$, we can give an inference rule for output prefix as

$$\langle \bar{a}(e_1, \cdots, e_n) : E, k, env \rangle \overset{\bar{a}(v_1, \cdots, v_n)}{\rightarrow} \langle E, k, env[(v_1, \cdots, v_n)/a] \rangle,$$

where $eval$ is an evaluator; for all $1 \leq i \leq n$, v_i is $eval(e_i, env)$.

Next, we consider a conditional agent with two arms. Let α be an element of the union set of names and co-names. Evaluating b to one of the boolean values $\{\texttt{true}, \texttt{false}\}$, we can give an inference rule for conditional agents as

$$\frac{E \overset{\alpha}{\rightarrow} E'}{\texttt{if (true) } (E) \ (F) \overset{\alpha}{\rightarrow} E'} \qquad \frac{F \overset{\alpha}{\rightarrow} F'}{\texttt{if (false) } (E) \ (F) \overset{\alpha}{\rightarrow} F'}.$$

Using operational semantics, the behavior of other agents is defined as shown in Figure 2.

3.2. Linear Temporal Logic

We use Linear Temporal Logic(LTL) to discuss the properties for workflows. We first assume that a trace has initial states and is a finite

$$\frac{\langle E, k, env \rangle \overset{\alpha}{\rightarrow} \langle E', k, env \rangle}{\langle E+F, k, env \rangle \overset{\alpha}{\rightarrow} \langle E', k, env \rangle} \qquad \frac{\langle F, k, env \rangle \overset{\alpha}{\rightarrow} \langle F', k, env \rangle}{\langle E+F, k, env \rangle \overset{\alpha}{\rightarrow} \langle F', k, env \rangle}$$

$$\frac{\langle E, k, env \rangle \overset{\alpha}{\rightarrow} \langle E', k, env \rangle}{\langle E|F, k, env \rangle \overset{\alpha}{\rightarrow} \langle E', k(\lambda x.x|F), env \rangle} \qquad \frac{\langle F, k, env \rangle \overset{\alpha}{\rightarrow} \langle F', k, env \rangle}{\langle E|F, k, env \rangle \overset{\alpha}{\rightarrow} \langle F', k(\lambda x.E|x), env \rangle}$$

$$\frac{\langle E, k, env[v_1/x_1, \cdots, v_n/x_n] \rangle \overset{\alpha}{\rightarrow} \langle E', k, env[v_1/x_1, \cdots, v_n/x_n] \rangle}{\langle P(v_1, \cdots, v_n), k, env \rangle \overset{\alpha}{\rightarrow} \langle E', k, env[v_1/x_1, \cdots, v_n/x_n] \rangle} \quad (P(x_1, \cdots, x_n) \overset{\text{def}}{=} E)$$

Fig. 2. Operational semantics of the processes calculus

sequence of states because workflows are finite. We write the length of trace $\sigma = s_0 s_1 \cdots s_n$ to $|\sigma|$ in which $|\sigma|$ is $n + 1$. We write the suffix of $\sigma = s_0 s_1 \cdots s_i \cdots s_n$ starting at i as $\sigma^{i\cdots} = s_i \cdots s_n$, and the ith state as σ^i.

We provide workflow properties by using the following notation. We assume a vocabulary $x, y, z, \cdots$ of variables for data values. For each state, variables are assigned a single value. A state formula is any well-formed first-order formula constructed over the variables. Such state formulae are evaluated on a single state to a true value. If the evaluation of state formula p becomes true over s, then we write $s[\![p]\!] = \mathtt{tt}$ and say that s satisfies p, where $\mathtt{tt}$ and $\mathtt{ff}$ are truth values, respectively denoting *true* and *false*. Let φ and ψ be temporal formulae, a temporal formula is inductively constructed as follows:

- a state formula is a temporal formula,
- the negation of a temporal formula $\neg\varphi$ is a temporal formula,
- $\varphi \vee \psi$ and $\varphi \wedge \psi$ are temporal formulae, and
- $\square\,\varphi$, $\Diamond\,\varphi$, $\circ\,\varphi$, and $\varphi\,\mathcal{U}\,\psi$ are temporal formulae.

We define semantics of temporal formulae over a trace. If trace σ satisfies property φ then we write $\sigma \models \varphi$.

- If p is a state formula, $\sigma \models p$ iff $\sigma^0[\![p]\!] = \mathtt{tt}$ and $|\sigma| \neq 0$.
- $\sigma \models \neg\varphi$ iff $\sigma \not\models \varphi$,
- $\sigma \models \varphi \vee \psi$ iff $\sigma \models \varphi$ or $\sigma \models \psi$,
- $\sigma \models \varphi \wedge \psi$ iff $\sigma \models \varphi$ and $\sigma \models \psi$,
- $\sigma \models \square\varphi$ iff for all $0 \leq i < |\sigma|$, $\sigma^{i\cdots} \models \varphi$,
- $\sigma \models \Diamond\varphi$ iff there exists $0 \leq i < |\sigma|$ such that $\sigma^{i\cdots} \models \varphi$,
- $\sigma \models \circ\varphi$ iff $\sigma' \models \varphi$ where $\sigma' = \sigma$ if $|\sigma| = 1$ and $\sigma' = \sigma^{1\cdots}$ if $|\sigma| > 1$,
- $\sigma \models \varphi\,\mathcal{U}\,\psi$ iff there exists $0 \leq k < |\sigma|$ s.t. $\sigma \models \psi$ and for all $j < k$, $\sigma \models \varphi$.

A formula φ is satisfiable if there exists a sequence σ such that $\sigma \models \varphi$. Given set of traces T and formula φ, φ is valid over T if for all $\sigma \in T$, $\sigma \models \varphi$.

3.3. *Relationships between Agents and Formulae*

In this subsection, we describe a relationship between algebraic models and LTL formulae. The modeling language enables to pass values via input prefix $\alpha(e)$ and output prefix $\overline{\alpha}(x)$ with the same name. Execution of $\alpha(e)$ causes a value v of e. Execution of $\overline{\alpha}(x)$ causes a single assignment to x.

Execution of two actions causes atomic assignment $x := v$; that is, communication between two agents produces a new state by changing the values of the variables. This is similar to the first paragraph in Section 3.3 of [16, page 290].

The assignment changes states. We represent the change as $s[v/x]$, which denotes a change in the values of x in s to v. A state is a mapping from variables to values. Assuming that $\mathrm{Var_E}$ is a set of variables that appears in prefixes in agent E with range V, $s : Var_E \rightarrow$ V. For example, the evaluation $s[\![x = y]\!]$ of $x = y$ at s becomes $s[\![x]\!] = s[\![y]\!]$, and at $s[v/x]$, $s[v/x][\![x]\!] = s[v/x][\![y]\!]$, i.e. $v = s[y]$.

Therefore, communication between agents produces a sequence of assignments which then produces a sequence of state changes called trace. Let a set of traces produced by agent E be T. If for all traces $\sigma \in T, \sigma \models \varphi$, then we say φ is valid over E and write $E \models \varphi$.

4. Workflow Model

Before providing a model of human-made faults, we characterize a workflow as follows. A workflow is informally regarded as a set of sequences of tasks. A task has a principal and an object. A performance of a task is transmission of information, in which information is transmitted in the form of messages. Messages cause send-actions in principals and receive-actions in objects. In addition, tasks have dependencies on each other. Dependency is indicated by an ordering of tasks. Tasks, principals, objects and message are just symbols. Symbols are assigned to actual meanings depending on skill, knowledge, cognitive processes, etc.

Formally, we characterize a workflow with five tuples of (C, T, O) where C is a set of principals and objects, T is a partial order set of tasks or messages and $O(\subseteq T \times T)$ is a set of orders of two tasks. For example, given the workflow for extracting blood samples in a hospital (as shown in Figure 1), we extract the following sets:

- $C =$ {patient, nurse, label, receipt, clerk, tube, laboratory},
- $T =$ {"give a clerk ID-card", "make system read ID-card", "give clerk two sheets", "give receipt to nurse",$\cdots$},
- $O =$ {("give a clerk ID-card", "make system read ID-card"), ("make system read ID-card", "give clerk two sheets"),$\cdots$}.

C and T are sets of symbols. Each symbol is assigned to an element of domain D by interpretation $I: C \cup T \rightarrow D$. D and I denote parts of cognitive processes, skills and knowledge of humans.

4.1. Mapping to Process Algebra

We map workflows to agents using the process algebra described in Section 3.1 above. The given mapping method is based on algorithm 1 of[13] and an idea presented in.[12] The mapping produces agents corresponding to principals and objects of tasks. Each element of $\mathcal{C}$ becomes an agent. For example, $Patient, Nurse, Receipt, Clerk, Tube,$ and $Lab.$

Moreover, the mapping produces a co-name and a name for each task because the performance of a task causes a send-action and a receive-action. The mapping produces co-names in agents for principals, and names in agents for objects. For example, as shown in part in Figure 3 for "give receipt to nurse" $\in \mathcal{T}$, output prefix $\overline{give\_receipt\_to\_nurse}(e)$ appears in $Clerk$ and input prefix $give\_receipt\_to\_nurse(e)$ appears in $Nurse$, where e is an expression over a set of values.

The orders of occurrence of names and co-names preserve orders between pairs of tasks. If for example, ("give receipt to nurse", "give label"),("give label", "prepare tube") $\in \mathcal{O}$ then we produce

$$\overline{give\_receipt\_to\_nurse}(receipt\_id\_Nurse, name\_on\_receipt\_Nurse) :$$
$$\overline{give\_label}(receipt\_id\_on\_label\_Nurse, name\_on\_label\_Nurse) :$$
$$\overline{prepare\_tube} : \cdots .$$

$$
\begin{aligned}
Nurse \stackrel{\text{def}}{=}\ &(give\_receipt\_to\_nurse(receipt\_id\_Nurse, name\_on\_receipt\_Nurse) : \\
&give\_label(receipt\_id\_on\_label\_Nurse, name\_on\_label\_Nurse) : \\
&\overline{prepare\_tube} : \\
&\overline{make\_system\_read\_label} : \\
&\overline{put\_label\_on\_tube}(name\_on\_label\_Nurse) : \\
&confirm\_label(patient\_name\_Nurse) : \\
&receive\_receipt(name\_on\_receipt\_for\_patient\_Nurse) : \\
&compare\_receipt(patient\_name\_Nurse) : \\
&\overline{extract\_blood} : \\
&\overline{take\_sample\_to\_lab}(name\_on\_receipt\_for\_patient\_Nurse, \\
&\qquad\qquad\qquad name\_on\_label\_Nurse) : \\
&Nurse)
\end{aligned}
$$

$$
\begin{aligned}
Clerk \stackrel{\text{def}}{=}\ &(give\_id\_card(patient\_name\_on\_card\_Clerk) : \\
&\overline{make\_system\_read\_card}(patient\_name\_on\_card\_Clerk) : \\
&\overline{give\_receipt}(receipt\_id\_Clerk, name\_on\_receipt\_Clerk) : \\
&\overline{give\_receipt\_to\_patient}(receipt\_id\_Clerk, name\_on\_receipt\_Clerk) : \\
&\overline{give\_receipt\_to\_nurse}(receipt\_id\_Clerk, name\_on\_receipt\_Clerk) : \\
&Clerk)
\end{aligned}
$$

Fig. 3. Sample model for error-free tasks regarding the blood extraction process of Figure 1

A complete workflow is represented by the composition of all agents. For example,

$$W \stackrel{\text{def}}{=} (Patient|Nurse|Clerk|Receipt|Tube|Lab).$$

A formal definition of agent *Nurse* is shown in Figure 3. The definition allows for recursion. We may be able to accept an opposite direction of several actions. For example, *compare_name_on_receipt* and *confirm_name* have the opposite direction from principals to objects, and vice versa. We can choose one of the directions to simplify the model.

Let a work flow W be $(\mathcal{C}, \mathcal{T}, \mathcal{O})$, we describe a map of W to the process algebra. $\mathcal{C}$ becomes a set of constant agents for principals and objects. Given a set of names N and a set of co-names $\overline{N}$, $\mathcal{T}$ becomes $N \cup \overline{N}$. $\mathcal{O}$ becomes action prefixes in the process algebra.

In the remainder of this study, we do not mention skills, knowledge, and cognitive processes of humans. these are represented by domain $\mathcal{D}$ and interpretation $\mathcal{I}$. We assume that all task sequences before injecting faults reach the goal of a workflow.

5. Injection of Human-Made Faults

We formalize human-made faults except for timing faults because the process algebra and logic that we use do not have a notion of time. The formalism produces agents for tasks in which human-made faults may occur in opposition to the correct meaning of tasks mentioned in Section 4. In this study, we treat omission faults, selection faults and sequence faults as human-made faults.

Given set of faulty tasks H and workflow model W, let a set of names in W be N and a set of co-names be $\overline{N}$. We next describe the injection of omission faults. Let $t \in H$ and $H \subseteq \mathcal{T}$. For each $t_1, t_2 \in \mathcal{T}$, if $(t_1, t), (t, t_2) \in \mathcal{O}$, then $\{(t_1, t_2)\}$ is added to $\mathcal{O}$. We therefore obtain $W_H = (\mathcal{C}, \mathcal{T}, \mathcal{O}')$, where $\mathcal{O}' = \mathcal{O} \cup \{(t_1, t_2)\}$. For faulty tasks in a workflow, we construct constant agents for them. Summation agents are constructed as follows: let an action for t be $\alpha \in N \cup \overline{N}$,

$$(\alpha(e) : STOP) + (STOP).$$

We next describe the injection of selection faults. Given two sets of tasks $H \subseteq \mathcal{T}$ and $H' \not\subseteq \mathcal{T}$. Let $t \in H$, $t' \in H'$. If $(t_1, t), (t, t_2) \in \mathcal{O}$, then we replace t by t'. We then obtain (t_1, t') and (t', t_2). Adding $\{(t_1, t'), (t', t_2)\}$ to $\mathcal{O}$, $\mathcal{O}' = \{(t_1, t'), (t', t_2)\} \cup \mathcal{O}$, and $\mathcal{T}' = H' \cup \mathcal{T}$. We then obtain

$W_{H,H'} = (\mathcal{C}, \mathcal{T}', \mathcal{O}')$. Let actions for faulty tasks be $\alpha(e_1)$ and $\alpha'(e')$. Using the summation operator, we construct the following agent.

$$\alpha(e_1) : STOP + \alpha'(e') : STOP.$$

Those faulty tasks with omission and selection faults can be represented by the following single agent.

$$(\alpha(e_1) : STOP) + (\alpha'(e') : STOP) + (STOP).$$

Finally, we describe the injection of sequence faults. Let $t_1, t_2 \in H$, then $\mathcal{O}$ becomes $\mathcal{O}' = \{(t_1, t_2), (t_2, t_1)\} \cup \mathcal{O}$. We can then obtain $\mathcal{W}_H = (\mathcal{C}, \mathcal{T}, \mathcal{O}')$. For tasks with the faults, we construct constant agents for them in a workflow model. Let agents for the faulty tasks be $Task\_t1$ and $Task\_t2$ and actions for them be $\alpha_1(e_1), \alpha_2(e_2) \in N \cup \overline{N}$ respectively, and then we have

$$Task\_t1 \stackrel{\text{def}}{=} (\alpha_1(e_1) : STOP),$$
$$Task\_t2 \stackrel{\text{def}}{=} (\alpha_2(e_2) : STOP).$$

Using composition, we construct the following agent:

$$Task\_t1 \mid Task\_t2.$$

For tasks with omission, selection and sequence faults, we can construct the following agent:

$$Task\_t1 \stackrel{\text{def}}{=} (\alpha_1(e_1) : STOP + \alpha'_1(e'_1) : STOP + STOP),$$
$$Task\_t2 \stackrel{\text{def}}{=} (\alpha_2(e_2) : STOP + \alpha'_2(e'_2) : STOP + STOP),$$

and $Task\_t1 \mid Task\_t2$.

Using these formalisms, we inject human-made faults into the model shown in Figure 3. We suppose $H = \{$"confirm label", "compare receipt"$\}$. Our formalism produces the following two agents: $Task\_confirm\_label$ and $Task\_compare\_receipt$. If nurses cause faults at those tasks, then composition of those agents replaces $confirm\_label$ and $compare\_name$ in $Nurse$. Figure 4 shows these injected agents. We obtain multiple traces from the agents and a single trusted service trace from Figure 3.

6. Robustness Test

We investigate the existence of sequences that cannot recover human-made faults using model checking. In Section 6.1 below, we provide a framework

$Task\_confirm\_label \overset{\text{def}}{=}$
$(confirm\_label(name\_on\_display\_TaskConfLabel) : STOP$
$+STOP)$
$Task\_compare\_receipt \overset{\text{def}}{=}$
$(receive\_receipt(name\_on\_receipt\_for\_patient\_TaskCompReceipt) :$
$\quad compare\_receipt(name\_on\_display\_TaskCompReceipt) : STOP$
$+STOP)$
$Nurse1 \overset{\text{def}}{=}$
$(\overline{extract\_blood} :$
$\overline{take\_sample\_to\_lab}(name\_on\_receipt\_for\_patient\_Nurse1,$
$\quad name\_on\_label\_Nurse1) : Nurse)$
$Nurse \overset{\text{def}}{=} (give\_receipt\_to\_nurse(receipt\_id\_Nurse, name\_on\_receipt\_Nurse) :$
$give\_label(receipt\_id\_on\_label\_Nurse, name\_on\_label\_Nurse) :$
$\overline{prepare\_tube} :$
$\overline{make\_system\_read\_label} :$
$\overline{put\_label\_on\_tube}(name\_on\_label\_Nurse) :$
$(Task\_confirm\_label \mid Task\_compare\_receipt \mid Nurse1))$

Fig. 4. Human error model of a nurse's tasks (see Figure 1)

for model checking, then in Section 6.2, we apply this technique to the example model given in Figure 4.

6.1. *Framework for Verification*

Robustness is an attribute that systems are often required to have. This attribute depends on external factors. We therefore define the robustness of workflows below.

Definition 6.1 (Robustness). *Let e be an error state formula, $\hat{e}$ an error state, and φ a formula. If error state $\hat{e}$ exists on σ and $(\sigma, \hat{e}) \models \Diamond\varphi$, then σ is robust on error e and we say that σ is (e, φ)-robust. If φ is valid over timelines obtained from W, then W is (e, φ)-robust.*

This definition intuitively means that a sequence of tasks σ reaches a goal, which satisfies φ from an error state.

We next focus on a technique for guaranteeing robustness. This technique consists of the detection of and recovery from errors. Recovery may be contained in an atomic task as a step of it. A task probably contains some step although we assume a task is atomic (in this case, error and recovery occur at same time). Conversely, a recovery task probably occurs after error. We therefore define the following two types of recovery—strong recovery and weak recovery. Strong recovery intuitively means that recovery r is true on the time error $\hat{e}$ happens. Weak recovery intuitively means that r becomes true after e. Strong recovery reflects a task including some steps recovering error, whereas weak recovery reflects error handling task.

Definition 6.2 (Strong Recovery). *Given timeline σ, if $\sigma \models [](e \rightarrow []r)$, then we say σ is strongly recoverable, where e and r are an error state formula and a recovery state formula, respectively.*

Definition 6.3 (Weak Recovery). *Given σ, if $\sigma \models \Box(\neg e) \vee \Diamond(e \wedge \Diamond r)$, then we say σ is weakly recoverable, wherein e and r are an error state formula and a recovery state formula, respectively.*

We abbreviate $\Box(\neg e) \vee \Diamond(e \wedge \Diamond r)$ at $e \triangleright r$.

Lemma 6.1. *Given σ. Let e_i be an error state formula, a recovery state formula r_i, if $\sigma^{\hat{r_i}\cdots} \models (\bigwedge_i r_i) \wedge \Diamond\varphi$ and $\sigma \models \bigwedge(e_i \triangleright r_i)$ then $\sigma \models (\bigwedge_i(e_i \triangleright r_i)) \ni \Diamond\varphi$*

Proof Sketch 1. Let e_i be an error state formula, a recovery state formula r_i. We suppose that $\sigma \models (e_i \triangleright r_i)$ holds over σ.

$$\models (e_i \triangleright r_i)$$
$$\text{iff} \models \Box(\neg e_i) \vee \Diamond(e_i \wedge \Diamond r_i)$$
$$\text{iff} \models \Box(\neg e_i) \text{ or } \models \Diamond(e_i \wedge \Diamond r_i)$$

In the case that $\Diamond(e_i \wedge \Diamond r_i)$ holds, there exists s_i such that e_i and $\Diamond r_i$ hold. Let all r_i hold at s_j where $j \geq i$, we suppose that $(\sigma, s_j) \models (\bigwedge_j r_j) \ni \Diamond\varphi$. Then, there exists s_k such that φ holds. Therefore, $\sigma \models (e_i \triangleright r_i) \ni \Diamond\varphi$. Supposing for all e_i, $\sigma \models (e_i \triangleright r_i) \ni \Diamond\varphi$, $\bigwedge_i \sigma \models (e_i \triangleright r_i) \ni \Diamond\varphi$.

In the other case in which $\neg e_i$ always holds, $\Diamond\varphi$ clearly holds because we suppose that a workflow before the injections of errors reaches its goal. ■

By Lemma 6.1, if there exists σ such that $\sigma \models \neg\Diamond\varphi$ then there exists e_i such that $\sigma \models \neg(e_i \triangleright r_i)$. This means that there are errors that cannot be recovered. Therefore, giving the negation, we will verify recoverability of workflows by model checking.

6.2. Model Checking

A designer of the workflow shown in Figure 1 above may believe that the workflow prevents nurses from mistaking patients because of two checks

Table 1. Result of model checking

numbers of patients	aspect of workspace	Failure
one	—	not appear
two	not isolate	appear
two	isolate	not appear

namely setp 9 to confirm and step 11 to compare. Those tasks are detection tasks in the workflow, and so fundamental that nurses do not mistake patients. Therefore, we provide $H = \{$ "confirm label", "compare name" $\}$. Figure 4 illustrates the injected models. We suppose that the rest of the tasks do not cause human-made faults.

A goal of the workflow for nurses is to take tubes and sheets without making any mistakes. Nurses guarantee that the blood of patients is not mixed up, or more specifically, they guarantee that the names on labels match those on sheets. When those names have the same value, the workflow is complete. Given an agent for laboratory $Lab \overset{\text{def}}{=}$ $(take\_sample\_to\_lab(name\_on\_receipt\_Lab, name\_on\_label\_Lab) : Lab)$, we now identify the property

$$\Box \Diamond (name\_on\_receipt\_Lab = name\_on\_label\_Lab). \tag{1}$$

We next investigate the recoverability of workflows using a model checking tool.[3] We give negation of (1): $\Diamond \Box \neg (name\_on\_receipt\_Lab = name\_on\_label\_Lab)$ and instances of the workflow model to the tool. We then investigate three cases. In the first case, one patient exists, in the second case, two patients exist and the workspaces are not isolated, in the third case, two patients exist and the workspaces are isolated. Isolation of workspaces is represented via scope of variables. We then obtain the results shown in Table 1. We conclude that "confirm label" and "compare name" are not enough to avoid making any mistakes. In addition, the workflow requires isolation of workspaces for each patient.

7. Conclusion

In this study, we discussed a verification technique for workflows using model checking. The technique provides a framework for the recoverability of workflows injected with human-made faults. As an example, we investigated the recoverability of workflows for taking blood samples in a hospital.

We formalized some human-made faults using process algebra, separating into the following five classes: omission faults, selection faults, sequence faults, timing faults and qualitative faults.[2] Our formalism treats sequence faults. We did not attempt handling any timing faults because the process algebra does not have a notion of time. Thus, we intend to use timed automata as part of our future work.

References

1. J. Reason, *Human Error* (Cambridge University Press, 1990).
2. A. D. Swain and H. E. Guttmann, *HANDBOOK OF HUMAN RELIABILITY ANALYSIS WITH EMPHASIS ON NUCLEAR POWER PLANT APPLICATIONS*, Draft Report NUREG/CR-1278, U.S. Nuclear Regulatory Commission Office of Nuclear Regulatory Research (Washington, DC, 1982).
3. PRESYSTEMS Inc., A Model Checker: nhk http://www4.ocn.ne.jp/~presys/index_en.html.
4. J. Rushby, Formal specification and verification of a fault-masking and transient-recovery model for digital flight-control systems, in *Formal Techniques in Real-Time and Fault-Tolerant Systems*, ed. J. Vytopil, Lecture Notes in Computer Science, Vol. 571 (Springer Berlin Heidelberg, 1991).
5. P. Krishnan, A semantic characterisation for faults in replicated systems, *Theoretical Computer Science* **128**, 159 (1994).
6. C. Bernardeschi, A. Fantechi and S. Gnesi, Model checking fault tolerant systems, *Software Testing, Verification and Reliability* **12**, 251 (2002).
7. S. Gnesi, G. Lenzini and F. Martinelli, Logical specification and analysis of fault tolerant systems through partial model checking, in *Proceedings of the International Workshop on Software Verification and Validation (SVV 2003)*, Mumbai, India, eds. S. Etalle, S. Mukhopadhyay and A. Roychoudhury, *Electronic Notes in Theoretical Computer Science (ENTCS)* **118** (Elsevier, Amsterdam, December 2003).
8. D. Manova, S. Ilieva, F. Lonetti, A. Bertolino and C. Bartolini, Towards automated robustness testing of BPEL orchestrators, in *Proceedings of the 12th International Conference on Computer Systems and Technologies*, (ACM, New York, NY, USA, 2011).
9. R. Milner, *Communication and Concurrency* (Prentice-Hall, Inc., Upper Saddle River, NJ, USA, 1989).
10. R. S. Aguilar-Savén, Business process modelling: Review and framework, *International Journal of Production Economics* **90**, 129 (2004).
11. W. M. P. v. d. Aalst, Verification of workflow nets, in *Proceedings of the 18th International Conference on Application and Theory of Petri Nets*, (Springer-Verlag, London, UK, 1997).
12. C. T. Karamanolis, D. Giannakopoulou, J. Magee and S. M. Wheater, Model checking of workflow schemas, in *Proceedings of the 4th International conference on Enterprise Distributed Object Computing*, (IEEE Computer Society, Washington, DC, USA, 2000).
13. F. Puhlmann, Soundness verification of business processes specified in the pi-calculus, in *On the Move to Meaningful Internet Systems 2007: CoopIS, DOA, ODBASE, GADA, and IS*, eds. R. Meersman and Z. Tari, Lecture

Notes in Computer Science, Vol. 4803 (Springer Berlin/Heidelberg, 2007). 10.1007/978-3-540-76848-7_3.

14. R. Hamadi and B. Benatallah, Recovery nets: Towards self-adaptive workflow systems, in *Proceedings of the 5th International Conference on Web Information Systems Engineering (WISE04)*, Lecture Notes in Computer Science Vol. 3306 (Springer-Verlag, 2004).

15. A. Pnueli, The temporal logic of programs, in *Proceedings of the 18th Annual Symposium on Foundations of Computer Science*, (IEEE Computer Society, Washington, DC, USA, 1977).

16. L. Lamport and F. B. Schneider, The "Hoare Logic" of CSP, and all that *ACM Transactions on Programming Languages and Systems (TOPLAS)* **6** (ACM, New York, NY, USA, April 1984).

COMPOSITIONAL CONSTRUCTION OF GROUP-WIDE META-LEVEL ARCHITECTURES

TAKUO WATANABE

Department of Computer Science, Tokyo Institute of Technology,
2-12-1 Ookayama, Meguroku, Tokyo, Japan
E-mail: takuo@acm.org

This work is an attempt to construct a new group-wide meta-level architecture based on the Actor model. The overall goal is to establish a solid semantic basis for reflection in concurrent systems. The main idea presented in this paper is a constraint-based abstract specification of meta-level actors. The proposed method provides a general model of group-wide reflection and results in a clearer semantics.

Keywords: Computational Reflection; Group-Wide Reflection; Meta-Level Architecture; Actor Model; Parallel Composition; CEK Abstract Machine.

1. Introduction

Actors[1] and concurrent objects[2] provide practical high-level abstraction for concurrent and parallel programming and are gaining popularity with the adoption of some programming languages or libraries such as Erlang, Scala or Akka. For some practical reasons such languages/libraries give programmers chances to mix actors with other concurrency primitives including threads, shared objects and locks.[3] Although using these primitives clearly breaks the abstraction, they also provide convenient features related to the collective behaviors of a group of actors: load-balancing, scheduling, resource management, fault-tolerance and so on. Implementing these features only with pure actors is generally impractical because numerous messages for underlying coordination protocols are apt to mingle with application messages.

To overcome such shortcomings of the pure actors, several coordination models have been proposed.[4-8] Also, *computational reflection* has been used for the purpose.[9-12] Especially, *group-wide reflection* (GWR)[13] in contrast to the sequential per-actor based reflection, allows each actor to have capabilities of reasoning about/acting upon the collective behavior of the group it belongs to. For example, group synchronization, application oriented message scheduling, mobility, name management can be realizable using GWR.[13]

The author recently proposed a new approach to GWR based on the parallel composition of per-actor meta-levels that realizes a uniform construction method for various types of meta-levels.[14] The operational semantics of the language used in the paper is organized in twofold; the semantics of the base language is given as a reduction system, while the meta-level is defined in the language itself. Unfortunately, this description hierarchy in the semantics complicates reasoning about systems written in the language.

In this paper, a different approach to formalize the composed meta-levels is proposed. The idea is to use constraint-based abstract specification of meta-level behaviors instead of concrete descriptions by defined languages. As a result, the composed meta-level is described in the same manner (by a transition relation) as the semantics of the base actor language. This simplifies the construction and results in clearer description of group-wide reflection.

The rest of the paper is organized as follows. The next section introduces a simple actor language used in this paper and Section 3 describes the operational semantics of the language. In Section 4, the meta-level composition and its semantics are defined. Section 5 concludes the paper.

2. A Simple Actor Language

2.1. *The Actor Model*

In the actor model, a computational system is modeled as a collection of autonomous entities called *actors*. Asynchronous one-to-one message passing is the only way of communication between actors. This means that actors do not share variables or states. A message is guaranteed to arrive at its destination within a finite but unbounded time. It is not required that the order of message dispatch between two arbitrary actors is preserved at their arrival.

A unique conceptual location called *mail address* (hereafter *address*) is associated with each actor. An actor can send messages to other actors only when it *knows about* (*i.e.*, has a reference of) the addresses of the destinations. The knows-about relation may change dynamically since messages can bring addresses.

On receiving a message, an actor may send messages to other actors or to itself, create new actors and/or change its behavior. The behavior of an actor is described as a function called *behavior function* that is applied to the message content when the actor receives a message. The change of the behavior is realized as a replacement of behavior functions. This represents the state change of an object in common object-oriented languages.

2.2. Our Actor Language

The language used in this paper is a simple untyped functional language extended with actor primitives. The abstract syntax is shown in Fig. 1. The metavariables e, x and c range over expressions, variables and built-in constants respectively. Built-in constants include Boolean values, numbers, unit[a], arithmetic and comparison functions and so on.

We call the sublanguage defined in lines 1–7 the *core language*. In addition to this, we use some syntactic extensions for tuples, pattern-argument functions, sequencing, conditional and letrec expressions (lines 8–13) for notational convenience. They can be encoded with the core language as usual. We use infix notations for some built-in functions to aid readability.

1	$e ::= c$	(constants)
2	$\mid x$	(variables)
3	$\mid (\lambda x.e)$	(functions)
4	$\mid (e\ e)$	(applications)
5	$\mid [e \Leftarrow e]$	(message sending expressions)
6	$\mid$ **new** e	(actor creation expressions)
7	$\mid$ **become** e	(become expressions)
8	$\mid (e,\dots,e)$	(tuples)
9	$\mid (\lambda p.e)$	(pattern-argument functions)
10	$\mid e\,;e$	(sequencing)
11	$\mid$ **if** e **then** e **else** e	(conditional expressions)
12	$\mid$ **letrec** $x = e$ **in** e	(letrec expressions)
13	$p ::= x \mid (p,\dots,p)$	(tuple patterns)

Fig. 1. The Abstract Syntax of the Language

---

[a]The singleton datatype whose sole value is written as ● in this paper.

The informal descriptions of the three actor primitives [_ $\Leftarrow$ _], new and become are described as follows:

[$e_1 \Leftarrow e_2$] sends a message to an actor. The arguments e_1 and e_2 should evaluate to the address of the destination and the message content respectively. The message content should be a *communicable value*; *i.e.*, it should not contain functions.

new e creates an actor with initial behavior specified with e that should evaluate to a behavior function. When the new actor receives a message, the function will be applied to the pair of the address of the actor and the message content. Thus a behavior function should look like $\lambda(s, x).e'$ where s corresponds to 'self' (or 'this') in common object-oriented languages. The created actor is initially in *dormant* mode; it does nothing until it receives a message.

become e replaces the behavior of the actor evaluating this expression with the new behavior function to which e evaluates and set the actor to dormant mode. The rest of the current computation (the continuation of this expression) in the actor is carried out by an *anonymous actor* that is not affected by this replacement. The new behavior is activated when the actor receives the next message. The behavior function should be defined to terminate for any argument; an infinite iteration should be implemented using self-targeted messages and become expressions.

Figure 2 shows an example of a recursive factorial actor. The variable fact is bound to the behavior function of the actor. An actor instance, obtained by evaluating new fact, accepts a message that is a tuple (n, c) of an integer and an actor that eventually receives the result; *i.e.*, c plays the role of a continuation in continuation-passing style. The expression

```
1  letrec fact = λ(self,(n,c)).
2        become fact;
3        if x = 0
4            then [c ⇐ 1]
5            else [self ⇐ (n − 1, new (λ(s,v).[c ⇐ n × v]))]
6  in
7        [new fact ⇐ (10, printer)]
```

Fig. 2. Recursive Factorial Actor

new $(\lambda(s,v).[c \leftarrow n \times v])$ evaluates to a continuation actor that receives $(n-1)!$ and then send $n!$ to c. By evaluating [new fact $\Leftarrow$ (10, printer)], the actor printer will receive the final result (10!).

3. The Operational Semantics of the Core Language

3.1. *The Semantics of the Sequential Sublanguage*

We first define the semantics of the sequential sublanguage (the core language without the actor primitives). For this purpose, we use a variant of CEK machine.[15]

In the following, $\mathbb{N}$ denotes the set of positive integers. We write $X \times Y$ and $X + Y$ to mean the Cartesian product and direct sum of sets X and Y respectively. X^* denotes the set of all finite sequences of elements of X. We write the empty sequence as ε and the concatenation of $s_1, s_2 \in X^*$ as $s_1 \cdot s_2$. $X \to_{\text{fin}} Y$ denotes the sets of finite functions from X to Y. The notation $f[x \mapsto v]$ stands for the function that is identical to f on all elements except x for which it gives v. $\text{Dom}(f)$ and $\text{Rng}(f)$ are the domain and range of f respectively. We write $\mathcal{F}(X)$ to denote the set of all finite subsets of X and $\mathcal{F}_\mathcal{M}(X)$ to denote the set of all finite multisubsets of X.

Fig. 3 describes the domains of the machine states (*MState*) and related domains including mail addresses (*Addr*) and communicable values (*CommVal*) mentioned in Section 2.1. Note that *Exp* and *Var* respectively denote the set of expressions and variables described in Fig. 1.

$$
\begin{aligned}
\sigma \in \textit{MState} \quad &::= \langle e, \rho, \kappa \rangle \mid \langle \kappa, v \rangle \mid \langle v \rangle \\
\rho \in \textit{Env} \quad &= \textit{Var} \to_{\text{fin}} \textit{Value} \\
\kappa \in \textit{Cont} \quad &::= \mathsf{mt} \mid \mathsf{ar}(e, \rho, \kappa) \mid \mathsf{fn}(f, \kappa) \mid \\
&\quad \mathsf{me}(e, \rho, \kappa) \mid \mathsf{sn}(a, \kappa) \mid \mathsf{na}(\kappa) \mid \mathsf{be}(\kappa) \\
v \in \textit{Value} \quad &= \textit{CommVal} + \textit{FunVal} \\
m \in \textit{CommVal} \quad &= \textit{Addr} + \textit{PrimVal} + \\
&\quad \textit{CommVal} \times \cdots \times \textit{CommVal} \\
a, (i, a) \in \textit{Addr} \quad &= \textit{BaseAddr} + (\mathbb{N} \times \textit{Addr}) \\
f \in \textit{FunVal} \quad &= \textit{PrimFun} + \textit{Closure} \\
\mathsf{cl}(x, e, \rho) \in \textit{Closure} \quad &= \textit{Var} \times \textit{Exp} \times \textit{Env} \\
e \in \textit{Exp} \quad & \\
x \in \textit{Var} \quad &
\end{aligned}
$$

Fig. 3. Machine States, Environments, Continuations and Values

$$\langle c, \rho, \kappa \rangle \mapsto_\lambda \langle \kappa, c \rangle$$
$$\langle x, \rho, \kappa \rangle \mapsto_\lambda \langle \kappa, \rho(x) \rangle$$
$$\langle (\lambda x.e), \rho, \kappa \rangle \mapsto_\lambda \langle \kappa, \mathsf{cl}(x, e, \rho) \rangle$$
$$\langle (e_1\ e_2), \rho, \kappa \rangle \mapsto_\lambda \langle e_1, \rho, \mathsf{ar}(e_2, \rho, \kappa) \rangle$$
$$\langle [e_1 \Leftarrow e_2], \rho, \kappa \rangle \mapsto_\lambda \langle e_1, \rho, \mathsf{me}(e_2, \rho, \kappa) \rangle$$
$$\langle \mathsf{new}\ e, \rho, \kappa \rangle \mapsto_\lambda \langle e, \rho, \mathsf{na}(\kappa) \rangle$$
$$\langle \mathsf{become}\ e, \rho, \kappa \rangle \mapsto_\lambda \langle e, \rho, \mathsf{be}(\kappa) \rangle$$

$$\langle \mathsf{mt}, v \rangle \mapsto_\lambda \langle v \rangle$$
$$\langle \mathsf{ar}(e, \rho, \kappa), f \rangle \mapsto_\lambda \langle e, \rho, \mathsf{fn}(f, \kappa) \rangle$$
$$\langle \mathsf{fn}(\mathsf{cl}(x, e, \rho), \kappa), v \rangle \mapsto_\lambda \langle e, \rho[x \mapsto v], \kappa \rangle$$
$$\langle \mathsf{fn}(f, \kappa), v \rangle \mapsto_\lambda \langle \kappa, \delta(f, v) \rangle \qquad (f \in PrimFun)$$
$$\langle \mathsf{me}(e, \rho, \kappa), a \rangle \mapsto_\lambda \langle e, \rho, \mathsf{sn}(a, \kappa) \rangle$$

Fig. 4.   The Semantics of the Sequential Sublanguage as a CEK Machine

We define the operational semantics of the sequential sublanguage as the transition relation $\mapsto_\lambda$ on *MState* as shown in Fig. 4. The semantics, expressed as a CEK machine, basically corresponds to a call-by-value λ-calculus.

3.2. The Semantics of the Actor Primitives

Now we define the operational semantics of the core language as a transition relation on actor configurations. The semantics is basically an adaptation of the one given by Agha *et al.*[16]

An *actor configuration* (hereafter, *configuration*) is a snapshot of an actor system (a group of actors) at a certain frame of reference. Fig. 5 describes the domains of configurations (*Conf*) and related structures. We

$$\langle A, T \rangle_X^R \in Conf \qquad = ActorMap \times \mathcal{F}_\mathcal{M}(Task) \times \mathcal{F}(Addr) \times \mathcal{F}(Addr)$$
$$(\langle A, T \rangle_X^R \text{ should satisfy the property defined in Definition 3.1})$$
$$A \in ActorMap = Addr \to_{\mathsf{fin}} ActorState$$
$$\varsigma, (q, \sigma, s) \in ActorState = Queue \times MState \times Mode$$
$$q \in Queue = Comm\,Val^*$$
$$s \in Mode = \{0, 1, 2\}$$
$$(a, m) \in Task = Addr \times Comm\,Val$$

Fig. 5.   Actor Configurations, Actor Maps and Tasks.

write $\langle A, T \rangle_X^R$ to denote an actor configuration[b]. A is a finite function called *actor map* that models the current collection of actors in the configuration. $A(a) = (q, \sigma, s)$ is the state of the actor with address a, where q, σ and s are the message queue, the machine state and the *mode* of the actor respectively. The mode is one of 0, 1 or 2, representing the dormant, active or anonymous mode of the actor respectively. T is the finite multiset of *tasks* — messages that have been sent but not yet received. A task (a, m) consists of the destination address a and a communicable value m as the message content. R and X are the finite sets of *receptionists* and *external actors* respectively. Receptionist are externally visible actors of the configuration. External actors are not included in A but referred to by actors in A.

Here we introduce some more notations. $\text{Act}(A)$ indicates the set of the addresses of non-anonymous actors in $A \in ActorMap$, defined as

$$\text{Act}(A) = \{a \in \text{Dom}(A) \mid A(a) = (q, \sigma, s) \wedge s \neq 2\}.$$

We write $addrs(v)$ to denote the set of all addresses referred within the value v. For example, $addrs((a_1, (10, a_2))) = \{a_1, a_2\}$ if $a_1, a_2 \in Addr$. We extend the domain of $addrs$ to *MState* and *Queue* so that we can calculate the set of all addresses referred by an actor. For $a_1, a_2 \in Addr$, we write $a_1 \overset{1}{\leadsto} a_2$ iff $a_1 = (i, a_2)$. The binary relation $\leadsto$ on *Addr* is defined as the reflexive transitive closure of $\overset{1}{\leadsto}$. In addition, $a \leadsto X$ means that $\exists a' \in X. a \leadsto a'$ if $X \subseteq Addr$. We write $\bullet$ to indicate the sole value of the unit type.

Fig. 6 shows the transition relation $\mapsto_\alpha$ on *Conf* that gives the operational semantics of the core language. In this semantics description, the fresh address generation $a' = \text{fresh}(a)$ means that the form of the generated address a' depends on a; i.e., $a' \in BaseAddr$ if $a \in BaseAddr$, and, on the other hand, if $a = (i, a_0)$, then $a' = (i', a_0)$ and i' is a fresh index.

A configuration should satisfy the following property. Proposition 3.1 shows that this property is an invariant over the transition. The proof can be done by straightforward case analysis on the rules in Fig. 6.

Definition 3.1 (Configuration Property). $\langle A, T \rangle_X^R \in Conf$ *satisfies* the configuration property *iff the following conditions hold:*

$$\forall a \in R. [a \leadsto \text{Act}(A)], \tag{1}$$

---

[b]This notation loosely follows that used by Agha et al.[16]

(SEQ) $\langle A[a \mapsto (q, \sigma_1, s)], T\rangle_X^R \mapsto_\alpha \langle A[a \mapsto (q, \sigma_2, s)], T\rangle_X^R$
$$(s \neq 0 \wedge \sigma_1 \mapsto_\lambda \sigma_2)$$

(NEW) $\langle A[a \mapsto (q, \langle \mathsf{na}(\kappa), f\rangle, s)], T\rangle_X^R$
$\mapsto_\alpha \langle A[a \mapsto (q, \langle \kappa, a'\rangle, s)][a' \mapsto (\varepsilon, \langle f\rangle, 0)], T\rangle_X^R$
$$(s \neq 0 \wedge a' = \mathrm{fresh}(a))$$

(BECM) $\langle A[a \mapsto (q, \langle \mathsf{be}(\kappa), f\rangle, 1)], T\rangle_X^R$
$\mapsto_\alpha \langle A[a \mapsto (q, \langle f\rangle, 0)][a' \mapsto (\varepsilon, \langle \kappa, \bullet\rangle, 2)], T\rangle_X^R$
$$(a' = \mathrm{fresh}(a))$$

(SEND) $\langle A[a \mapsto (q, \langle \mathsf{sn}(a', \kappa), m\rangle, s)], T\rangle_X^R$
$\mapsto_\alpha \langle A[a \mapsto (q, \langle \kappa, \bullet\rangle, s)], \{(a', m)\} \cup T\rangle_X^R$
$$(s \neq 0 \wedge a' \rightsquigarrow \mathrm{Dom}(A) \cup X)$$

(RECV) $\langle A[a \mapsto (q, \sigma, s)], \{(a, m)\} \cup T\rangle_X^R$
$\mapsto_\alpha \langle A[a \mapsto (q \cdot m, \sigma, s)], T\rangle_X^R$ $(s \neq 2)$

(ACC) $\langle A[a \mapsto (m \cdot q, \langle f\rangle, 0)], T\rangle_X^R$
$\mapsto_\alpha \langle A[a \mapsto (q, \langle \mathsf{fn}(f, \mathsf{mt}), (a, m)\rangle, 1)], T\rangle_X^R$

(ROUTE) $\langle A, \{((i, a), m)\} \cup T\rangle_X^R \mapsto_\alpha \langle A, \{(a, (i, m))\} \cup T\rangle_X^R$
$$((i, a) \notin \mathrm{Dom}(A)) \wedge a \rightsquigarrow \mathrm{Dom}(A)))$$

(IN) $\langle A, T\rangle_X^R \mapsto_\alpha \langle A, \{(a, m)\} \cup T\rangle_{X \cup (addrs(m) \setminus Dom(A))}^R$
$$(a \in R \wedge addrs(m) \cap \mathrm{Dom}(A) \subseteq R)$$

(OUT) $\langle A, \{(a, m)\} \cup T\rangle_X^R \mapsto_\alpha \langle A, T\rangle_X^{R \cup (addrs(m) \cap Dom(A))}$
$$(a \not\rightsquigarrow \mathrm{Dom}(A)) \wedge a \rightsquigarrow X)$$

Fig. 6.   The Semantics of the Core Language

$$\forall a \in X. [a \not\rightsquigarrow \mathrm{Dom}(A)], \tag{2}$$

$$\forall (q, \sigma, s) \in \mathrm{Rng}(A). \forall a \in addrs(q) \cup addrs(\sigma). [a \rightsquigarrow \mathrm{Act}(A) \cup X], \tag{3}$$

$$\forall (a', m) \in T. \forall a \in \{a'\} \cup addrs(m). [a \rightsquigarrow \mathrm{Act}(A) \cup X], \tag{4}$$

$$\forall a, a' \in \mathrm{Dom}(A) \cup X. [a \rightsquigarrow a' \implies a = a']. \tag{5}$$

Proposition 3.1. *If* $\langle A_1, T_1\rangle_{X_1}^{R_1}$ *satisfies the configuration property and* $\langle A_1, T_1\rangle_{X_1}^{R_1} \mapsto_\alpha \langle A_2, T_2\rangle_{X_2}^{R_2}$, *then* $\langle A_2, T_2\rangle_{X_2}^{R_2}$ *satisfies the configuration property.*

4. Compositional Construction of Meta-Level Actors

4.1. *Actor Groups*

As defined in Fig. 3, a mail address is either a single value in *BaseAddr* or a pair of a positive integer and an address. This address structure is used for organizing actor groups. Let a be an address. If $a \in BaseAddr$, we call it a *base address*. If $a = (i, a')$, we call i and a' the *local index* and *group address* of a respectively. An *actor group* is a collection of actors that share a common group address. For example, suppose that we have six actors with the addresses $(1, a_1)$, $(1, (2, a_1))$, $(2, (2, a_1))$, $(3, a_1)$, a_2 and $(1, a_3)$ where $a_1, a_2, a_2 \in BaseAddr$. The actors with addresses $(1, a_1)$ and $(3, a_1)$ belong to the group a_1, and the actors $(1, (2, a_1))$ and $(2, (2, a_1))$ belong to $(2, a_1)$. The group $(2, a_1)$ belongs to a_1 and is called a subgroup of a_1. The actor a_2 does not belong to any group, and the actor $(1, a_3)$ is the sole member of a_3. Fig. 7 depicts the example.

The configuration property (Definition 3.1 (5)) enforces that if an address is used as a group address of some actor or group, no actor with the address is allowed to exist. For example, a_1, a_3 and $(2, a_1)$ in the above example cannot be the addresses of actors.

Note that if an actor that belongs to a group creates an actor, the new actor also belongs to the same group. This is imposed by the characteristics of the fresh name generation mentioned in Section 3.2.

4.2. *Composition of Actor Groups*

In this subsection, we define the composition of an actor group. The purpose of the composition is to construct a single actor with which the group can be replaced.

We first introduce a configuration of a group to be composed. Let $a \in Addr$ and $I \in \mathcal{F}(\mathbb{N})$. Consider a configuration $\langle A, T \rangle_X^R \in Conf$ where

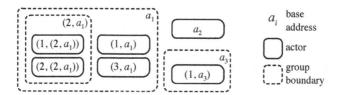

Fig. 7. Actor Groups

$\text{Dom}(A) = \{(i, a) \mid i \in I\}$. This means that every actor in this configuration belongs to the same group with group address a.

Next we discuss how a composed version of the configuration $\langle A, T \rangle_X^R$ should be defined. Because the group must be replaced by a single actor, the actor map of the composed version, denoted by $\mathbf{A}$, should satisfy that $\text{Act}(\mathbf{A}) = \{a\}$ and $\text{Dom}(\mathbf{A}) \cap \text{Dom}(A) = \varnothing$. In $\mathbf{A}$, a is used as the address of the sole (non-anonymous) actor in $\mathbf{A}$. We call $\mathbf{A}$ the *composed actor map* of A (wrt a) and the actor with the address a the *composed actor*.

Let us consider the configuration $\langle \mathbf{A}, T \rangle_X^R$ obtained by replacing the actor map of the original configuration with the composed one. From **(ROUTE)** in Fig. 6, messages targeted to group member actors in A are redirected to the composed actor in $\mathbf{A}$. Thus it is possible that the composed actor can behave as if it were a member of the original group. We expect that we can use $\langle \mathbf{A}, T \rangle_X^R$ instead of $\langle A, T \rangle_X^R$; *i.e.*, $\mathbf{A}$ should model (simulate, or interpret) A.

4.3. *Abstract Definition of the Meta-Level Behaviors*

It is possible to construct the composed actor in various ways, for example, by defining the behavior function of the composed actor from scratch,[13] or by composing individual (per-actor) meta-level actors.[14] In those previous work, meta-level actors are described concretely by the defined languages, while the semantics of the defined languages themselves are defined formally using other methods. Unfortunately, such difference of descriptions complicates reasoning about systems written in the languages.

To tackle the issue, we propose a method based on *abstract definition* of meta-level actors. We first introduce the notion of abstract meta-base relations on actor maps. Then we preset a set of constraints on $\mapsto_\alpha$ that defines the behavior of meta-level actors without using concrete description by the defined language (the core language).

Let A be an actor map where $\text{Dom}(A) = \{(i, a) \mid i \in I\}$ and $\mathbf{A}$ be the composed actor map of A wrt a. We write $\mathbf{A} \models_a A$ to mean that $\mathbf{A}$ models A; *i.e.*, $\mathbf{A}$ is the meta-level representation of A. Note that we don't state any concrete definition of $\models_a$. The notation $\mathbf{A}[\![i \mapsto \varsigma]\!]$ denotes the composed actor map that is identical to $\mathbf{A}$ except that it models the actor with address (i, a); *i.e.*, $\exists A \in \textit{ActorMap}. [\mathbf{A}[\![i \mapsto \varsigma]\!] \models_a A \wedge A((i, a)) = \varsigma]$ where $\varsigma \in \textit{ActorState}$.

Now we define the behavior of $\mathbf{A}$ as the meta-level of A. Fig. 8 defines the set of constraint rules on $\mapsto_\alpha$ that makes $\mathbf{A}$ to be the meta-level of A. The notation $\mapsto\!\!\!\twoheadrightarrow_\alpha$ denotes the reflexive transitive closure of $\mapsto_\alpha$. The

(SEQ)
$$\frac{\langle \mathbf{A}_1[\![i \mapsto \varsigma]\!], T_1\rangle_{X_1}^{R_1} \mapsto_\alpha \langle \mathbf{A}_2[\![i \mapsto \varsigma]\!], T_2\rangle_{X_2}^{R_2} \quad \sigma_1 \mapsto_\lambda \sigma_2}{\langle \mathbf{A}_1[\![i \mapsto (q, \sigma_1, s)]\!], T_1\rangle_{X_1}^{R_1} \mapsto_\alpha \langle \mathbf{A}_2[\![i \mapsto (q, \sigma_2, s)]\!], T_2\rangle_{X_2}^{R_2}}$$
$$(\varsigma = (q, \sigma_1, s) \wedge s \neq 0)$$

(NEW)
$$\frac{\langle \mathbf{A}_1[\![i \mapsto \varsigma]\!], T_1\rangle_{X_1}^{R_1} \mapsto_\alpha \langle \mathbf{A}_2[\![i \mapsto \varsigma]\!], T_2\rangle_{X_2}^{R_2}}{\langle \mathbf{A}_1[\![i \mapsto (q, \langle \mathsf{na}(\kappa), f\rangle, s)]\!], T_1\rangle_{X_1}^{R_1}}$$
$$\mapsto_\alpha \langle \mathbf{A}_2[\![i \mapsto (q, \langle \kappa, (i', a)\rangle, 0)]\!][\![i' \mapsto (\varepsilon, \langle f\rangle, 0)]\!], T_2\rangle_{X_2}^{R_2}$$
$$(\varsigma = (q, \langle \mathsf{na}(\kappa), f\rangle, s) \wedge s \neq 0 \wedge (i', a) = \mathrm{fresh}((i, a)))$$

$(BECM)$
$$\frac{\langle \mathbf{A}_1[\![i \mapsto \varsigma]\!], T_1\rangle_{X_1}^{R_1} \mapsto_\alpha \langle \mathbf{A}_2[\![i \mapsto \varsigma]\!], T_2\rangle_{X_2}^{R_2}}{\langle \mathbf{A}_1[\![i \mapsto (q, \langle \mathsf{be}(\kappa), f\rangle, 1)]\!], T_1\rangle_{X_1}^{R_1}}$$
$$\mapsto_\alpha \langle \mathbf{A}_2[\![i \mapsto (q, \langle f\rangle, 0)]\!][\![i' \mapsto (\varepsilon, \langle \kappa, \bullet\rangle, 2)]\!], T_2\rangle_{X_2}^{R_2}$$
$$(\varsigma = (q, \langle \mathsf{be}(\kappa), f\rangle, 1) \wedge (i', a) = \mathrm{fresh}((i, a)))$$

$(SEND)$
$$\frac{\langle \mathbf{A}_1[\![i \mapsto \varsigma]\!], T_1\rangle_{X_1}^{R_1} \mapsto_\alpha \langle \mathbf{A}_2[\![i \mapsto \varsigma]\!], T_2\rangle_{X_2}^{R_2}}{\langle \mathbf{A}_1[\![i \mapsto (q, \langle \mathsf{sn}(a', \kappa), m\rangle, s)]\!], T_1\rangle_{X_1}^{R_1}}$$
$$\mapsto_\alpha \langle \mathbf{A}_2[\![i \mapsto (q, \langle \kappa, \bullet\rangle, s)]\!], \{(a', m)\} \cup T_2\rangle_{X_2}^{R_2}$$
$$(\varsigma = (q, \langle \mathsf{sn}(a', \kappa), m\rangle, s) \wedge s \neq 0 \wedge a' \rightsquigarrow \{a\} \cup X_1 \cup X_2)$$

$(RECV)$
$$\frac{\langle \mathbf{A}_1[\![i \mapsto \varsigma]\!], T_1\rangle_{X_1}^{R_1} \mapsto_\alpha \langle \mathbf{A}_2[\![i \mapsto \varsigma]\!], T_2\rangle_{X_2}^{R_2}}{\langle \mathbf{A}_1[\![i \mapsto (q, \sigma, s)]\!], \{((i, a), m)\} \cup T_1\rangle_{X_1}^{R_1}}$$
$$\mapsto_\alpha \langle \mathbf{A}_2[\![i \mapsto (q \cdot m, \sigma, s)]\!], T_2\rangle_{X_2}^{R_2}$$
$$(\varsigma = (q, \sigma, s) \wedge s \neq 2)$$

(ACC)
$$\frac{\langle \mathbf{A}_1[\![i \mapsto \varsigma]\!], T_1\rangle_{X_1}^{R_1} \mapsto_\alpha \langle \mathbf{A}_2[\![i \mapsto \varsigma]\!], T_2\rangle_{X_2}^{R_2}}{\langle \mathbf{A}_1[\![i \mapsto (m \cdot q, \langle f\rangle, 0)]\!], T_1\rangle_{X_1}^{R_1}}$$
$$\mapsto_\alpha \langle \mathbf{A}_2[\![i \mapsto (q, \langle \mathsf{fn}(f, \mathsf{mt}), ((i, a), m)\rangle, 1)]\!], T_2\rangle_{X_2}^{R_2}$$
$$(\varsigma = (m \cdot q, \langle f\rangle, 0))$$

Fig. 8. Constraint Rules for Meta-Level Actor Behaviors

following lemma says that if $\mathbf{A}$ is defined to satisfy the rules in Fig. 8, it keeps the meta-base relation $\models_a$ along the transitions.

Lemma 4.1. *Let A_k be actor maps where $\mathrm{Dom}(A_k) = \{(i, a) \mid i \in I_k\}$ for $k \in \{1, 2\}$ and let $\mathbf{A}_1$ be a composed actor map of A_1 wrt a that is defined to satisfy the rules in Fig. 8. If $\mathbf{A}_1 \models_a A_1$ and $\langle A_1, T_1\rangle_{X_1}^{R_1} \mapsto_\alpha \langle A_2, T_2\rangle_{X_2}^{R_2}$, then there exists a composed actor map $\mathbf{A}_2$ of A_2 such that $\langle A_1, T_1\rangle_{X_1}^{R_1} \mapsto \to_\alpha \langle \mathbf{A}_2, T_2\rangle_{X_2}^{R_2}$ and $\mathbf{A}_2 \models_a A_2$.*

Proof. By induction on the structure of the rules in Fig. 8. □

5. Concluding Remarks

In this paper, we propose a new method for defining meta-level behaviors of actor groups. Our proposal is based on a parallel composition of actor groups and a constraint-based abstract specification of meta-level behaviors. The method provides uniform construction of meta-levels in group-wide reflection (GWR) without using concrete description by the defined languages. For future work, we plan to develop a framework of reasoning meta-level behaviors based on this proposal.

Acknowledgments

This work is partly supported by JSPS KAKENHI Grant No. 24500033.

References

1. G. Agha, *Actors: A Model of Concurrent Computation in Distributed Systems*, MIT Press, 1986.
2. A. Yonezawa, J.-P. Briot and E. Shibayama, Object-oriented concurrent programming in ABCL/1, in *OOPSLA '86*, 258–268, ACM, 1986.
3. S. Tasharofi, P. Dinges and R. E. Johnson, Why do Scala developers mix the actor model with other concurrency models?, in *ECOOP '13*, 302–326, LNCS 7920, Springer, 2013.
4. S. Frølund, *Coordinating distributed objects: an actor-based approach to synchronization*, MIT Press, 1996.
5. C. Varela and G. Agha, A hierarchical model for coordination of concurrent activities, in *COORDINATION '99*, 166–182, LNCS 1594, Springer, 1999.
6. S. Ren, Y. Yu, N. Chen, K. Marth, P.-E. Poirot and L. Shen, Actors, roles and coordinators — a coordination model for open distributed and embedded systems, in *COORDINATION '06*, 247–265, LNCS 4038, Springer, 2006.
7. P. Dinges and G. Agha, Scoped synchronization constraints for large scale actor systems, in *COORDINATION '12*, 89–103, LNCS 7274, Springer, 2012.
8. J. De Koster, T. Van Cutsem and T. D'Hondt, Domains: Safe sharing among actors, in *AGERE!@SPLASH 2012*, 11–22, ACM, 2012.
9. T. Watanabe and A. Yonezawa, Reflection in an object-oriented concurrent language, in *OOPSLA '88*, 306–315, ACM, 1988.
10. G. S. Blair, G. Coulson, P. Robin and M. Papathomas, An architecture for next generation middleware, in *Middleware '98*, 191–206, Springer, 1998.
11. N. Venkatasubramanian, C. Talcott and G. Agha, A formal model for reasoning about adaptive QoS-enabled middleware, in *FME 2001*, 197–221, LNCS 2021, Springer, 2001.

12. T. Suzuki, K. Pinte, T. Van Cutsem, W. De Meuter and A. Yonezawa, Programming language support for routing in pervasive networks, in *PERWARE 2011*, 226–232, IEEE, 2011.

13. T. Watanabe and A. Yonezawa, An actor-based metalevel architecture for group-wide reflection, in *Foundations of Object-Oriented Languages*, 405–425, LNCS 489, Springer, 1991.

14. T. Watanabe, Towards a compositional reflective architecture for actor-based systems, in *AGERE!@SPLASH 2013*, 19–24, ACM, 2013.

15. M. Felleisen and D. P. Friedman, Control operators, the SECD-machine, and the lambda-calculus, in *IFIP TC 2/WG2. 2 Working Conf. on Formal Description of Programming Concepts Part III*, 193–219, 1986.

16. G. Agha, I. A. Mason, S. F. Smith and C. Talcott, A foundation for actor computation, *Journal of Functional Programming*, 7(1), 1–72, 1997.

AN APPLICATION PROGRAMMING INTERFACE FOR THE COMMUNICATION AND STORAGE PROTOCOL FOR THE TALA EMPATHIC SPACE[*]

GREGORY CU

*Center for Empathic-Human Computer Interactions,
Computer Technology Department, De La Salle University, Taft Avenue,
Manila, 1004, Philippines*

JOSE MARI R. CIPRIANO

*Center for Empathic-Human Computer Interactions,
Computer Technology Department, De La Salle University*

MICHAEL JOSEPH GONZALES

*Center for Empathic-Human Computer Interactions,
Software Technology Department, De La Salle University*

KEVIN MARTIN TANALGO

*Center for Empathic-Human Computer Interactions,
Software Technology Department, De La Salle University*

CHRISTIAN KAY B. MAGDAONG

*Center for Empathic-Human Computer Interactions,
Computer Technology Department, De La Salle University*

MICA PAULINE TIU

*Center for Empathic-Human Computer Interactions,
Software Technology Department, De La Salle University*

JERICHO ROMEO U. LONGALONG

*Center for Empathic-Human Computer Interactions,
Software Technology Department, De La Salle University*

[*] This work is supported the Philippine Department of Science and Technology-Philippine Council for Industry and Energy Research and Development.

The TALA Empathic Space is a physical, computing space that contains modules and sensors which recognizes the feelings of its occupant and responds to it by deploying changes in the environment. The space is composed of different modules and devices that collect and process data for it to be able to adapt by providing changes on the ambient settings. The COSMOS protocol provides a way on how devices and applications communicate and transfer data between devices in the empathic space. The protocol also provides an organized method for storing and accessing distributed data. Moreover, the empathic space also contains nodes which are devices or applications connected to a network and capable of sending and receiving data. COSMOS defines generic object called cosmos object, which is used to send commands and data for node to node communication and accessing data readily available on the network. COSMOS also provides an Application Programming Interface (API) that enables the user to device functions and commands for nodes usage and data acquisition and reception. With the growing devices and numerous data within the TALA Empathic Space, a user needs a convenient way to observe processes and outputs and manage the tools within the space. With the use of the COSMOS API, developers can create applications or systems that can control and manage the on-going transactions between devices and data in the empathic space. A dashboard system is capable of managing the device and gathering multiple, simultaneous data within the space. The TALA Dashbaord (TADa) is developed using the COSMOS API to provide users a manageable interface in accessing the devices and data available in the empathic space. The TADa system aims to provide different type of users - the Administrator who is able to control all devices, the Concierge to stream data, and the User who can simply view information — the system is able to adjust its accessibility per user.

1. Introduction

The TALA Empathic space aims to understand multi-modal emotions and develop human-centered systems which enable computers to detect human effect and adapts to the user's needs (Estrada, et. al., 2010). The Empathic Space has sensors, actuators, cameras and microphones used for data gathering and environment manipulation. Collected data from the space are processed and used as a basis in decision making of systems in the space. The applications developed in the empathic space can extract data from the devices as well as transfer, stream and store data in other systems. This process requires a standardized protocol that facilitates the communication of devices and method of data handling between these devices.

The COSMOS communication and storage protocol serves as a middleware that handles the simultaneous device access and provides a structured and organized method of handling data across the local area network (LAN) of the empathic space. This protocol serves as a mediator for device communication and data transfer for simultaneous processing. The COSMOS protocol functionalities are made available to the developer through the use of an Application Programming Interface (API). The API provides methods and classes to develop applications which can register and access devices, and be able to transfer and store data within the local network. This provides the developers the control and for the devices and data flow inside the empathic space.

Through the use of the COSMOS API developers are able to develop an application to monitor the different devices and functionalities available in the TALA empathic space. A dashboard is an easy-to-read, real-time user interface showing a graphical presentation of the current status (snapshot) and historical trends of an organization's Key Performance Indicators (KPIs) to enable instantaneous and informed decisions to be made at a glance (McFadden, 2012). A dashboard can be implemented for the TALA Empathic Space through the use of the COSMOS API, to monitor the live of performance of the devices and locate specifics files or data in the local network. This empathic space is a physical computing system that adds value to ambient intelligent spaces by considering empathy when inferring user and context features and initiating interactions (J. Cu & R. Trogo, 2012). Without the dashboard, data is very difficult to be monitored and users cannot see the state of the empathic space at any point in time. A dashboard enable users to manage and control the system and collect data from the empathic space — acting as a key to gaining information from the ambient intelligence within the space.

2. Review of Related Works

2.1. *Centralized Data Acquisition Unit for the Empathic Space*

Central Data Acquisition Unit is a procedure data management through "collective structures" that serves as the data management medium of data collected inside the empathic space (Estrada, et. al., 2010). The data acquisition unit caters to both low-level and high-level structures of data extracted from various hardware devices like sensors and microphones. The CDAU, as it is called, provides an efficient interconnection between high-level and low-level structures and providing ease of access to its data. The elaboration of devices like the layout of sensors, sensor data processing and interfacing, as well as data collection and management are also discussed. Results of the test runs of the devices as well as data collection procedures were presented such as the accuracy of occupant presence recognition and detection.

2.2. TALA Empathic Space: Integrating Affect and Activity Recognition into a Smart Space

The empathic space named TALA that does not involve obtrusive means of automatically detecting a presence of an entity in an empathic space. Instead, it recognizes the presence of an occupant automatically, through constant learning of its patterns. Different datasets were involved, like Identity Dataset, Affect Dataset and Activity Dataset, used to identify patterns of possible occupants and discrepancy factors in the empathic space (Cu, et. al., 2010). Identity recognition techniques such as facial mapping are also discussed, as well as affecting data that may alter the processing of data for a normal occupant. Results of tests as well as discrepancies in the data are also presented.

2.3. MOD-G Protocol: A Communication Protocol for the Empathic Network

MOD-G is an empathic network protocol that allows each every node in the network to interact (Bartolome, Rivera, Rosalin & Tan, 2010). It also enables data access for every user through its defined Application Programming Interface (API) which has its commands for receiving and sending data. Even though they did not implemented well the algorithms they used, the model and design that they applied were in high level of network nodes tolerance and convergence. On the contrary, scalability of the API was not implemented properly because of the dependencies on the protocol itself.

3. System Architecture

3.1. System Overview of the COSMOS Protocol

The COSMOS protocol set-up is composed of a node middleware, an API for applications and a utility program for device and resource management. The node middleware is responsible for device and node-to-node communication and storage processes between nodes. A host node can contain cameras, microphones and sensor devices. The node middleware allows registered devices to be accessed by other host nodes that are part of the LAN. The node middleware is also responsible for storage processes that include file transfer, locating other host node that contains copies of the same requested file and allow multiple nodes to serve a file request. The API is used to create applications that

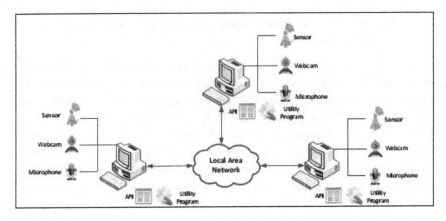

Fig. 1. System Set-up

access the functionalities available within the node middleware. This allows developers to utilize the resources available in the LAN. The utility program facilitates ease of registration of devices and access of files for developers to use.

3.2. *System Architecture of the COSMOS Protocol*

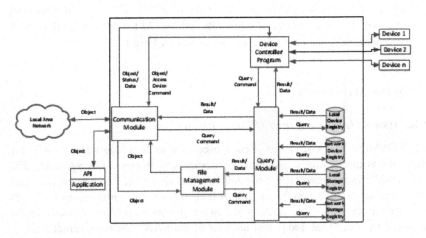

Fig. 2. Set-up of the COSMOS Node Middleware

3.3. *COSMOS API*

The COSMOS Application Programming Interface (COSMOS API) is the defined set of objects and methods that developers can use to create applications that utilizes the resources available in the said laboratory. The API provides a standard approach to communicate and make use of registered devices, nodes and files that are part of the Local Area Network. The COSMOS API includes retrieving data from devices such as, sensor data, camera data and audio data. Data received is in the form of bytes which can be transformed to a specified format. The COSMOS API is also use to send and received files that are part of the network. This also provides a way for developers to learn and retrieve the names of registered devices and files in given node.

The COSMOS API is responsible in communicating with the COSMOS Middleware. This allows the developer to communicate with the network that provides resources for its applications. Developers are required to use the API to fully access these resources in the Local Area Network.

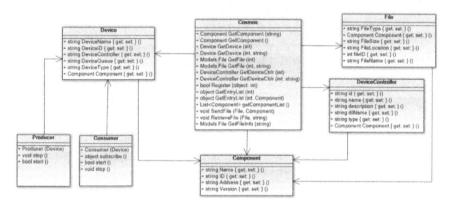

Fig. 3. COSMOS API Class Diagram

3.4. *TADa System Overview*

TADa, short for the TALA Dashboard, is a web-based system that serves as the primary interface for data management in the TALA Empathic Space through the use of the COSMOS protocol. These data, ranging from videos to audios and from gestures to body temperatures, are gathered by the various sensors in the space. TADa provides a way for TALA users to view all these data, live streamed or archived, in just a single application. To stream data, devices must be added to TADa's registry and this is done using the dashboard itself. Device status and settings can also be viewed and configured by authorized users. Aside from these, TADa can control certain settings in the environment of the TALA Empathic Space such as music volume and room temperature.

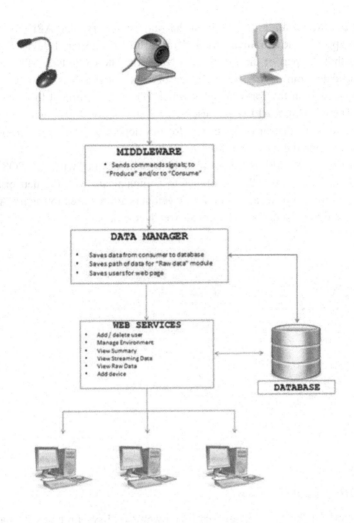

Fig. 4. TADa's System Architecture

3.5. *TADa System Architecture utilizing the COSMOS Protocol*

The architectural design consists of three main modules namely the Middleware which consists of the API and the Middleware of COSMOS itself which is responsible for getting data from the devices connected to a host node. The Middleware can get data from installed devices and it can be broadcasted to other members of the local network. Users of the Empathic Space can create applications, like TADa, that can make use of the resources using the API of

COSMOS. The Data Manager catches, saves, and throws data to the web service directly and to the database of TADa. The Data Manager module receives commands from the Middleware to produce data from a chosen device, or to consume data from a chosen device. When data from a device is consumed, it is automatically saved into the database to be used by the Web Services module for different features of the web page.

Using the COSMOS API, the TADa dashboard can add and access the device through a web interface that are available for the users of the empathic space. Data, such as video, audio and sensor files are also made available using the web interface of the TADa system. These functionalities are implementation of the COSMOS API.

Fig. 6. TADa Web Interface

Using the COSMOS API, the TADa dashboard can add and access the device through a web interface that are available for the users of the empathic space. Data, such as video, audio and sensor files are also made available using the web interface of the TADa system. These functionalities are implementation of the COSMOS API.

View Raw Data

Date

From ⬜ ▾ to ⬜ ▾

Time

From 00 ▾ 00 ▾ to 00 ▾ 00 ▾

Devices

⬜ ▾ Select Device

Show Result

2013730_195.avi

© 2013 TADa About · Contact Us

Back to top

4. Initial Testing and Findings

4.1. *Real Time Streaming*

Testing Real Time Streaming is done through the use of the middleware and the Device Control Program to access a Camera. On a separate node, there is an application that displays the frames captured by the webcam. The test is run 5 times for 10 seconds, creating an average. The test was conducted for 5 times, and based on the results on testing the Streaming capabilities of the COSMOS protocol, we achieved an average of 9.94 frames per second (FPS). Although the average FPS output of the camera was about 10.1 FPS when used locally and our output was lower than 10.1, this was the best frame rate achieved with the network traffic.

Table 1. Frames per second test using the COSMOS Protocol

Trial #	Output Rate (FPS)
1	10.1
2	10.0
3	9.7
4	10.1
5	9.8
Average	9.94

4.2. File Management

This test measures the capability of the COSMOS Protocol to transfer files over the network as well as the speed. When a file is prepared for transfer, the host which will service the request will use a Queue, which name, in form a random string coming from the requesting host, to send File Objects which contain the payload carrying the file segments, controlled by a buffer which size is 512 kilobytes. The file segments will be sent continuously, until the command type field in the payload changes and tells the protocol of the end of file. The speed of the file transfer is measured by dividing the total size of the file to the total time, in seconds that the file transfer was completed.

Table 2 File Transfer rate using the COSMOS Protocol

Trial	File Size	Transfer Rate
1	188 MB	2.40 MBps
2	240 MB	2.41 MBps
3	400 MB	2.42 MBps
4	800 MB	2.40 MBps
5	1 GB	2.40 MBps

4.3. Simultaneous Multiple Device Streaming

To test the capability of the COSMOS Protocol to facilitate simultaneous multiple device streaming, a minimum of three to four hosts, with connected web cameras and microphones connected using the COSMOS Protocol, and an application that streams data from the devices that makes use of the COSMOS API which are individually run on the hosts are used for the test. One host will act as the source or producer of the data stream, while all of the hosts will act as subscribers to the source of the stream. The effect of the number of clients or subscribers to the source of stream on the streaming rate is also observed. The test is done in five trials per increasing number of consumers, where the application that streams the data runs for 30 seconds. The streaming rate for all five trials is averaged to get the average streaming rate. For multiple consumers, the streaming rate is averaged for all trials.

4.4. Audio and Video Synchronization

To test the capability of the COSMOS Protocol to synchronize the streaming of image and sound data, two workstations that are wired to the CEHCI network with a connected webcam and microphone as well as a running application developed using the COSMOS API that streams the data objects will be used for the test. A computer will serve both as a producer and consumer of the stream, while another computer will only act as a consumer of the stream. In order to test the synchronization of image and sound, a volunteer from the CEHCI laboratory will show a piece of paper where the word "COSMOS" is written and will show and say the word in front of the workstation where the camera and microphone will stream the captured data. The time when the application captured the image and sound data is logged through timestamps, where the timestamp is up to the nearest millisecond due to the fast arrival of image and data objects. The proximity of the images and sound objects' timestamps to each other will then be compared for both workstations to see during what duration a word was shown and heard, in order to test its synchronization. The test is done in five trials, where the duration of every action of showing and speaking the word is around three to four seconds for both computers. The DateTime and StopWatch classes of the .NET framework are used to get the milliseconds, wherein the current elapsed ticks of the application are added to the current running ticks of the system clock of the application to get the nearest millisecond when the data object was captured.

Table 3 Tabulated Results of Average Streaming Rate per Increasing Number of Consumers

Number of Consumers	Trial 1 (Output in Average FPS)	Trial 2 (Output in Average FPS)	Trial 3 (Output in Average FPS)	Trial 4 (Output in Average FPS)	Trial 5 (Output in Average FPS)
1	9.33	8.40	8.90	9.03	9.10
2	5.57	5.67	5.70	5.58	5.90
3	4.21	4.34	4.15	4.12	4.15
4	3.31	3.80	3.38	3.12	2.98

Table 4 Tabulated Results of Start and End Duration of Captured Frames and Byte Data for Producer and Consumer / Subscriber Host

Trial Number	Start Time of Stream Segment Capture (in milliseconds)	Start Duration of Captured Frame Data (in milliseconds)	End Duration of Captured Frame Data (in milliseconds)	Start Duration of Captured Byte Data (in milliseconds)	End Duration of Captured Byte Data (in milliseconds)	End Time of Stream Segment Capture (in milliseconds)
1	1.12	1.126	4.224	1.121	4.229	4.23
2	7.21	7.218	11.323	7.212	11.328	11.33
3	14.31	14.317	17.414	14.312	17.418	17.42
4	20.41	20.415	23.504	20.412	23.508	23.51
5	26.32	26.324	29.114	26.321	29.119	29.12

Based from the testing done in the CEHCI laboratory, it is observed that sound data is captured faster by the application compared to bitmap data, because of the small size of the byte data sent continuously to the device queue, compared to the larger size of the bitmap data. There is a significant delay in the arrival time of the data objects in milliseconds, but this is because the byte objects are sent in small segments of 1KB each and may have different timestamps with each other, while the bitmap frames are sent as one segment of data. The capture timestamp of the bitmap frames are synchronized with the capture timestamp of the byte data in terms of seconds, but differ in milliseconds because of the sound byte data being sent in small segments.

5. Conclusion and Problems Encountered

5.1. *COSMOS API and TADa*

The API is able to provide the functionalities necessary to implement a dashboard that can monitor the live state of the empathic space. The dashboard is able access a device and gets feedback from it through streaming. Adding new devices is made available through the dashboard website. Through the COSMOS Protocol and the COSMOS API, the functionalities of the empathic space are made available using the TADa Dashboard. The application programming interface provides flexibility and ease-of-use for developers in developing researches in the empathic space. Through the TADa Dashboard, COSMOS Protocol and the Application Programming Interface, the empathic space is fully available to all researches in the empathic space.

5.2. *COSMOS Protocol*

Utilizing the ActiveMQ technology in the research allowed us to simplify the work and improve the protocol. The ActiveMQ technology uses the Queuing algorithm for its messages, allowing for it to all be simply filed properly and organized, and we would not need to worry much about the sequencing. It also allowed for us to ensure that each message would arrive to the different nodes on the COSMOS Network. ActiveMQ also allowed for simpler implementation of streaming which allowed for multiple consumer nodes to connect to the device for streaming. The use of Topics that was based on subscriptions allowed for this to be simple and easier to implement.

Since ActiveMQ framework is used for the communication module, the back bone module of the system, most of the issues and limitations of the system were concerned with activeMQ. The system's middleware should able to listen continuously for coming requests/commands from the network and at the same time from the API continuously. ActiveMQ can listen through a certain queue with used of sockets at a certain period of time until the connection it established expires. It does have a default time span to when the connection it established expires. ActiveMQ does not have a function that determines if the connection it established through a certain queue already expired and it is also hard to implement a method that knows the connection status of ActiveMQ. Since a time span can be set for the ActiveMQ can listen at a certain queue, setting also a constant time span to terminate the connection and establish a new connection is what the system answers for this kind of limitation.

Acknowledgement

This project was supported by the Department of Science and Technology-Philippine Council for Industry and Energy Research and Development (DOST-PCIERD) and De La Salle University – Center Empathic and Human Computer Interaction (DLSU-CEHCI) under the project "Development of a Scalable Computing System for an Ambient Intelligent Empathic Space", within the program entitled "Towards the Development of a Self-improving and the Ambient Intillegent Empathic Space: Data-centric, Multimodal Empathic Modeling from a Pluridisciplinary Perspective".

References

1. Estrada, A. Magdaong, R., Manalo, D., Oblepias, Cu. G. (2010). Centralized Data Acquisition Unit for the Empathic Space, Center for Human-Computer Interactions, De La Salle University-Manila
2. Bartolome, J. M., Rivera, D. A., Rosalin, O., Tan, G. (2010). MOD-G Protocol: A Communication Protocol for the Empathic Network, Center for Empathic and Human Computer Interaction, De La Salle University – Manila Philippines
3. Cu, *et al.* (2010). The TALA Empathic Space: Integrating Affect and Activity Recognition into a Smart Space, Center for Human-Computer Interactions, De La Salle University-Manila
4. J. Cu, G. C. P. I., R. Cabredo, & R. Trogo, M. S. (2012). The TALA empathic space: Integrating affect and activity recognition into a smart space.
5. McFadden, P. (2012, May 10). What is a dashboard really?
6. Apache. ActiveMQ open source messaging system. [accessed 2013 August 2]; Available from: http://activemq.apache.org/

AN OBJECT-ORIENTED LANGUAGE FOR PARAMETERISED REACTIVE SYSTEM SPECIFICATION BASED ON LINEAR TEMPORAL LOGIC

Kenji Osari, Takuya Murooka, Kiyotaka Hagiwara, Takahiro Ando[†], Masaya Shimakawa, Sohei Ito[‡], Shigeki Hagihara and Naoki Yonezaki

Department of Computer Science,
Graduate School of Information Science and Engineering,
Tokyo Institute of Technology,
Meguro-ku, Tokyo 152-8552, Japan

[†]*Department of Advanced Information Technology,*
Faculty of Information Science and Electrical Engineering,
Kyushu University, Nishi-ku, Fukuoka 819-0395, Japan

[‡]*Department of Fisheries Distribution and Management,*
National Fisheries University,
Shimonoseki, Yamaguchi 759-6595, Japan

We describe an object-oriented language, called T, for reactive system specifications based on linear temporal logic (LTL). Because the language is object-oriented, the specifications can be modular, and the modules are related by "is-a" and "has-a" relations. Furthermore, we can use parameterised specifications. We introduced the syntax and semantics of the language T, and report a compiler that interprets a specification written in T into an equivalent LTL formulation. Finally, we discuss the advantages of T and the compiler compared to other languages.

Keywords: Object-oriented Specification Language; Reactive system; Parameterized system; Linear Temporal Logic.

1. Introduction

There are many safety-critical systems in common usage, including systems that control nuclear power plants and air traffic-control systems. Such systems respond to requests from an environment with the appropriate timing, and are considered reactive systems.

In the formal development of reactive systems, linear temporal logic (LTL) is a commonly used specification language. By expressing the specifications of systems in LTL, if the specification has flaws, we can detect the cause of the flaws by the methods proposed in Ref. 1–3. Furthermore, after the specifications have been corrected, by checking whether they are realisable, we can automatically synthesise programs that satisfy the specifications.[4,5]

Several tools have been proposed for synthesising programs from LTL specifications, including Lily,[6,7] AcaciaPlus,[8,9] Unbeast.[10,11] The specifications should include all of the constraints of the behaviour of the systems and all of the assumptions of the environment; therefore, the scale of the specifications tends to be large. To provide large-scale specifications, we require a modular specification language. Furthermore, if the systems are parameterised, e.g., an n-floor m-lift elevator control system, or a n-process distributed system, so are the specifications. In such cases, it is extremely useful to have a formal specification language.

TRIO+[12] is an object-oriented extension of TRIO, which is a first-order temporal logic. In TRIO+, TRIO formulae are implemented in a modular manner as classes, and is-a and has-a relations can be defined between classes. However, TRIO+ is not aiming to be a specification language of reactive systems, but to be that of general time-critical systems. That is, specifications written in TRIO+ do not distinguish requests caused by an environment and responses of a system. Furthermore, formula-typed parameters are not allowed in TRIO+, and this is a matter of concern for specifying reactive systems.

AspectLTL[13] is a module-based extension of temporal logic, where LTL formulae are modularised as aspects, and these aspects modify transition systems that are described in SMV format.[14] From the modified transition systems, we can synthesise systems that behave within a given set of constraints that are represented by the transition systems. However, AspectLTL is not object-oriented, and parameterised specifications cannot be specified in AspectLTL. Therefore AspectLTL is not appropriate for large-scale parameterised specifications.

In this paper, we report an object-oriented language for reactive system specifications based on LTL. This language, called T, is object-oriented, and so we can provide specifications in a modular fashion, where the modules are related by the is-a and has-a relations. Furthermore, the specifications can be parameterised. We describe the syntax and semantics of the language, and report a compiler that transforms a specification written in T into an equivalent LTL formulation. Because the resulting LTL formulae have the same meaning as the specifications written in T, by verifying that the LTL formulae are satisfiable and realizable, we can verify that the same is true of the specification written in T, and so can automatically synthesise a program that satisfies the specifications written in T.

The remainder of this paper is organised as follows. In Sec. 2, we introduce the notion of a reactive system and LTL as a specification language, and discuss some of the problems faced when defining practical specifications using LTL. In Sec. 3, we describe the design philosophy of the language; in Sec. 4, we define the syntax; in Sec. 5, we give the semantics; and in Sec. 6, we detail an implementation of a T compiler. In Sec. 7, we discuss the advantages of the language and the compiler. Section 8 concludes the paper.

2. Reactive System and Specification

In this section, we introduce reactive systems and LTL as a specification language. We also discuss some problems that exist when providing specifications using LTL.

2.1. Reactive systems

A reactive system is a system that responds to requests from an environment with appropriate timing.

Definition 2.1 (Reactive system). *A reactive system RS is a triple* $\langle X, Y, r \rangle$, *where X is a set of events caused by an environment, Y is a set of events caused by the system and* $r : (2^X)^+ \mapsto 2^Y$ *is a reaction function.*

We call events caused by the environment 'input events', and those caused by the system 'output events'. $(2^X)^+$ is the set of all finite sequences of input events. A reaction function r relates sequences of sets of previously occurring input events to a set of current output events.

2.2. Language for describing reactive system specifications

The timing of the input and output events is a critical element of reactive systems. Modal logic is widely used in computer science, and temporal logic has been widely applied to the analysis of reactive systems, following the work of Manna and Pnueli.[15] A propositional LTL[16] with an "until" operator is a suitable language for describing the timing of events. Here, we use LTL to describe the specifications of reactive systems. We treat input events and output events as atomic propositions.

2.2.1. *Syntax*

Formulae in LTL are inductively defined as follows:

- Atomic propositions are formulae, i.e., input events and output events are formulae.
- $f \wedge g$, $\neg f$, Xf, fUg are formulae if f and g are formulae.

Intuitively, $f \wedge g$ and $\neg f$ represent 'both f and g hold' then 'f does not hold' respectively. The notation Xf states that 'f holds at the next time', while fUg represents 'f always holds until g holds'. The notation $f \vee g$, $f \rightarrow g$, $f \leftrightarrow g$, $\top$, fRg, fWg, Ff and Gf are abbreviations for $\neg(\neg f \wedge \neg g)$, $\neg(f \wedge \neg g)$, $\neg(f \wedge \neg g) \wedge \neg(\neg f \wedge g)$, $\neg\bot$, $\neg(\neg fU\neg g)$, $gR(f \vee g)$, $\top Uf$, $\neg F\neg f$ respectively, where $\bot$ is an atomic proposition representing 'falsity'.

2.2.2. *Semantics*

Behaviour is an infinite sequence of sets of events. Let i be an index such that $i \geq 0$. The i-th set of behaviour σ is represented by $\sigma[i]$. When a formula f holds for the i-th set of behaviour σ, we write $\sigma, i \models f$, and inductively define this relation as follows.

- $\sigma, i \models p$ iff $p \in \sigma[i]$
- $\sigma, i \not\models \bot$
- $\sigma, i \models f \wedge g$ iff $\sigma, i \models f$ and $\sigma, i \models g$
- $\sigma, i \models \neg f$ iff $\sigma, i \not\models f$
- $\sigma, i \models Xf$ iff $\sigma, i+1 \models f$
- $\sigma, i \models fUg$ iff $\exists j \geq 0.((\sigma, i+j \models g)$ and $\forall k(0 \leq k < j. (\sigma, i+k \models f)))$

We say σ satisfies f and write $\sigma \models f$, if $\sigma, 0 \models f$. We say f is satisfiable if there exists a σ that satisfies f.

It is important for reactive system specifications to satisfy realisability. The realisability requires that there exist a reactive system such that, for any input events of any timing, the reactive system produces output events such that the specification holds.

Definition 2.2 (Realizability[4,5]). *A specification Spec is realisable if the following holds:*

$$\exists RS \forall \tilde{a}(behave_{RS}(\tilde{a}) \models Spec),$$

where $\tilde{a}$ is an infinite sequence of sets of input events, i.e., $\tilde{a} \in (2^X)^\omega$. $behave_{RS}(\tilde{a})$ is the infinite behaviour by RS for $\tilde{a}$ defined as follows. If $\tilde{a} = a_0 a_1 \ldots$,

$$behave_{RS}(\tilde{a}) = (a_0 \cup b_0)(a_1 \cup b_1) \ldots,$$

where b_i is a set of output events caused by RS, i.e., $b_i = r(a_0 \ldots a_i)$, and $\cup$ is the union operator of two sets.

If a specification is not realisable, it must be modified. A number of methods for detecting the causes of the flaws have been reported in Ref. 1–3. Using these methods, we can obtain strategies for correcting the specifications. After they have been modified accordingly, using the methods proposed in Ref. 4,5, we can convert a realisable specification into a transition system, which represents a program. Several tools for synthesizing transition systems from LTL specifications have been proposed, including Lily,[6,7] AcaciaPlus,[8,9] and Unbeast.[10,11] These tools check whether a specification is realisable, and generate a transition system from a realisable specification.

2.3. Specifying a reactive system in LTL

In practical situations, there are a large number of specifications for reactive systems that should be parameterised, and may have complex structures. However, because LTL is merely a logical system, it is neither modular nor parameterised. Therefore, the scale of the specifications written in LTL tends to be large. We show a specification of a buffer controller in Appendix A. This specification is a sample specification shown in AcaciaPlus.[9] In this specification, the timing constraints to transfer items from 2 sender processes to 7 receiver processes are given. As shown in Appendix A, the scale of these specifications written in LTL is large. This is a general problem for specifying reactive systems in LTL. In the following sections, we develop an object-oriented language for parameterised reactive system specifications based on LTL.

3. Design of the Language

In the language T, specifications of reactive systems are divided into modules called classes, and the behavioural constraints are specified in the classes. There are two kinds of relations between classes: is-a and has-a relations.

Because the language is parameterised, classes can have two kinds of parameters: integer parameters and formula parameters. Formula parameters are used for abstraction of constraints in the class. Integer parameters are used to give the number of event propositions or instances defined in the class. By giving arguments (integer values and formulae) for the parameters, the class can be instantiated. Using parameterised formulae in conjunction with integer parameters, parameterised specifications, such as the control system for an n-floor elevator system, can be specified in T.

To describe numerical values using temporal logic with only true/false propositions, it is necessary to encode the numerical values to true/false using binary counters. The specification of the binary counters should not be included in the specifications of systems. To exclude the specification of binary counters from the system, we allow numerical values to be included in a specification written in T.

The language should have the following characteristics:

- Input/output event propositions are defined in each class. This makes it easy to describe or modify specifications.
- The structure of the specifications should be intuitive, and it should be straightforward to reuse parts of them.
- The syntax for parameterised formulae should be provided. It must be possible to define parameterised specifications.
- Integer variables can be used both for integer parameters and numerical-valued propositions.
- A sum-up function can be used in the specifications. This function takes an array of propositions as an input, and outputs the number of propositions whose values are true.
- Macros can be specified.

4. Syntax of T

To describe a specification of a system using the language T, we define classes, which are modular sets of specifications, and define an instance, called a system instance, which is the top-level instance representing the whole system. In this section, we describe the syntax of the classes and the system instance. We also show the syntax of formulae for specifying constraints and assumptions in classes.

4.1. *Classes*

In classes, we define input/output event propositions, instances of other classes, the timing constraints of the system behaviour, and assumptions about the behaviour of the environment. Because T is object-oriented, we can define the is-a relation (i.e., the superclass-subclass relation) between classes. Subclasses inherit all of the event propositions, instances, constraints, and assumptions defined in their superclasses. Multiple inheritance is allowed, and we can specify multiple superclasses. To resolve the names of event propositions and instances in the superclasses correctly, we cannot define event propositions or instances that have the same name. Furthermore, the language T does not support overriding; it is prohibited to define events or instances that have the same name as those that are defined in the superclasses. It is also prohibited to override constraints and assumptions that are defined in the superclasses.

4.1.1. *Class definition*

We summarise the syntax of classes in Fig. 1. `ClassName` is the name of a class. The first character of the name must be a letter. In the following parentheses, the parameters of the class are specified. If f is declared in `formula f`, it is a formula parameter. When a class with a formula parameter is instantiated, a formula is passed as an argument. For example, when

```
class ClassName(formula f, ..., const n): ParentClasses{
 var:
  VarDecl;
   ...
 instance:
  InstanceDecl;
   ...
 macro:
  MacroDecl;
   ...
 initial:
  Formula;
   ...
 physical:
  Formula;
   ...
 service:
  Formula;
   ...
 control:
  Formula;
   ...
 assume:
  Formula;
   ...
}
```

Fig. 1.   Class definition

a class A, which is defined by A(formula f), is instantiated by a:A(f=not p), the argument not p is passed as a parameter to f. If n is declared in const n, it is an integer parameter. When a class with an integer parameter is instantiated, an integer value is passed as an argument. This parameter n can be used to determine the length of the instance array that is defined in this class, and can also be used as an argument to instantiate another class.

ParentClasses is a comma-separated list of names of superclasses. If multiple superclasses are specified, it is prohibited to use event propositions and instances that have the same name as that defined in the superclasses.

Between braces { and }, we can specify the contents of the class. We call of these terms (e.g., var: and instance:) 'part specifiers', and call the area between the part specifiers a 'part'. The syntax of each part is defined as follows.

4.1.2. *var part*

In the var part, we define input/output event propositions (for both binary values and numerical values). For the proposition of numerical values, we also define a numerical range. For example, we can define event propositions as follows.

```
prop x;
req prop y;
int a: 1..5;
req int b: 1..10;
```

Using prop x and req prop y, we define the output event proposition x, and the input event proposition y. Using int a:1..5 and req int b:1..10, we define the output event proposition a with a numerical value between 1 and 5, and the input event proposition b with a numerical value between 1 and 10.

Propositions can be defined using arrays, as shown below. Each proposition in the array shown in the example below can be referred to using indices, i.e., x[1],...,x[10].

```
prop x[1..10];
int a[1..3]: 1..5;
prop x2[1..3][1..10]; // multi-dimensional array
```

The notation start..end, e.g., 1..10 is called an interval notation. start..end represents a range i such that $start \leq i \leq end$, and start...end represents a range i such that $start \leq i < end$. The boundaries *start* and *end* are terms that consist of numerical values (e.g., 0,100), integer parameters, and mathematical operators (+,-,*,/,%).

4.1.3. *instance part*

In the instance part, we define instances owned by the class. The syntax of the instance declaration is as follows.

```
instanceName: ClassName(Parameter1=Argument1, ..., ParameterN=ArgumentN);
```

Each integer parameter argument is a term that consists of numerical values, integer parameters, iterators, or mathematical operators (+,-,*,/,%). Each argument of a formula parameter is a formulae, defined in Sec. 4.3. For example, if we instantiate a class A with arguments x and y and 10 with parameters g and m, we specify the following, where ins is the name of the instance.

```
ins: A(g=(x and y), m=10);
```

In a similar manner to propositions, instances can be defined using an array as follows.

```
ins[1..10]: A(g=(x and y), m=10); //ins[1]-ins[10] are instances
ins2[i in 1..10]: A(g=(x and y), m=i); // iterator i is used. ins2[i] is a result of
                                        // instantiation by A(g=(x and y), m=i);
```

Unlike propositions, however, we can use iterators in arguments to make it possible to pass different values as arguments. To define an iterator, we declare the iterator as i in 1..10.

We can refer to propositions defined in a class of an instance through the name of the instance. For example, we can refer to the proposition p of the instance ins by ins.p.

4.1.4. *macro part*

In the macro part, we define abbreviations of constraints or numerical values as macros. A macro defined in this part can be used in formulae as well as event propositions or integer parameters. For example, the following macros MAX and a_zero represent the numerical value 100 and the constraint a==0, respectively.

```
MAX = 100;
a_zero = (a == 0);
```

4.1.5. *initial/physical/service/control part*

In these parts, we define constraints that should be satisfied in the class using formulae defined in Sec. 4.3. In the initial part, we define constraints of the initial state. In the physical part, we define the physical constraints. In the service part, we define the essential constraints for realising an objective. In the control part, we define constraints for realising the objective efficiently. Let us consider a specification of an elevator control system as an example. In the initial part, we may specify such a constraint as 'no buttons are pushed at the initial state'. In the physical part, may we specify a constraint such as 'the lift cannot be located on different floors simultaneously'. In the service part, may we specify a constraint such as 'the lift must arrive at the floor for which the request button was pushed'. In the control part, we may specify a constraint that 'the lift stops at the floors for which the buttons have been pressed in ascending order if the lift is ascending'.

Whichever part the constraints are specified in, the class has the same meaning. However, by providing these parts, we can include an intention in the specifications.

4.1.6. *assume part*

In the assume part, we specify the assumptions for the behaviour of an environment using formulae defined in Sec. 4.3. For example, in the specification of the elevator control system, we may provide an assumption that 'the door-close button can be pressed an infinite number of times'.

4.2. *System instance*

As a class definition is merely a common description of its instances, we should specify how the top-level class will be instantiated. In the language T, we specify this as follows.

```
system:
  ClassName(Parameter1=Argument1, ..., ParameterN=ArgumentN);
```

4.3. *Formulae*

Constraints and assumptions in classes are specified by formulae. We can specify the following formulae.

Table 1. Operators in T.

operator in LTL	operator in T	operator in LTL	operator in T
$\top$	TOP	$\bot$	BOT
$\neg\varphi$	not φ		
$\varphi \wedge \psi$	φ and ψ	$\varphi \vee \psi$	φ or ψ
$\varphi U \psi$	φ U ψ	$\varphi W \psi$	φ W ψ
$\varphi R \psi$	φ R ψ		
$\varphi \rightarrow \psi$	φ -> ψ	$\varphi \leftrightarrow \psi$	φ <-> ψ
$G\varphi$	G φ	$F\varphi$	F φ
$X\varphi$	X φ		

$$\varphi ::= \text{TOP}|\text{BOT}| < \text{event proposition} > |\varphi_{and}|\varphi_{or}|\varphi_{Exp}$$

$$|(\text{G}|\text{F}|\text{X}|\text{not})\varphi$$

$$|\varphi(\text{U}|\text{W}|\text{R}|\text{and}|\text{or}|->|<->)\varphi$$

The operators G,F,X,not,U,W,R,and,or,->,<-> are operators used in LTL, as shown in Table 1.

The order of operators is as follows.

(strong) unary operators $G, F, X, \neg$
| binary temporal operators(U, W, R)
(week) binary operators $\wedge, \rightarrow, \vee, \leftrightarrow$.

AND/OR formulae We call $\varphi_{and}, \varphi_{or}$ introduced in the definition of formulae φ AND-formulae and OR-formulae, respectively. Intuitively, AND-formulae and OR-formulae represent $\bigwedge_i \varphi_i$ and $\bigvee_i \varphi_i$, respectively. For example, AND(i in 1..3){p[i] or q[i]} represents the formula (p[1] or q[1]) and (p[2] or q[2]) and (p[3] or q[3]). The syntax of AND/OR-formulae is as follows.

$$\varphi_{and} ::= \text{AND (i in } Interval(:\text{i} \circ E)?)\{\varphi\}$$

$$\varphi_{or} ::= \text{OR (i in } Interval(:\text{i} \circ E)?)\{\varphi\}$$

Interval is an interval. The boundaries of the interval are terms that consist of numerical values, integer parameters, iterators, and mathematical operators (+,-,*,/,%). ':io E' is a condition about iterator i, and the resulting formula represents connecting φ_i such that the iterator i satisfies the condition, with and/or. 'o' represents a binary relation (==, !=, >, >=, <, <=). E is a term that consists of numerical values, integer parameters, iterators, and mathematical operators $(+,-,*,/,\%)$. The condition ':io E' may be omitted and, in such cases, the resulting formulae represent connecting all φ_i with **and/or**.

In the example specification of an elevator control system, using AND/OR-formulae, we can define the specification as 'a lift is located in one floor' as follows.

```
class Elevator(const n){
var:
 prop location[1..n]; // location[i]: 'the lift is located on floor i'
physical:
 // the lift cannot be located on different floors simultaneously.
 G(AND(i in 1..n){location[i] -> AND(j in 1..n:j!=i){not location[j]}});
 // the lift is located on some floor.
 G(OR(i in 1..n){location[i]});
 }
```

Comparisons We call φ_{Exp} introduced in the definition of formulae φ comparison formulae. Using a comparison formula, we can compare terms involving numerical constraints with numerical values. The syntax of comparison formulae and terms is as follows.

$$\varphi_{Exp} ::= Exp(==, !=, >, >=, <, <=)Exp$$

$$Exp ::= < \text{numerical value} > | < \text{numerical symbol} > | Exp(+|-|*|/|\%)Exp$$

$$| Exp_{sum} | Exp_{sharp}$$

where a numerical symbol is an integer parameter, a numerically valued proposition or an iterator. The operators $+,-,*,/$ and $\%$ are mathematical operators.

The SUM term Exp_{sum} introduced in the definition of terms Exp are called SUM terms. An SUM term represents $\sum_i Exp_i$. For example, SUM(i in 0..3){n[i]} represents n[0]+n[1]+n[2]+n[3], if n[i] is defined by int n[0..3]:1..10;. The syntax of SUM terms is as follows.

$$Exp_{sum} ::= \text{SUM} (\text{ i in } Interval(:i \circ E)?)\{Exp\}$$

The sum-up function Exp_{sharp} introduced in the definition of terms Exp, which are called sum-up functions. A sum-up function represents the number of propositions that are true. For example, if p is an array of propositions defined by prop p[1..3];, #(p) represents the number of propositions among p[1],p[2],p[3] that are true. Hence #(p)=>1 indicates that at least one p[i] is true. The syntax of a sum-up function is as follows.

$$Exp_{sharp} ::= \#(\ < proposition >\ )$$

A sum-up function is also available for multi-dimensional arrays of propositions. For example, if p is a multi-dimensional array defined by p[1..3][1..2], if #(p)>=1, it follows that at least one p[i][j] among p[1][1],p[1][2],p[2][1], p[2][2],p[3][1],p[3][2] is true.

If p is not an array, but a proposition, #(p) is 1 if p is true, and #(p) is 0 if p is false.

4.4. Example specification in T

Here we show a specification of a control system of lamps with buttons. This specification consists of a Lamp class representing a lamp, a Button class representing a button, and a LButton class representing a button connected to a lamp.

The Lamp class has a parameter 'formula lampOn', which describes whether the lamp is lit. In this class, the output event proposition lamp is defined by prop lamp;, which represents a lit lamp. G(lampOn <->lamp) is a constraint that should be satisfied in this class. This constraint indicates that lampOn is satisfied if and only if the lamp is lit.

```
//lampOn: whether or not the lamp is lit.
class Lamp(formula lampOn){
 var:
 //lamp: output event proposition that the lamp is lit.
 prop lamp;
 service:
 //If the condition lampOn is satisfied, the lamp is lit,
 //otherwise the lamp is not lit.
 G(lampOn <-> lamp);
}
```

In the Button class, the input event proposition push is defined by req prop push;. The output event propositions on and timeout are also defined. push indicates that the button is pushed. on indicates that the button is valid. timeout indicates that the button has timed out. off is a macro that describes off = not on;. Two constraints are defined in the initial part and the service part, which indicate that, in the initial state, the button is not valid, and that if the button is pushed, it is valid until it times out. The two assumptions are also defined in the assumption part, which indicates that, in the initial state, the button is not pushed, and that if button is pushed, it will be released.

```
class Button(){
 var:
  //push: input event proposition indicating that the button is pushed.
  req prop push;
  //on: output event proposition indicating that the button is valid.
  //timeout: output event proposition indicating that the button has timed out
  prop on,timeout;
 macro:
  off = not on;
 initial:
  //In initial state, the button is not valid.
  off;
 service:
  //if the button is pushed, it is valid until it has timed out.
  G(push -> (on U timeout));
 assume:
  // In the initial state, the button is not pushed.
  not push;
  // If the button is pushed, it will be released.
  G(F(not push));
 }
```

Because the LButton class is defined as a subclass of the Button class, it inherits all of the event propositions, macros, constraints and assumptions from the Button class. Furthermore, in LButton, the Lamp class is instantiated by lamp:Lamp(lampOn=on);. This means that a lit lamp signifies that the button is valid.

```
class LButton():Button{// The LButton class inherits all of the attributes of
                       // the Button class.
 instance:
  //Lamp is instantiated by the argument for parameter lampOn.
  //The name of the instance is lamp.
  lamp:Lamp(lampOn=on);
 }
```

In the system instance, the class LButton is instantiated.

```
system:
LButton();
```

The class diagram of this specification is shown in Fig. 2.

5. Semantics of T

5.1. *Preliminary*

A specification written in T is interpreted to create a set of LTL formulae. First, macros are expanded to include their definition. We now introduce several notations to provide interpretation. $c' \in c.Parents$ indicates that c' is a superclass of c. $\varphi \in c.Guarantee$ indicates that a constraint φ is specified

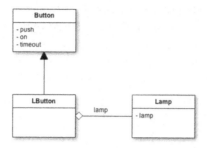

Fig. 2. A class diagram of the specification of the control system for lamps with buttons.

in a class c. $\varphi \in c.Assume$ indicates that an assumption φ is specified in a class c. $\langle c', id, arg, \{\langle i_1, I_1 \rangle, \cdots, \langle i_n, I_n \rangle\}\rangle \in c.Instances$ indicates that an instance id is defined in a class c, where c' is a class of the instance id, arg is a set of arguments for instantiation of id. If no argument is passed in the instantiation, arg is $\emptyset$. $\langle i_k, I_k \rangle$ represents an iterator i_k and an interval I_k, which are used when id is defined as an array of instances. If an iterator is not used for the definition, i_k is *null*. If id is not defined as an array, $\{\langle i_1, I_1 \rangle, \cdots, \langle i_n, I_n \rangle\}$ is represented by ϵ.

For example, an instance is defined by `elevators[i in 3..8]`: `Elevator(n=i);` in class c, $\langle \texttt{Elevator}, \texttt{elevators}, \{\texttt{n} \mapsto \texttt{i}\}, \{\langle \texttt{i}, 3..8 \rangle\}\rangle \in$ $c.Instances$ holds.

5.2. Semantics

Now, we formally define specifications written in T and the interpretation of those specifications.

Definition 5.1 (specification). *Spec is a definition of a system instance and a set of classes, and is represented by* $Spec = \langle \{c_1, \cdots, c_n\},$ $\langle System, \epsilon, arg, \epsilon \rangle \rangle$, *where a system class System is the class of a system instance. System* $\in \{c_1, \cdots, c_n\}$ *holds.*

Definition 5.2 (interpretation of specification). *Let Spec* $=$ $\langle \{c_1, \cdots, c_n\}, \langle System, \epsilon, arg, \epsilon \rangle \rangle$. *The interpretation* $[\![Spec]\!]$ *of specification Spec is defined as the interpretation* $[\![System]\!]_{arg,\epsilon}^{c_1,\cdots,c_n}$ *of a system instance of the class System, where the set of arguments is arg, and the name of the instance is* ϵ

Now we define $[\![c]\!]_{arg,id}^{c_1,\cdots,c_n}$, which represents the interpretation of the instance (named id), which is the result of instantiation of c with arguments arg. $[\![c]\!]_{arg,id}^{c_1,\cdots,c_n}$ is LTL formulae defined as follows.

Definition 5.3 (interpretation of instance). *Let c be a class, arg be a set of arguments used in the instantiation of c, id is the name of the resulting instance. $[\![c]\!]_{arg,id}^{c_1,\dots,c_n}$ is an LTL formula of the form $\bigwedge_{\varphi_A \in A(c,arg,id)} \varphi_A \to \bigwedge_{\varphi_g \in G(c,arg,id)} \varphi_G$, where $A(c,arg,id)$ is a set of assumptions of the environmental behaviour, and $G(c,arg,id)$ is a set of constraints for system behaviour, so that we have:*

$$G(c,arg,id) = \{Merge(arg,id)(\varphi)|\varphi \in c.Guarantee\}$$

$$\cup \bigcup_{\tilde{c}\in c.Parents} G(\tilde{c},arg,id)$$

$$\cup \bigcup_{\langle\tilde{c},\tilde{id},\tilde{arg},\epsilon\rangle\in Instances(c,arg,id)} G(\tilde{c},\tilde{arg},\tilde{id})$$

Let arg be $arg = \{n_1 \mapsto Exp_1,\dots,n_x \mapsto Exp_x, p_1 \mapsto \psi_1,\dots,p_y \mapsto \psi_y\}$; $arg(\varphi)$ is defined by $arg(\varphi) = \varphi[Exp_1/n_1,\dots,Exp_x/n_x,\psi_1/p_1,\dots,\psi_y/p_y]$. For example, if $arg = \{$p $\mapsto$ (a and b), q $\mapsto$ (c or d)$\}$, then $arg(G($p->F(q)$))$ is $G(($a and b$)$->F$(($c or d$)))$. Similarly, let I be interval. $arg(I)$ is defined as an application of arg by I. For example, if $arg = \{$n $\mapsto 10\}$, $arg(1..$n$)$ is $1..10$.

Merge is defined by $Merge(arg,id) = arg \cup \{s \mapsto id.s|s \notin dom(arg)\}$. For example, let arg be $\{$p $\mapsto$ a and b, n $\mapsto 10\}$. $Merge(arg,$button$)($ $G($p->AND(i in 1..n)$\{$q[i]$\}))$ is $G(($a and b$)$->AND(i in 1..10)$\{$button.q[i]$\})$.

$Instances(c,arg,id)$ is a set of instances (named id) that result from instantiation of a class c with argument arg. $Instances_a$ is a set of instances defined as an array, and $Instances_n$ is a set of instances that is not defined as an array. These are defined as follows.

$$Instances(c,arg,id) = Instances_n(c,arg,id) \cup Instances_a(c,arg,id)$$
$$Instances_n(c,arg,id) =$$
$$\{\langle\tilde{c},id.\tilde{id},\tilde{arg}\circ Merge(arg,id),\epsilon\rangle|\langle\tilde{c},\tilde{id},\tilde{arg},\epsilon\rangle \in c.Instances\}$$
$$Instances_a(c,arg,id) =$$
$$\{\langle\tilde{c},id.\tilde{id}[d_1]\cdots[d_n],\tilde{arg}\circ\mathbb{D}[i_1 \mapsto d_1,\dots,i_n \mapsto d_n]\circ Merge(arg,id),\epsilon\rangle$$
$$|\langle\tilde{c},\tilde{id},\tilde{arg},\{\langle i_1,I_1\rangle,\dots,\langle i_n,I_n\rangle\}\rangle \in c.Instances \wedge d_k \in [\![arg(I_k)]\!]\},$$

where an interval I is interpreted as the set of its elements. For example, $[\![1..3]\!]$ is $\{1,2,3\}$. $\mathbb{D}[i_1 \mapsto d_1,\dots,i_n \mapsto d_n]$ represents a function that maps i_k into d_k.

Similar to the definition of $G(c,arg,id)$, $A(c,arg,id)$ is also defined by changing c.Guarantee into c.Assume.

Intuitively, $G(c,arg,id)$ represents LTL formulae that are the constraints for the instance (named id) that results from the instantiation of a class c with arguments arg. $G(c, arg, id)$ is defined by the union of (i) $\{Merge(arg, id)(\varphi)|\varphi \in c\ Guarantee\}$: the set of LTL formulae defined in c, (ii) $\bigcup_{\tilde{c} \in c.Parents} G(\tilde{c}, arg, id)$: the set of LTL formulae that are the result of interpretation of the super classes of c, and (iii) $\bigcup_{\langle \tilde{c}, id, \tilde{arg}, \epsilon \rangle \in Instances(c, arg, id)} G(\tilde{c}, \tilde{arg}, \tilde{id})$: the set of LTL formulae, obtained by attaching the prefix $\tilde{id}$ to the result of interpretation of the classes of instances defined in c. The inclusion of (ii) in $G(c, arg, id)$ corresponds to inheritance of the constraints defined in super classes.

$A(c, arg, id)$ has the same intuitive meaning as one of the $G(c, arg, id)$, except for changing the constraints to assumptions.

5.3. Interpretation example

Here we show the interpretation of the specification of a control system of lamps with buttons described in Sec. 4.4.

No constraints are defined in *LButton*. *LButton* has a super class *Button* and an instance *lamp*, which is the result of instantiation of *Lamp* class with an argument $lampOn \mapsto on$. Therefore, we have

$$G(LButton, \emptyset, \epsilon) = \emptyset \cup G(Button, \emptyset, \epsilon)$$
$$\cup\, G(Lamp, \{lampOn \mapsto on\}, lamp).$$

The constraints $not\ on$, $G(push \rightarrow on\ U\ timeout)$ are defined in the *Button* class, which has neither its super class nor its instance. Therefore, we have

$$G(Button, \emptyset, \epsilon) = \{not\ on, G(push \rightarrow on\ U\ timeout)\} \cup \emptyset \cup \emptyset$$

The *Lamp* class has the constraint $G(lampOn \leftrightarrow lamp)$. The *Lamp* class has neither its super class nor its instance. Therefore, we have

$$G(Lamp, \{lampOn \mapsto on\}, lamp)$$
$$= \{Merge(\{lampOn \mapsto on\}, lamp)(G(lampOn \leftrightarrow lamp))\} \cup \emptyset \cup \emptyset$$
$$= \{G(on \leftrightarrow lamp.lamp)\}.$$

Hence, we also have

$$G(LButton, \emptyset, \epsilon) = \{not\ on, G(push \rightarrow on\ U\ timeout),$$
$$G(on \leftrightarrow lamp.lamp)\}.$$

$A(LButton, \emptyset, \epsilon)$ is obtained in a similar manner to that described above. Because *LButton* has no assumptions, we have

$$A(LButton, \emptyset, \epsilon) = \emptyset \cup A(Button, \emptyset, \epsilon)$$
$$\cup\, A(Lamp, \{lampOn \mapsto on\}, lamp).$$

138

The assumptions *not push*, $G(F(not\ push))$ are defined in the *Button* class, i.e.,

$$A(Button, \emptyset, \epsilon) = \{not\ push, G(F(not\ push))\} \cup \emptyset \cup \emptyset.$$

The *Lamp* class has neither assumption, its super class nor its instance.

$$A(Lamp, \{lampOn \mapsto on\}, lamp) = \emptyset \cup \emptyset \cup \emptyset$$

Therefore

$$A(LButton, \emptyset, \epsilon) = \{not\ push, G(F(not\ push))\}$$

and we have

$$[\![LButton]\!]_{\emptyset, \epsilon}^{LButton, Button, Lamp}$$
$$= A(LButton, \emptyset, \epsilon) \to G(LButton, \emptyset, \epsilon)$$
$$= (not\ push \wedge G(F(not\ push)))$$
$$\to (not\ on \wedge G(push \to on\ U\ timeout) \wedge G(on \leftrightarrow lamp.lamp))$$

6. The T Compiler

We implemented a T compiler, which converts specifications *Spec* written in T into LTL formulae φ, according to the semantic rules of T defined in Sec. 5. The resulting LTL formulae have the same meaning as the original specification, i.e., $[\![Spec]\!]$ is φ. These LTL formulae are of the input format of AcaciaPlus.[9] The T compiler was implemented using Java and Python, and required 1100 lines of Java source code and 900 lines of Python source code.

Because the target LTL formulae are pure LTL formulae, it is necessary to encode numerical-valued propositions into true/false ones. The T compiler has a function for such encoding. Because it is also necessary to represent sum-up functions using pure propositional formulae, the T compiler encodes sum-up functions into the equivalent pure propositional formulae.

7. Advantages of T

We show the specification of a buffer controller using the language T in Appendix B. This specification has the same meaning as the specification written in LTL, shown in Appendix A. That is, the result of interpretation of the specification written in T is just the same as that written in LTL. However, the specification written in T is considerably simpler than that written in LTL, and easier to understand. Furthermore, because the numerical variables used as parameters of the class are available in T, it is possible to provide parameterised specifications, and this improves reusability.

There are various methods and tools for analysing specifications written in LTL, including methods for detecting the causes of the flaws reported in Refs.1–3, and tools for synthesizing programs from LTL specifications, which include Lily,[6,7] AcaciaPlus,[8,9] and Unbeast.[10,11] By applying these methods and tools to the LTL formulae produced by the T compiler, these methods and tools become applicable to the specifications written in T.

8. Conclusion

We have described an object-oriented language called T for reactive system specifications based on LTL. We gave the semantics for specification in T, and implemented a compiler that converts specifications written in T into LTL formulae of a suitable form to use as input to Acacia. Using T, we can specify specifications modularly. This means that, in each class, we can specify input/output event propositions and timing constraints, as well as assumptions of the events. Hence, the language makes it easier to define specifications. Even if specifications are complex and consist of a large number of modules, it is possible to define the whole of the specifications efficiently and in a manner that is intuitive and easy to understand. In addition, numerical variables and integer values can be used in the specifications. The sum-up function and SUM-formulae are also available. Using these notations, we can intuitively define specifications that refer to numerical values, because we do not need to transform numerical values into true/false values using counters. Furthermore, we can use numerical variables as parameters of classes. It is also possible to define parameterised specifications to improve reusability.

Acknowledgment

This work was supported by Grant-in-Aid for Scientific Research(C) (24500032). We would like to thank the reviewers for their valuable comments and suggestions to improve the quality of the paper.

Appendix A. Specification of Buffer Controller written in LTL

Figure A1 shows a specification of a buffer controller written in LTL, which is shown as an example of AcaciaPlus.[9] This specification is large, and several constraints are omitted for brevity.

```
LTL formula file:
  [spec_unit s2b_0]
  assume s2b_req0=0;
  assume G((s2b_req0=1 * b2s_ack0=0) -> X(s2b_req0=1));
  assume G(b2s_ack0=1 -> X(s2b_req0=0));
  b2s_ack0=0;
  G( (s2b_req0=0 * X(s2b_req0=1)) -> X(b2s_ack0=0 * X(F(b2s_ack0=1))) );
  G( (b2s_ack0=0 * X(s2b_req0=0)) -> X(b2s_ack0=0) );
  G(b2s_ack0=0 + b2s_ack1=0);

  [spec_unit s2b_1]
  assume s2b_req1=0;
  assume G((s2b_req1=1 * b2s_ack1=0) -> X(s2b_req1=1));
  assume G(b2s_ack1=1 -> X(s2b_req1=0));
  b2s_ack1=0;
  G( (s2b_req1=0 * X(s2b_req1=1)) -> X(b2s_ack1=0 * X(F(b2s_ack1=1))) );
  G( (b2s_ack1=0 * X(s2b_req1=0)) -> X(b2s_ack1=0) );
  G(b2s_ack0=0 + b2s_ack1=0);

  [spec_unit b2r_0]
  assume r2b_ack0=0;
  assume G(b2r_req0=0 -> X(r2b_ack0=0));
  assume G(b2r_req0=1 -> X(F(r2b_ack0=1)));
  b2r_req0=0;
  G(r2b_ack0=1 -> X(b2r_req0=0));
  G((b2r_req0=1 * r2b_ack0=0) -> X(b2r_req0=1));
  G((b2r_req0=1 * X(b2r_req0=0)) -> X( b2r_req0=0 U (b2r_req0=0 * b2r_req6=1)));
  G(  (b2r_req0=0 * b2r_req1=0 * b2r_req2=0 * b2r_req3=0 * b2r_req4=0 * b2r_req5=0)
    + (b2r_req1=0 * b2r_req2=0 * b2r_req3=0 * b2r_req4=0 * b2r_req5=0 * b2r_req6=0)
    + (b2r_req2=0 * b2r_req3=0 * b2r_req4=0 * b2r_req5=0 * b2r_req6=0 * b2r_req0=0)
    + (b2r_req3=0 * b2r_req4=0 * b2r_req5=0 * b2r_req6=0 * b2r_req0=0 * b2r_req1=0)
    + (b2r_req4=0 * b2r_req5=0 * b2r_req6=0 * b2r_req0=0 * b2r_req1=0 * b2r_req2=0)
    + (b2r_req5=0 * b2r_req6=0 * b2r_req0=0 * b2r_req1=0 * b2r_req2=0 * b2r_req3=0)
    + (b2r_req6=0 * b2r_req0=0 * b2r_req1=0 * b2r_req2=0 * b2r_req3=0 * b2r_req4=0));
  G((s2b_req0=1+s2b_req1=1) -> X(F(b2r_req0=1+b2r_req1=1+b2r_req2=1+b2r_req3=1+b2r_req4=1+b2r_req5=1+b2r_req6=1)));

  [spec_unit b2r_1]
  assume r2b_ack1=0;
  assume G(b2r_req1=0 -> X(r2b_ack1=0));
  assume G(b2r_req1=1 -> X(F(r2b_ack1=1)));
  b2r_req1=0;
  G(r2b_ack1=1 -> X(b2r_req1=0));
  G((b2r_req1=1 * r2b_ack1=0) -> X(b2r_req1=1));
  G((b2r_req1=1 * X(b2r_req1=0)) -> X( b2r_req1=0 U (b2r_req1=0 * b2r_req0=1)));
  G(  (b2r_req0=0 * b2r_req1=0 * b2r_req2=0 * b2r_req3=0 * b2r_req4=0 * b2r_req5=0)
    + (b2r_req1=0 * b2r_req2=0 * b2r_req3=0 * b2r_req4=0 * b2r_req5=0 * b2r_req6=0)
    + (b2r_req2=0 * b2r_req3=0 * b2r_req4=0 * b2r_req5=0 * b2r_req6=0 * b2r_req0=0)
    + (b2r_req3=0 * b2r_req4=0 * b2r_req5=0 * b2r_req6=0 * b2r_req0=0 * b2r_req1=0)
    + (b2r_req4=0 * b2r_req5=0 * b2r_req6=0 * b2r_req0=0 * b2r_req1=0 * b2r_req2=0)
    + (b2r_req5=0 * b2r_req6=0 * b2r_req0=0 * b2r_req1=0 * b2r_req2=0 * b2r_req3=0)
    + (b2r_req6=0 * b2r_req0=0 * b2r_req1=0 * b2r_req2=0 * b2r_req3=0 * b2r_req4=0));
  G((s2b_req0=1+s2b_req1=1) -> X(F(b2r_req0=1+b2r_req1=1+b2r_req2=1+b2r_req3=1+b2r_req4=1+b2r_req5=1+b2r_req6=1)));

  # [spec_unit b2r_2]
  # ... Omitted
  # [spec_unit b2r_3]
  # ... Omitted
  # [spec_unit b2r_4]
  # ... Omitted
  # [spec_unit b2r_5]
  # ... Omitted

  [spec_unit b2r_6]
  assume r2b_ack6=0;
  assume G(b2r_req6=0 -> X(r2b_ack6=0));
  assume G(b2r_req6=1 -> X(F(r2b_ack6=1)));
  b2r_req6=0;
  G(r2b_ack6=1 -> X(b2r_req6=0));
  G((b2r_req6=1 * r2b_ack6=0) -> X(b2r_req6=1));
  G((b2r_req6=1 * X(b2r_req6=0)) -> X( b2r_req6=0 U (b2r_req6=0 * b2r_req5=1)));
  G(  (b2r_req0=0 * b2r_req1=0 * b2r_req2=0 * b2r_req3=0 * b2r_req4=0 * b2r_req5=0)
    + (b2r_req1=0 * b2r_req2=0 * b2r_req3=0 * b2r_req4=0 * b2r_req5=0 * b2r_req6=0)
    + (b2r_req2=0 * b2r_req3=0 * b2r_req4=0 * b2r_req5=0 * b2r_req6=0 * b2r_req0=0)
    + (b2r_req3=0 * b2r_req4=0 * b2r_req5=0 * b2r_req6=0 * b2r_req0=0 * b2r_req1=0)
    + (b2r_req4=0 * b2r_req5=0 * b2r_req6=0 * b2r_req0=0 * b2r_req1=0 * b2r_req2=0)
    + (b2r_req5=0 * b2r_req6=0 * b2r_req0=0 * b2r_req1=0 * b2r_req2=0 * b2r_req3=0)
    + (b2r_req6=0 * b2r_req0=0 * b2r_req1=0 * b2r_req2=0 * b2r_req3=0 * b2r_req4=0));
  G((s2b_req0=1+s2b_req1=1) -> X(F(b2r_req0=1+b2r_req1=1+b2r_req2=1+b2r_req3=1+b2r_req4=1+b2r_req5=1+b2r_req6=1)));

  group_order = FLAT;

Partition of atomic signals file:
  .inputs s2b_req0 s2b_req1 r2b_ack0 r2b_ack1 r2b_ack2 r2b_ack3 r2b_ack4 r2b_ack5 r2b_ack6
  .outputs b2s_ack0 b2s_ack1 b2r_req0 b2r_req1 b2r_req2 b2r_req3 b2r_req4 b2r_req5 b2r_req6
```

Fig. A1. A specification of buffer controller written in LTL, shown as a sample specification of AcaciaPlus[9]

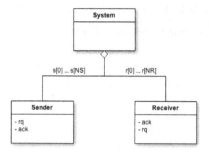

Fig. B.1.   The class diagram of a specification of a buffer controller.

```
// from /examples/buffer/gb_s2_r7.ltl

class Sender(){
  var:
    req prop rq;
    prop ack;
  assume:
    not(rq);
    G((rq and not(ack)) -> X(rq));
    G(ack -> X(not(rq)));
  service:
    not(ack);
    G((not(rq) and X(rq)) -> X(not(ack) and X(F(ack))));
    G((not(ack) and X(not(rq))) -> X(not(ack)));
}


class Receiver(){
  var:
    req prop ack;
    prop rq;
  assume:
    not(ack);
    G(not(rq) -> X(not(ack)));
    G(rq -> X(F(ack)));
  service:
    not(rq);
    G(ack -> X(not(rq)));
    G((rq and not(ack)) -> X(rq));
}

class System(const NS, const NR){
  instance:
    s[0...NS]: Sender();
    r[0...NR]: Receiver();
  service:
    // from s2b_0 and s2b_1
    // G( b2s_ack0=0 + b2s_ack1=0); <- this means
    G(AND(i in 0...NS){s[i].ack -> AND(j in 0...NS:j!=i){not(s[j].ack)}});

    // from b2r_0, b2r_1, b2r_2
    AND(i in 0...NR){G((r[i].rq and X(not(r[i].rq)))
                        -> X(not(r[i].rq) U (not(r[i].rq) and r[(i-1+NR)%NR].rq)))};
    G(OR(i in 0...NR){AND(j in 0...NR:j!=i){not(r[j].rq)}});
    G(OR(i in 0...NS){s[i].rq} -> X(F(OR(i in 0...NR){r[i].rq})));
}

system:
  System(NS=2, NR=7);
```

Fig. B.2.   A specification of buffer controller system written in T

Appendix B. Specification of Buffer Controller written in T

A specification of the same buffer controller written in T is shown in Fig. B.2, and the class diagram of this specification is shown in Fig. B.1. This specification has the same meaning as that in Appendix A, i.e., the result of interpretation of this specification with the T compiler is the specification shown in Appendix A.

References

1. S. Hagihara, Y. Kitamura, M. Shimakawa and N. Yonezaki, Extracting environmental constraints to make reactive system specifications realizable, in *Proceedings of the 2009 16th Asia-Pacific Software Engineering Conference*, APSEC '09 (IEEE Computer Society, Washington, DC, USA, 2009).
2. K. Chatterjee, T. A. Henzinger and B. Jobstmann, Environment assumptions for synthesis, in *Proceedings of the 19th international conference on Concurrency Theory (CONCUR 2008)*, Lecture Notes in Computer Science Vol. 5201 (Springer, 2008).
3. W. Li, L. Dworkin and S. A. Seshia, Mining assumptions for synthesis, in *MEMOCODE*, 2011.
4. M. Abadi, L. Lamport and P. Wolper, Realizable and unrealizable specifications of reactive systems, in *Proceedings of 16th International Colloquium on Automata, Languages, and Programming*, Lecture Notes in Computer Science Vol. 372 (Springer, 1989).
5. A. Pnueli and R. Rosner, On the synthesis of a reactive module, in *Proceedings of the 16th ACM SIGPLAN-SIGACT symposium on Principles of programming languages*, 1989.
6. B. Jobstmann and R. Bloem, Optimizations for LTL synthesis, in *Formal Methods in Computer Aided Design, 2006. FMCAD '06*, 2006.
7. *Lily - a LInear Logic sYnthesizer*. http://www.iaik.tugraz.at/content/research/design_verification/lily/.
8. A. Bohy, V. Bruyère, E. Filiot, N. Jin and J.-F. Raskin, Acacia+, a tool for LTL synthesis, in *Proceedings of the 24th international conference on Computer Aided Verification*, CAV'12 (Springer-Verlag, Berlin, Heidelberg, 2012).
9. *Acacia+: LTL Realizability Check and Winning Strategy Synthesis using Antichains*. http://lit2.ulb.ac.be/acaciaplus/.
10. R. Ehlers, Symbolic bounded synthesis, in *Proceedings of the 22nd international conference on Computer Aided Verification*, CAV'10 (Springer-Verlag, Berlin, Heidelberg, 2010).
11. *Unbeast - Symbolic Bounded Synthesis*. http://www.react.uni-saarland.de/tools/unbeast/.
12. A. Morzenti and P. San Pietro, Object-oriented logical specification of time-critical systems, *ACM Trans. Softw. Eng. Methodol.* **3**, 56 (January 1994).

13. S. Maoz and Y. Sa'ar, Aspectltl: an aspect language for ltl specifications, in *Proceedings of the tenth international conference on Aspect-oriented software development*, AOSD '11 (ACM, New York, NY, USA, 2011).

14. *The SMV System.* http://www.cs.cmu.edu/modelcheck/smv.html.

15. Z. Manna and A. Pnueli, Axiomatic approach to total correctness of programs, *Acta Informatica* **3**, 243 (1974).

16. A. Pnueli, The temporal semantics of concurrent programs, *Theoretical Computer Science* **13**, 45 (1981).

BUILDING POLICIES FOR SUPPORTIVE FEEDBACK IN SELF-DIRECTED LEARNING SCENARIOS

P. S. INVENTADO*,†, R. LEGASPI, K. MORIYAMA,

K. FUKUI and M. NUMAO

*The Institute of Scientific and Industrial Research, Osaka University,
Ibaraki, Osaka 567-0047, Japan
* E-mail: inventado@ai.sanken.osaka-u.ac.jp
www.ai.sanken.osaka-u.ac.jp*

†*Center for Empathic Human-Computer Interactions,
College of Computer Studies, De La Salle University, Manila, 1004, Philippines*

Students often face difficulty in self-directed learning scenarios (e.g., studying, research) because they need to control many aspects of the learning session. They need to decide what to learn, how long to perform a learning task, when to shift to a different learning task and manage distractions apart from others. We observed from our previous research that self-reflection and self-evaluation helped students manage their own learning. However, majority of the students only evaluated one or two major aspects of the learning session that they think needed to be changed or improved (e.g., need to spend less time in non-learning related activities, need to focus on only one learning task at a time). If students would look further into their learning session, they would discover more behaviors that also need to be re-evaluated. In this paper we discussed reinforcement learning-based methods for discovering good learning behavior which can be used by future systems to suggest to students possible ways to improve their behavior.

Keywords: Self-directed learning; Self-regulated learning; Reinforcement learning; Profit sharing.

1. Introduction

Although students learn a lot from formal instruction, an important aspect of learning is learning on one's own. Teachers often give students homework, projects or research assignments not only for them to learn more, but to foster their ability to learn on their own which also prepares them for life after graduation and for life-long learning. However, there are many challenges in learning alone such as the need to manage time, to manage different learning goals, to identify and perform activities that lead to the achievement of learning goals, to manage motivation and affect, to avoid distractions and much more.

Research has shown that self-regulation processes such as self-reflection and self-evaluation are effective in helping students improve their learning behavior and learn better.[1] Unfortunately, it is not very common for students to engage in these processes because of the already high cognitive load they experience. In our previous work, we developed a software tool called Sidekick Retrospect which minimized the cognitive load from performing self-reflection and self-evaluation by delaying these processes after the learning session.[2] Students used the software to review their learning behavior by going through screenshots of themselves and their desktop while they learned. Although the results were promising, we observed that students usually reflected and evaluated only on major events or aspects of the learning session. If students also spent time reflecting on the other aspects of the learning episode, it might be possible for them to improve their learning behavior better and faster.

In this paper, we discuss our work in identifying effective and ineffective student learning behavior so that future systems can help students focus on other important aspects of their learning behavior which they would otherwise not spend time evaluating or reflecting on.

2. Related Work

There are already existing tools that have been developed to help students learn to self-regulate. Process Coordinator is an inquiry-based learning system for the Physics domain that helps students self-regulate.[3] Specifically, as the students progressed in the learning task within the tool, the system gave students hints to help them check their understanding or suggested tasks that helped them understand the lesson better. The tool also allowed students to keep track of their progress in achieving their learning goal.

MetaTutor is a hypermedia learning environment developed for the Biology domain.[4] It helps students self-regulate by providing them with tools to perform self-regulation strategies and also to keep track of the different self-regulation strategies they have used and can use. While the student studied, the system suggested learning strategies that students could employ so they could learn better.

The novelty of our work is that we are working on supporting self-regulation in self-directed learning environments. Unlike existing research that constrain support within a specific domain and content, we allow students to have complete control over their learning. This allows students to learn in natural settings and get support regardless of the domain. We also subscribe to a retrospective approach of self-reflection and self-evaluation wherein these processes happen after the learning session. We hope that this will lessen the cognitive load while learning and still allow students to learn about their behavior and adjust it accordingly.

3. Learning Behavior Data

We used the data in our previous work[2] for evaluating our methodologies in identifying effective and ineffective learning behavior. The data was collected from one male undergraduate student, one male master's student and two female doctoral students who all engaged in research activities as part of their academic requirements. They were aged between 17 and 30 years old wherein three of them were taking Information Science while one doctoral student was taking Physics. During the data collection period, two of the students were writing conference papers and two made Power Point presentations about their research. Students had control over how they conducted their learning activities and did not receive any direct support from their supervisor.

Data was collected in five separate two-hour learning sessions from each student over a span of one week. Students freely decided on the time, location and type of activities they did but were required to learn in front of a computer that ran our software which recorded their learning behavior. All students were already using a computer in doing their research so the setup was natural and they did not have to change how they usually learned.

At the beginning of each learning session, students inputted their learning goals into the system. The system then logged the applications they used, took screenshots of their desktop and captured image stills from their webcam with corresponding timestamps. After a learning episode, students were shown a timeline that displayed the desktop screenshots and image stills depending on the position of their mouse on the timeline. This helped students recall what happened during the learning episode so they could annotate it. Although annotation takes much time and effort, it encouraged students to evaluate and reflect more about their learning behavior.

Students made annotations by selecting a time range on the interface and inputting their intentions, activities and affect. Intentions were either goal related or non-goal related, relative to the goals the students set at the beginning of the learning session. Activities referred to any activity done while learning which was either on the computer (e.g., using a browser) or outside of it (e.g., reading a book). Two sets of affect labels were used for annotating affective states. Goal-related intentions were annotated as delighted, engaged, confused, frustrated, bored, surprised or neutral and were based on emotions commonly observed in learning.[5] Non-goal related intentions however, were annotated as delighted, sad, angry, disgusted, surprised, afraid or neutral. The affective states considered for learning-related activities were used because they gave more contextual information about the students' learning activity. However, this same set might not have captured other emotions outside of the learning context so Ekman's basic emotions[6] were used to annotate them. After annotation, students were asked to rate their learning effectiveness using a scale of 1 to 5.

We first pre-processed the data we gathered so they would fit into the algorithms that we used. Although students already annotated the activities they performed while learning, many of them were similar and only differed in the applications used (e.g., browsing websites with Google Chrome vs. Mozilla Firefox). Instead of treating these separately, we used the students' activity and intention annotations to categorize their activities into six types: information search [IS] (e.g., using a search engine), view information source [IV] (e.g., reading a book, viewing a website), write notes [WN], seek help from peers [HS] (e.g., talking to a friend), knowledge application [KA] (e.g., paper writing, presentation creation, data processing) and off-task [OT] (e.g., playing a game).

We then proceeded in creating data instances using students' annotations and their categories. One instance contained the activity category, activity start time, activity duration and corresponding affect.

4. Uncovering Learning Policies

Our methodology for identifying effective behavior is based on the reinforcement learning (RL) problem wherein the goal is for an agent to identify the rules for selecting the best action to take in a given state that will lead to the highest reward.[7] In our case, the goal was to create personalized rules that identified the best activity for a student to perform in a given learning state that will maximize learning effectiveness. In this study, we used the students' self-rating of learning effectiveness for the learning session as the reward that will be maximized. We used two different reinforcement learning techniques to observe the different policies that would be developed. Each one is described in detail in the following subsections.

4.1. *Profit Sharing*

Profit sharing is a model-free RL approach that is capable of converging even in domains that do not satisfy the Markovian property.[8] We decided to use this approach primarily because we deal with human behavior in a non-deterministic and uncontrolled environment. Profit sharing's reinforcement mechanism allows it to learn effective, yet sometimes non-optimal, policies quickly. This is ideal for our situation because we want future systems that will use our approach to be able to use the policy with minimal data.

Profit sharing differs from other RL techniques because it reinforces effective rules instead of estimating values from succeeding sequential states. A rule consists of an observation-action pair (O_t, A_t) which means performing action A_t when O_t is observed. In our case, O_t refers to the state when a student is learning (i.e., activity category, activity duration, affective state). In this paper we use the term observation and state interchangeably. An episode n is a finite sequence of rules wherein the entire sequence is awarded the reward R based on its outcome. After each episode, the weights of each rule in the sequence is updated using (1) where function $f(R, t)$ is a credit assignment with t being the rule's distance from the goal. Note that it is possible for a rule's weight to be updated more than once if it appears more than once in a sequence. The set of all rules and their corresponding weights is called a policy. In profit sharing, a policy is rational or guaranteed to converge to a solution when the credit assignment function satisfies the rationality theorem (2) with L being the number of possible actions. In our work, we used a modified version of the rational credit assignment function (3), which was adapted from[8] so that the rules' weights will be bound by the reward value.

$$W_{n+1}(O_t, A_t) \leftarrow W_n(O_t, A_t) + f(R, T) \tag{1}$$

$$\forall t = 1, 2, 3, \ldots, T \quad L\sum_{j=0}^{t} f(R, j) < f(R, t) \tag{2}$$

$$f_{n+1}(R, t) = (R - W_n(O_t, A_t))(0.3)^{T-t} \tag{3}$$

For implementing this algorithm, we used a table to store the weight value assigned to each observation-action pair. Using the pre-processed data, the equations discussed above were applied on each observation-action pair in each episode then the weight values of the corresponding entry in the table was updated accordingly. In order to easily distinguish this approach, we will refer to it as PS-TBL.

4.2. Profit Sharing with Linear Function Approximation and Eligibility Traces

Although PS-TBL works well for a relatively small amount of features, it has difficulty handling many features as well as numeric features because it results in state explosion. In our work for example, we had to discretize activity duration into short, medium and long so it could be handled by PS-TBL.

One way to remove the constraints in using table-based implementations is the use of function approximators. It is usually a supervised machine learning algorithm that learns the weights associated to a state. These kinds of algorithms solve the problem of handling large or infinite state spaces in RL problems. In this work, we used Matsui and colleagues' extension to PS-TBL that used linear function approximation, gradient descent and eligibility traces.[9] This time, we will use the term PS-LFAET to refer to this algorithm.

Unlike our representation in PB-TBL, we experimented with the same set of features except the activity duration wherein we used the actual value in seconds instead of discretizing it. The rest of the categorical features were converted into binary features. This allowed us to compare the performance between the two approaches while leveraging on PS-LFAET's capability to handle continuous features.

Matsui and colleagues' implementation was a modification of the linear, gradient-descent Sarsa(λ) with binary features outlined in.[7] We slightly modified the PS-LFAET algorithm further by removing the policy control section because in our case, we only learned the policies. The pseudocode of the algorithm we used is shown in Fig. 1. In the pseudocode, $\overrightarrow{\theta}$ refers to the weight vector assigned to each feature, k is a small arbitrary constant, $\overrightarrow{e}$ refers to the eligibility trace, γ refers to the decay factor, α refers to the step-size for learning and β refers to the learning rate. In our experiments we set $\gamma = 0.2$ and $\beta = 0.2$.

5. Results and Analysis

The data from each student was used to build personalized learning policies. One learning session corresponded to one episode and one instance of the data corresponded to one step in the reinforcement learning algorithm. This produced four different learning policies wherein each policy was updated five times (i.e., five episodes). The resulting policies created by each type of reinforcement algorithm is discussed in the following subsections.

$$\vec{\theta} \leftarrow k\vec{1}$$

Repeat for each episode:

$$\vec{e} \leftarrow \vec{0}$$

Repeat for each step of an episode:

$$\vec{e} \leftarrow \gamma\vec{e}$$

$F_a \leftarrow$ set of features in s,a

Forall i in F_a:

$$e(i) \leftarrow e(i) + 1$$

$$\alpha \leftarrow \frac{1}{\sum_{i=1}^{n}\theta(i)}$$

$$\vec{e}_t \leftarrow \beta\vec{e}_{t-1} + \vec{\theta}_t$$

$$\vec{\theta} \leftarrow \vec{\theta} + \alpha r\vec{e}$$

$$s \leftarrow s'$$

Fig. 1.   Pseudocode for modified PS-LFAET algorithm

Table 1.   Subset of profit sharing rules

State	Action	Reward
Engaged, View Info Source, short	Apply Knowledge	0.360000
Engaged, View Info Source, short	View Info Source	0.004154
Confused, View Info Source, short	View Info Source	0.441939
Confused, View Info Source, short	Apply Knowledge	2.34E-05
Confused, View Info Source, short	Off-task	9.16E-15
Engaged, Apply Knowledge, long	Off-task	1.830000
Engaged, Apply Knowledge, long	Seek Help	0.009720
Engaged, Apply Knowledge, long	View Info Source	2.13E-06
Delight, Off-task, short	Apply Knowledge	0.389484
Delight, Off-task, short	View Info Source	2.00E-18
Delight, Off-task, short	Seek Help	9.57E-26

5.1. *PS-TBL*

The learning policies generated by PS-TBL consisted of rules based on the state and action representation we used. Table 1 shows a subset of the generated rules from one student. Take note that this policy is only a subset of around 60 rules built after five sessions. We assume that the state space has not yet been fully explored and the number of rules will still increase as more episodes are encountered.

Rules can easily be understood wherein putting together all rules describing the same state would describe which action would give the best reward when performed. The rules generated seemed to be logical wherein the first set of rules in the example may indicate that applying knowledge of a concept may be more effective than just reading about the concept. The second set can be interpreted as reading new material that is more understandable is better than forcing yourself to understand a confusing one. The last two sets are interesting because they describe a scenario wherein it was more effective for the student to take a break after spending a long time learning as they would eventually resume learning. Other generated rules were less intuitive but the policy's quality may improve further with more data.

Most research on reinforcement learning evaluate performance through simulations with thousands of episodes. However, this is not easy in our case because it is difficult to simulate learning behavior. We instead evaluated the performance of our policies by comparing how much of the policy the student actually followed. We assumed that since the policy maximized a student's learning effectiveness rating, the more the student followed the policy, the higher their effectiveness rating should also be.

We tested this by using the data from the current session to build the policies. Next, the ratio of the number of times a student followed the policy over the total number of steps in the sequence was compared against the students' learning effectiveness rating. Figure 2, shows the comparison between the two as well as the difference between them indicated by the

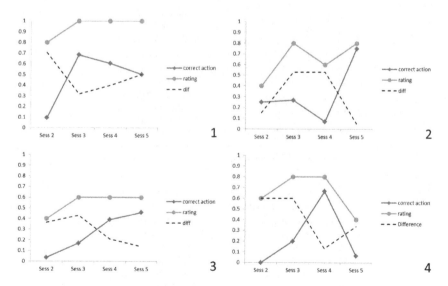

Fig. 2. Comparison between student ratings and the number of times they followed a policy

dotted line in the graphs. We can see that there seemed to be a correlation between the number of times the student followed the policy and the student's learning effectiveness rating. The difference between the two also seemed to decrease over time, or was at least less than the initial difference. This means that if we can encourage students to follow the policy, their learning effectiveness may improve.

5.2. *PS-LFAET*

As mentioned earlier, we represented activity duration as a single numeric feature in PS-LFAET. All the other categorical features were converted into binary features. If activity duration were also discretized, then the number of weights would just be the same as the number of rules in the table version.

Table 2 shows a subset of the weights generated by PS-LFAET from a total of 55 features. This is five less than the number of states used in the table representation.

Table 2. Weight values identified by linear function approximator

Duration	Weight
Action: Apply Knowledge	
Duration	19.370804120460775
Task = Relax	5.432052893832781
Task = Apply Knowledge	7.147558999219834
Task = Search	3.0788653447627436
Task = View Info Source	9.274572986789638
Affect = Neutral	10.113768354131865
Affect = Engaged	3.893589983031738
Affect = Confused	5.248619907779905
Affect = Bored	4.924993431565708
Affect = Delighted	0.7520785480957715
Action: View Info Source	
Duration	18.424851115665614
Task = Relax	6.638692790347588
Task = Apply Knowledge	4.061630468614316
Task = Search	1.731023625119618
Task = View Info Source	7.455867888384675
Affect = Neutral	11.783225211875068
Affect = Engaged	3.2053059318631867
Affect = Confused	1.6179389970351024
Affect = Bored	2.5286660768735434
Affect = Delighted	0.7520785548192918

Interpreting the results of linear function approximation was more difficult compared to using a table representation because many different combi-
nations were formed using the weights. However, we can identify the reward
for performing an action in a particular state by computing its weighted
sum. For example, given the state <Engaged, View Info Source, short>
from Table 1 and assuming that short maps to 0.05, the reward for performing the action Apply Knowledge would be 14.1285 and the reward for
performing View Info Source would be 11.571. This has the same result
as PS-TBL's policy wherein Apply Knowledge was also the better action.
There were also interesting rules derived from the policy such as higher
weight values were given when the student performed an Apply Knowledge
action coming from a bored or confused state. This can be interpreted as
testing a concept allowed the student to understand it better and engaged
him more rather than just reading about it.

We used the same evaluation process as in PS-TBL wherein we see in
Fig. 3 that there also seemed to be correlations between students' self-rating
and the number of times they followed the policy. The number of subjects
and the number of learning sessions we used in the experiment made it
difficult to make a conclusion as to which approach was better. However,
the flexibility of PS-LFAET seems to make it a good option given that

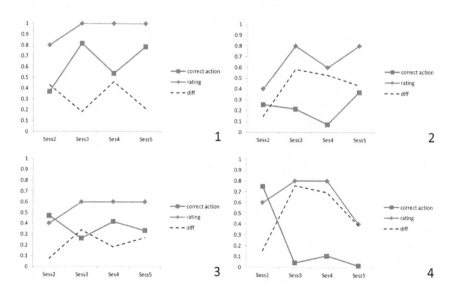

Fig. 3. Comparison between student ratings and the number of times they followed a
policy

it can perform as well as PS-TBL. We can also extend PS-LFAET more easily wherein we can use numeric features (e.g., time elapsed since the start of the session) without the need to discretize them. On top of this, using PS-LFAET also has the advantage of being able to generalize states which have not yet been encountered. The weighted sum can approximate a reward using other features' weights which is not possible in PS-TBL.

The disadvantage of PS-LFAET however is that it is more difficult to interpret. In PS-TBL's representation, feedback can be designed based on the exact value of categorical features. In PS-LFAET however, it is difficult to design feedback based on ranges of values for numeric features.

6. Conclusion and Future Work

In this paper we have discussed an extension to our previous work wherein we used the annotated data from students' self-reflection and self-evaluation to uncover effective learning behaviors. We were able to do this by using a reinforcement learning approach which identified behaviors (i.e., observation and action pairs) that led to better learning effectiveness. Future versions of our system, or other systems that adopt our approach, can use the list of effective and ineffective behaviors to analyze students' learning behavior in the current session and identify which activities may have caused effective (or ineffective) learning. These can then be used to design feedback that can help the student change his/her behavior accordingly. We feel that this approach is more effective than using rules from background knowledge or experts because the policy was built from the student's own learning history. Feedback given to students becomes more personal and more meaningful to them.

The results of both PS-TBL and PS-LFAET are promising however, there is still a need to find a way to discover effective or ineffective learning behavior faster. It would be beneficial for students to get meaningful feedback as soon as possible rather than after many episodes. Currently we are exploring the use of better features and reward measures that can distinguish between effective and ineffective behavior. We are also considering jump starting students' policies using background knowledge or inputs from experts to help speed up the process. Using other students' policies to supplement policy creation which mimics a "learning from others" type of mechanism may also be a good way to improve the approach.

There are still many issues that need to be resolved in this research but once completed, it will allow support for students in almost any domain and will help them learn how to learn. Overall, we hope that using the software will result in better learning experiences for students and help them become life-long learners.

Acknowledgment

This research is supported in part by the Management Expenses Grants for National Universities Corporations through the Ministry of Education, Culture, Sports, Science and Technology (MEXT) of Japan, by the Global COE (Centers of Excellence) Program of MEXT, and by KAKENHI 23300059. We would also like to thank the students who participated in our data gathering session.

References

1. B. J. Zimmerman, Self-regulated learning and academic achievement: An overview, *Educational psychologist* **25**, 3 (1990).
2. P. S. Inventado, R. Legaspi, R. Cabredo and M. Numao, Student learning behavior in an unsupervised learning environment, in *20th International Conference on Computers in Education*, (Singapore, 2012).
3. S. Manlove, A. W. Lazonder and T. Jong, Software scaffolds to promote regulation during scientific inquiry learning, *Metacognition and Learning* **2**, 141 (2007).
4. R. Azevedo, R. S. Landis, R. Feyzi-Behnagh, M. Duffy, G. Trevors, J. M. Harley, F. Bouchet, J. Burlison, M. Taub, N. Pacampara, M. Yeasin, A. K. M. M. Rahman, M. I. Tanveer and G. Hossain, The effectiveness of pedagogical agents' prompting and feedback in facilitating co-adapted learning with MetaTutor, in *Intelligent Tutoring Systems*, (Montreal, Canada, 2012).
5. S. D. Craig, A. C. Graesser, J. Sullins and B. Gholson, Affect and learning: An exploratory look into the role of affect in learning with AutoTutor, *Journal of Educational Media* **29**, 241 (2004).
6. P. Ekman, Are there basic emotions?, *Psychological Review* **99**, 550 (1992).
7. R. Sutton and A. Barto, *Reinforcement Learning: An Introduction (Adaptive Computation and Machine Learning)* 1998.
8. S. Arai and K. Sycara, Effective learning approach for planning and scheduling in Multi-Agent domain, in *6th International Conference on Simulation of Adaptive Behavior*, (MIT Press, Paris, France, 2000).
9. T. Matsui, N. Inuzuka and H. Seki, Profit sharing with linear function approximation, in *16th Annual Conference of Japanese Society for Artificial Intelligence*, (Tokyo, Japan, 2002).

DATA COLLECTION WITH PRIORITIZATION FOR WIRELESS SENSOR NETWORKS

ARLYN VERINA ONG

De La Salle University, 2401 Taft Avenue
Manila, 1004, Philippines

GREGORY CU

De La Salle University, 2401 Taft Avenue
Manila, 1004, Philippines

Wireless sensor networks (WSN) are a popular platform to support applications that require data collection from multiple sources. Using wireless networks to provide the communication infrastructure for these sensors makes the data from sensors prone to delays and loss due to the shared nature of a wireless medium. In applications where heterogeneous sensors are crucial for data collection, sensors generate data with different levels of importance and delivery requirements. This study presents a data collection method for WSNs that provides a classification scheme for sensors, and a prioritization method used to complement a TDMA-based medium access control algorithm to arbitrate data transmission among these sensors.

1. Introduction

A wireless sensor networks or a WSN is a network where devices interact via radio signals to provide monitoring and control services to an environment [1]. The elimination of the need for extensive wiring in WSNs contributes to easier installation of new devices, better mobility and portability. Because of this, WSNs have become a popular platform for different types of automated systems that require a sensor-rich infrastructure.

Typical wireless sensor networks consist of multiple low-powered nodes that monitor the environment in a target application. Nodes are characterized by relatively small form factors and the ability to operate with portable power sources for easy deployment. As such, these networks may be constrained by limited bandwidth for communications, low processing power memory resources, and best effort data delivery services.

Depending on the target application, wireless sensor networks may be composed of a heterogeneous mix of different sensor types, each monitoring a different aspect of the environment to provide the appropriate feedback to the application. These sensors exhibit varying data stream characteristics in terms of delay tolerance, throughput and network reliability requirements [2].

As an example, in an automated home, sensors that monitor environment variables like temperature, lighting and humidity may be configured to do periodic monitoring, thereby regularly consuming network bandwidth. At the same time, these may tolerate less reliability and longer delivery delays since only gradual changes are expected in the monitored variables. On the other hand, certain sensors like those involved in security systems may remain idle majority of the time, but will need high reliability and minimal delay when events are detected due to the critical nature of the aspects that they monitor.

With the potential variations in the data to be collected, coupled with the limited resources available to WSNs, a form of traffic management scheme is needed to provide appropriate prioritization to ensure that the sensor network satisfies the delivery requirements of different data sources [2]. Current mainstream WSN communication protocols such as ZigBee [3] and its underlying transmission protocol IEEE 802.15.4 standard [4] provide only best effort delivery, with no mechanisms to recognize traffic types and allocate the appropriate network resources in response to their delivery requirements. The low bandwidth of the network and the best effort delivery services these protocols may cause data losses and delays during periods of high network activity, impacting the delivery of potentially critical or urgent data.

Data collection algorithms developed for WSNs are designed to excel at one aspect at the expense of another. Some algorithms aim for longer battery life at the expense of delivery speed [5] or accuracy [6]. Others aim for reliable data routing [7]. Further still, some data collection algorithms are used in a network where all sensors are of the same type [8]. These do not categorize traffic for the purpose of providing the delivery requirements of each data flow.

This paper introduces a data collection algorithm for wireless sensor networks that provides a prioritized data handling mechanism. Section 2 describes the data priority scheme used. Section 3 introduces the underlying transmission protocol and details the data handling method used. Section 4 presents the simulation parameters and results of tests conducted. Finally Section 5 concludes this paper.

2. Data Priority Levels

Three data priority levels are defined for traffic categorization. Priority levels are designed to be statically assigned to a sensor; and hence, any need to increase or decrease the priority level of a sensor will have to be donemanually. All data originating from the sensor are associated with the same priority level.

It is assumed that a physical sensor node may house multiple sensors as well. The priority level assigned to a sensor is significant in terms of transmission priority among sensors on the same node and among different sensor nodes. Table 1 describes the three priority levels as well as the intended usage of each level in terms of the type of data expected from a sensor.

Table 1. Sensor priority levels and intended usage.

Priority	Intended Usage
Low	Sensors that transmit routine data, where moderate data losses are tolerable and latency is not critical
Mid	Sensors that can tolerate some data loss and moderate latency
High	Sensors that transmit critical data, where data must be reliably delivered to the sink and latency must be minimal

3. Traffic Prioritization and Handling

To perform traffic prioritization, a time division-based medium access control (MAC) protocol is used to arbitrate shared wireless transmission medium usage among the different sensor nodes in the network. The prioritization scheme used in conjunction with the MAC protocol controls how the network time is allocated to nodes for sensor data transmission.

3.1. *Medium Access Control*

The MAC algorithm used is a modification of the Advertisement-based Time Division Multi-Access (ATMA) protocol designed by Surjya et al [9]. Recurring transmission frames divide network time into an advertisement and a data phase, which are further divided into advertisement and data slots, respectively.

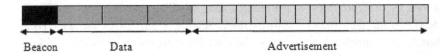

Beacon   Data   Advertisement

Figure 1. MAC protocol transmission frame.

To transmit data, sensor nodes must send out advertisements on randomly selected advertisement slots to reserve transmission slots for the data phase of the succeeding transmission round. Once a data slot is allocated, the transmitting node has exclusive use of the medium during its scheduled slot. Figure 1 illustrates the division of time within a transmission frame.

The modification to the MAC protocol centralizes the allocation and scheduling of data slots for requesting sensor nodes on a node is designated as network coordinator. Sensor nodes direct advertisements to the coordinator; which keeps track of all advertisements received within a transmission frame. Once the current frame ends, the coordinator broadcasts a beacon containing information on the number of data slots, as well the ID of the sensor node assigned to transmit data on each of the allocated slots at the onset of the next frame. Sensor nodes receiving the beacon use the information to determine data transmission order, as well as the schedule of the next advertisement phase for further data slot requests if needed.

3.2. *Transmit Prioritization*

Transmit prioritization is applied among sensors housed on a single node as well as among sensor nodes waiting to use the medium.

Regardless of the number of sensors housed on a single node, the node may service the transmission of data only one sensor at a time. Data produced by any sensor are placed into data queues for sending. These data packets are tagged with the data priority level associated with the originating sensor, as well as with a timestamp indicating the time that the data was generated.

The prioritization scheme assumes finite memory for a wireless sensor node. The data queue is a bounded priority queue where data packets awaiting transmission are ordered in descending priority level. Among packets of equal priority, ordering is done according to ascending time of creation. In case the packet at the head of the transmit queue is currently being serviced for transmission, its position as head is maintained and the insertion of a new data packet affects only the order of the rest of the queue.

The task of prioritizing data transmissions among sensor nodes is relegated to the coordinator node given its control over the allocation of data slots in the network. When a sensor node requests for data slots through advertisements, the priority level and the timestamp of the packet at the head of its data queue are included in the advertisement sent to the coordinator. Once the coordinator has collected one transmission frame worth of advertisements from different sensor nodes, the order of the data slots to be scheduled for the succeeding frame is arranged according to the same scheme of decreasing priority level followed by increasing timestamp.

In this sense, sensor nodes that have requested data slots for higher priority sensors are scheduled to transmit earlier than those of lower priority level. On the same note, data that was generated earlier will also be transmitted across the network earlier compared to others of equal priority.

4. Performance Evaluation

To evaluate the performance of the algorithm, a wireless sensor network is simulated to transmit data using the defined priority levels and traffic handling mechanism. The tests include three major test scenarios which differ in the manner that sensors generate data. Each scenario is tested with 50000 bps network bandwidth assuming a fully reliable transmission medium over 2 hours of simulation time. Simulated sensors fire at random intervals following an exponential distribution with mean values between 5 to 120 seconds.

The first test scenario assumes a network where sensors are not interrelated with each other and fire independently of each other. This mimics a setup where sensors are spaced far apart and the firing of a sensor does not affect any other sensors in the network.

The second test scenario assumes a network where sensors are interrelated but only a single sensor is housed per node. This scenario mimics a setup where sensors are deployed in close proximity of each other, with sensor groups firing simultaneously when a triggering event occurs within the monitored area.

Similar to the second scenario, the third scenario also simulates interdependent sensors; however the setup is modified so that multiple sensors located close to each other are housed on a single node. Each scenario is run with multiple tests varying the ratio of sensor count per priority level.

4.1. *Reliability*

In the tests conducted, transmission reliability is measured as the percentage of data packets that reach their destination out of all packets that were transmitted. Figures 2, 3 and 4 show the results for the first, second, and third scenarios, respectively.

Test scenarios 1 and 2 both present networks where only a single sensor is housed per node. Results from these scenarios show that data from all priority levels have 100% transmission reliability from source to destination node. The transmission rate of data frames is fast enough such that with only a single sensor placing data into the transmit queue of each sensor node, data moves out of the queue quickly; and queues are almost always empty.

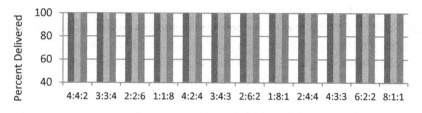

Figure 2. Transmission reliability per priority level (Scenario 1).

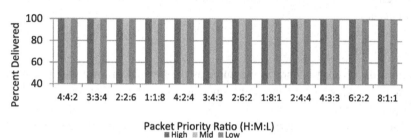

Figure 3. Transmission reliability per priority level (Scenario 2).

On the other hand, test scenario 3 has multiple sensors on a single node firing nearly at the same time when an event occurs. This immediately places several data packets into the queue when an event occurs; leading to queues filling up more quickly on each node. Once the queue is full, incoming high priority data cause lower priority data frames on the tail end of the queue to be discarded.

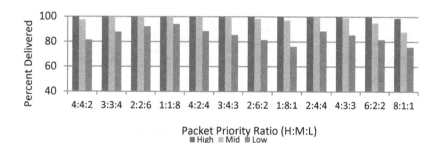

Figure 4. Transmission reliability per priority level (Scenario 3).

In Figure 4, transmission success for low priority or mid priority data drops significantly as the number of higher priority sensors present in the network increases. On the other hand, high priority data reliability drops only when network is composed of mostly high priority sensors; and queues cannot always accommodate all high priority traffic. With the number of sensors simulated in the test scenario, it is still possible for low priority data to be transmitted even if higher priority sensors make up a large ratio of network sensors; however, the transmit reliability of these low priority data drops significantly. At lower bandwidths, a high activity network with mostly high and mid priority sensors may cause starvation of low priority data as they are almost always discarded from queues.

4.2. *Latency*

Average data packet latency is measured as the time taken for a data packet to reach the sink, which includes the queuing time of the data packet and its transport time [10].

Scenario 1 is characterized by an even demand for network resources over time due to independently firing sensors; hence at any one time, only a few sensors request for data slots from the coordinator. While the trendillustrated in Figure 5 mostly shows that higher priority data experience lower latency, differences in average packet latency among data priority levels occur only in thousandths of a second. With a single sensor per node, only the order of data slots as scheduled by the coordinator affects frame latency. Each transmission frame has only a few data slots; and sensor nodes can transmit early into a frame even if data is of a low priority level.

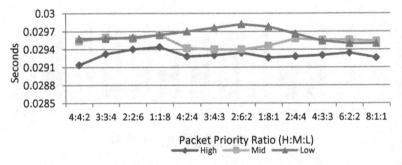

Figure 5. Average packet latency per priority level (Scenario 1).

A slightly higher latency for mid priority sensor data compared to low priority data may be observed in the graph for the instance where high priority data make up 60% of network traffic. As data traffic for this scenario exhibits an even distribution of demand for network resources, the slight increase can be attributed to the random sensor firing which can cause mid priority sensors to fire in slightly more frequent intervals compared to low priority sensors, leading to longer waiting times.

The second and third scenarios are characterized by sudden bursts of high network activity when events occur as these involve multiple sensors simultaneously each time. In scenario 2, latency is primarily affected by the scheduling of data slots by the network coordinator. There is a noticeable difference in average latency among data packets of different priority levels as shown in Figure 6. This is because lower priority data are scheduled for transmission on later data slots within the same frame.

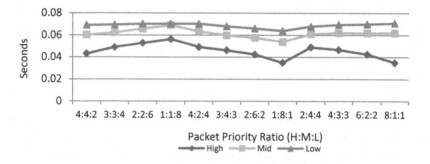

Figure 6. Average packet latency per priority level (Scenario 2)

Similarly in scenario 3 shown in Figure 7, average latency differs among packets of different priority level. This is primarily caused by the ordering of packets when placed into the queue of the node where the originating sensor is attached. As lower priority packets are pushed back in the queue when higher priority packets are inserted, waiting time in the queue is prolonged. The differences among priority levels are significantly more evident than the first 2 scenarios as each node transmits only one packet per transmission frame. Any packet waiting in the queue has to wait for subsequent transmission frames before transmission.

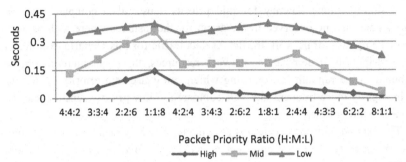

Figure 7. Average packet latency per priority level (Scenario 3).

In both second and third scenarios, high priority data exhibits the least latency when it constitutes the minority of data in the network. The lower number of high priority sensors presents little waiting time for high priority sensors. On the opposite end, low priority data exhibits the most latency among all priority levels since it is always scheduled at the last available data slots in a transmission round.

4.3. *Throughput*

Throughput is measured as the number of data packets successfully delivered by the network from source to destination over a unit of time.

Figure 8 shows results for Scenario 1. There are no differences in transmission reliability and minimal differences in latency among different priority levels. As such, the only observable trend is that for each priority level, throughput increases as the number of sensors increases mainly due to traffic volume.

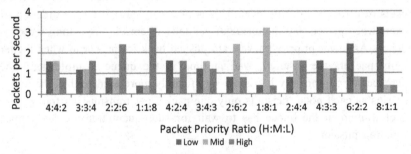

Figure 8. Throughput per priority level (Scenario 1).

In Figures 9 and 10, representing data for the second and third scenarios, differences in transmission reliability and latency at each priority level affect the overall throughput of data for the priority level. Throughput is still primarily affected by traffic volume, as it increases for a priority level when a larger number of sensors in the network happen to be assigned to that level. It can be observed though, that at instances when there are an equal number of sensors for two different priority levels, those at the higher priority level still have higher throughput. Examples of these instances are the test where mid priority data make up 20%, while high and low priority data both make up 40% each of network traffic.

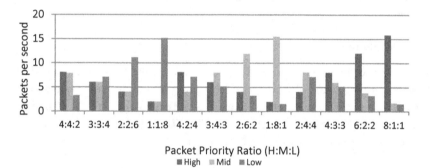

Figure 9. Throughput per priority level (Scenario 2).

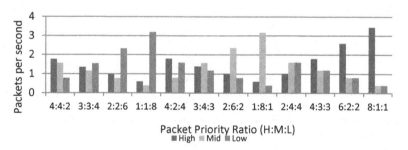

Figure 10. Throughput per priority level (Scenario 3).

5. Conclusion

The three-level classification scheme allows sensors in a WSN to be assigned to either low, mid or high priority level depending on the criticality of the data that they generate. Priority queuing directs data queues on nodes to prioritize thesending of higher priority data; and to begin discarding lower priority data first in case of resource shortage.

In addition, a centralized and contention-free MAC protocol is used to provide prioritized granting of network time nodes that need to transmit over the network. These mechanisms allow the data collection method to scale data transmission reliability, latency and throughput depending on data priority. The effect of this is most evident in networks characterized by bursty traffic patterns.

Care must be taken when using the proposed method to assign priority levels to sensors in networks where bandwidth is heavily utilized or where several high activity sensors are housed on a single node. If the ratio of sensors per priority level is not properly planned, there is a potential for resource starvation for low priority sensors.

Acknowledgments

The authors of this paper would like to acknowledge the Philippine Council for Industry, Energy and Emerging Technology Research and Development *(PCIEERD)* of the Department of Science and Technology, and the Center for Empathic Human-Computer Interactions (*CEHCI*) of De La Salle University for the invaluable support provided to this research.

References

1. Karl, H., Willig, A.: Protocols and architectures for wireless sensor networks. Wiley (2005).
2. Xia, F: QoS challenges and opportunities in wireless sensor/actuator networks. Sensors 8, 1099–1110 (2008).
3. The ZigBee Alliance: ZigBee specification: ZigBee document 053474r17. ZigBee Standards Organization (2008).
4. IEEE: IEEE Standard 15.4 wireless medium access control and physical layer for low-rate wireless personal area networks. New York (2003).
5. Incel, O. D., Ghosh, A., Krishnamachari, B.: Scheduling algorithms for tree-based data collection in wireless sensor networks. Computer Engineering 99, 1–15 (2011).
6. Dang, N., Bozorgzadeh, E., Venkatasubramania, N.: QuARES: quality-aware data collection in energy harvesting sensor networks. 2011 International Green Computing Conference and Workshops, 1–9 (2011).
7. Janacik, P., Matthews, E., Orfanus, D.: Self-organizing data collection in wireless sensor networks. IEEE 24th International Conference on Advanced Information Networking and Applications Workshops (WAINA), 662–667 (2010).
8. Kumar, M., Verma, S.: Querying video sensor networks. Third International Conference on Wireless Communication and Sensor Networks, 50–54 (2007).

9. Surjya, R., Demirkol, I., Heinzelman, W.: ATMA: Advertisement-based TDMA protocol for bursty traffic in wireless sensor networks. IEEE Global Tele communications Conference (GLOBECOM 2010), 1–5 (2010).
10. Lee H.J., Kim M.S., *et al.*: QoS parameters to network performance metrics mapping for SLA monitoring. Asia-Pacific Network Operations and Management Symposium Conference, (2002).

HEALTH INFORMATION SEARCH PERSONALIZATION WITH SEMANTIC NETWORK USER MODEL

IRA PUSPITASARI[†]

The Institute of Scientific and Industrial Research, Osaka University,
Mihogaoka 8-1 Ibaraki, Osaka 5670047, Japan

KEN-ICHI FUKUI, KOICHI MORIYAMA and MASAYUKI NUMAO

The Institute of Scientific and Industrial Research, Osaka University,
Mihogaoka 8-1 Ibaraki, Osaka 5670047, Japan

The emergence of e-patient has encouraged people to be more literate about healthcare subject. However, health information seeking remains problematic for most non-medical professionals (consumers). Most consumers are not knowledgeable with medical terminology. The diversity of consumer's familiarity with health domain also leads to frustration since the information presented may fall outside the consumer's comprehension level. This research aims to assist consumers obtain understandable health information by designing adaptive personalization approach in health information retrieval system. The proposed approach constructs user model dynamically based on the interaction with search engine. The user model captures contextual attributes and the familiarity level with health topic in a weighted semantic network. A node represents a topic of interest and its familiarity level and a weighted-link shows semantic similarity between nodes, which refers to Unified Medical Language System Semantic Network.

1. Introduction

The emergence of e-patient has encouraged people of non-medical professionals (consumers) to be more proactive about healthcare education and health decision making. More consumers are progressively using the Internet to search for health information. Numerous Consumer Health Informatics (CHI) portals and medical search engines have been developed to accommodate the rising needs of health information, such as Medline Plus, Healthline, and WebMD.

Despite the growth of Consumer Health Informatics systems, searching for relevant and understandable health information remains problematic for most consumers. Searching for health information requires a certain degree of cognitive effort to construct the query keywords, filter the search results, and

---

[†]Email: ira@ai.sanken.osaka-u.ac.jp

understand the selected result. Most consumers only have a vague idea and cannot describe their health situation clearly because of unfamiliarity with medical domain [1, 2, 10]. Oftentimes, the submitted queries do not accurately reflect the searcher's information needs. Another challenging matter is the difficulty in selecting relevant and understandable article from the retrieved results since the information varies from general health feature to complex medical paper [1, 15].

When searching for health information, different consumers may have different needs. The distinctive need among consumers is determined by several factors, such as individual background, user's knowledge, and user's interest. However, many CHI applications and health information retrieval systems do not consider these specific needs [2, 9]. A consumer who searches for "*cold symptoms*" may refer to a viral infectious disease of the upper respiratory tract or *Chronic Obstructive Lung Disease*. Other two consumers who search for "*arrhythmia*" and "*irregular heartbeat*" respectively may expect different retrieved documents.

Given the challenges in health information seeking for consumers, a personalization approach is required to assist consumers obtain relevant and understandable health information. This paper presents the framework of personalization approach in health information retrieval system using semantic network user model. The design of the proposed framework is explained with the following structure. Section 2 describes the related works on health information retrieval system and personalization approach. Section 3 explains the design of the proposed system. Section 4 and 5 discuss the user model development. Last section concludes the preliminary work and presents the follow-up works.

2. Related Works

This section presents related works on existing health information retrieval system, semantic network based user model, and dynamic user modeling.

2.1. *Health Information Retrieval System*

To accommodate the rising need for online health information seeking, researchers and healthcare providers have developed medical specialized search engine, such as Intelligent Medical Search Engine [11], MedSearch [10], MedicoPort [1], Project STEPPS [3], and Consumer Health Technologies for diabetes aging population [9]. All systems provide medical terminology assistance for the searchers.

According to Luo *et al.* [10], health information searchers opt to formulate readable and understandable long query in natural language and to receive all kinds of medical knowledge related to their situation. The researchers developed medical search engine MedSearch, which accepts long queries in plain English. The search engine then extracts the representative keywords from the submitted query. Based on the modified query, MedSearch returns diversified search result and suggests related medical phrases with proper ranking and annotation.

In the subsequent research work [11], Luo developed Intelligent Medical Search Engine (iMed). Users need personalized guidance during medical search process because of their unfamiliarity with medical terminology [11]. iMed uses predefined questionnaire to capture user's information need. Based on user's response, iMed automatically forms the medical query; structures the entire search results into multilevel hierarchy; and suggests related medical phrases.

The medical search system in MedicoPort used Unified Medical Language System (UMLS) resources to increase the effectiveness of medical search for non-medical professional searchers. The system utilized UMLS Specialist Lexicon for its crawler to index and generate concept. The query formulator and concept generator of MedicoPort used UMLS Metathesaurus and UMLS Semantic Network to expand user query, reformulate query terms, rank the search result, and filter irrelevant documents.

Another approach of medical specialized search engine is a personalized system. LeRouge *et al.* [9] used the user-centered design concept as methodological tools to design Consumer Health Technologies devices for aging population who suffered from diabetes. Other researchers have proposed strategy to provide personalized information retrieval by integrating electronic patient records with health-related content on the Internet. The project of Structured Evaluated Personalized Patient Support used electronic patient data to construct user profiles and to retrieve health information based on the profiles [3].

2.2. *Semantic Network based User Model*

A personalized system aims to provide appropriate tailored content and services to individual user [2, 4, 6]. The system collects information about the user, constructs the correct user model, and applies the model to deliver adaptive service / content. One technique to represent a user model in a personalized system is a semantic network user model. In semantic network representation, the attribute of the user model is maintained in a network structure of terms and related terms [4, 6]. To define the semantic relationships in the network, the system refers to a thesaurus dictionary. The network consists of nodes and links.

The main node holds weighted term that represents user's attribute, whereas the associated node contains semantically related terms. The node and its associated nodes are connected via weighted links, which represent the frequency of co-occurrence in a document.

An example of semantic network user model implementation is InfoWeb, a filtering system for online digital library documents [5]. InfoWeb records the user information needs in a semantically based user profile. Firstly, the semantic network contains unlinked concept nodes in which each node holds a single, representative weighted term for corresponding concept. As more information about the user is collected, the profile is enriched with satellite nodes and the link between concept nodes. The satellite node contains additional weighted keyword associated with the concept node. The link represents the association between concept nodes.

In another work, Micarelli *et al.* developed Web-based Information Filtering System (WIFS). WIFS is a content-based information-filtering module, capable of selecting html/text documents on computer science collected from the Web according to the user's interests [12]. The semantic network in WIFS represents user's interest. The planet (main node) holds a weighted topic term and the satellites (associated node) contain the co-occurring terms, which appear in the relevant documents. The weighted arc between the planet and its satellites represents the affinity rate.

2.3. *Dynamic User Modeling*

Users may change their attributes (e.g. interest, the purpose of using the system, the progress of level of understanding) from time to time [2, 6]. A personalized system applies dynamic user modeling to accommodate change in user attributes. In dynamic user modeling, the system applies updating mechanism to maintain the accuracy of the user model. The mechanism can be invoked by the system via decaying or aging technique or triggered upon a certain user action, such as an explicit user relevance feedback on display content [4, 6].

Some research works have developed adaptive system with dynamic user modeling, such as adaptive web search [13], OntoSearch [8], and Web-based Information Filtering System (WIFS) [12]. In adaptive web search system, Sugiyama *et al.* [13] implemented periodic decaying of interest to update the user model to its newest value. In OntoSearch, the researchers built a semantic search engine with spreading activation procedure to keep track the shifting of user interest over time. The latter system, WIFS, implements multiple updates (both implicit and explicit) to its user model. Users can update the model by

172

providing explicit relevance feedback to the topic interest and retrieved documents. Then, the system applies renting mechanism by decreasing the weights of corresponding topic and links in its user model.

3. The Framework of Personalized Health Information Retrieval System

The proposed personalization approach consists of two main subsystems, the user modeling system and the filtering system. The user modeling system constructs the user model dynamically based on the interaction with a particular search engine. The adaptive user model module extracts representative terms from consumer's query and webpage visited, classifies the extracted terms into a list of weighted topics of interest using Health Topic Reference, and determines the familiarity level for each topic of interest. The query analyzer classifies the consumer's query (general term query or advanced medical query), expands the query if necessary, and sends modified query to search engine. To generate relevant modified query, the query analyzer exploits the contextual attribute from the user model and the resources from Unified Medical Language System (UMLS). After retrieving the search result, the filtering system re-ranks the documents based on the similarity of retrieved-document, the consumer's query, and the consumer's familiarity level with the current health topic.

The overall system architecture is illustrated in Figure 1.

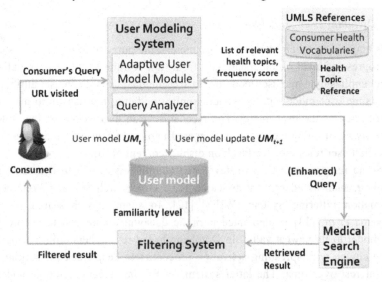

Figure 1 The System Framework

4. The Attributes of User Model

User model serves as the basis of personalization approach in any adaptive system. The user model may include information about demographic profiles, interest, background knowledge, or individual traits, depending on the purpose of the system. In health information retrieval system, contextual attributes and the familiarity level with health topic are the key sources to provide sufficient personalization. The contextual attribute determines the searching needs. To this work, the contextual attribute consists of a list of topic of interest and estimated delineation of health background condition. The latter information may contribute to significant improvements in system's performance. For example, an article about gestational diabetes is reasonably more relevant for a pregnant woman who searches for "*diabetes mellitus symptoms*" than for a senior age man who submits the same keyword to the same system.

Health information seeking involves unfamiliar medical terminology within various health topics for most consumers. A consumer may be knowledgeable about a certain health topic (e.g. digestive system) but completely unfamiliar with other topics (e.g. immune system, endocrine related diseases). The information in medical domain also varies from general article to one that requires high proficiency to understand. Therefore, the system must consider the familiarity level when processing the consumer's query.

The user modeling system in the proposed approach defines the contextual attributes and the familiarity level implicitly. Topic of interest can be extracted from query keywords and webpages visited. On the other hand, health condition background and familiarity level are difficult to be assessed accurately without explicit annotation from the consumer. Using patient record (Electronic Medical Record) is the most practical way to obtain accurate information about health condition background. However, this technique leads to privacy and security problem because patient record may not always be available to third party healthcare system and most people object the idea of giving access to personal medical record. Searching history and past queries may give clue about potentially health condition background of a consumer.

For the familiarity level, one approach to estimate the attribute value is by analyzing consumers searching behavior. According to [7, 14, 15], domain expert users and non-expert users search differently in term of query features, searching strategy, and result selection. In line with findings from previous researches and studies, our preliminary study about characterizing the effect of consumer familiarity in health information seeking showed that the familiarity level affected consumers' searching behavior, in terms of query keywords selection, the pattern of query reformulation pattern, and webpages visited. We exploit this finding in our personalization framework to build the familiarity level classification and to determine the familiarity level of each consumer.

In summary, Table 1 lists the sources of the consumer attributes.

Table 1 Attributes of the User Model

Attribute	Data Source
Interest	Consumer's query, webpages visited.
Health Condition	Search history, past queries.
Background	
Familiarity level	Query keywords, query reformulation pattern within single searching session, webpages visited, and frequency score.

5. Semantic Network User Model

The proposed approach constructs user model dynamically based on the interaction with search engine. The user model captures contextual attributes and familiarity with health topic in a weighted semantic network. A node represents a topic of interest and its familiarity level. To assign the correct label topic for each node, the system extracts representative terms from the consumer's query and webpages visited, then maps the terms to Health Topic Reference. After selecting the correct label for new node, the system assigns the initial value. To define the familiarity level, the user modeling system performs classifier selection. A weighted-link between nodes represents semantic similarity between health topics, which refers to Unified Medical Language System Semantic Network. The score in each link is calculated using Wu and Palmer [16] formulation as follows.

$$wup(a,b) = \frac{2 * depth(LCS(a,b))}{depth(a) + depth(b)} \tag{1}$$

where:

wup(a,b): Semantic similarity measure between concept a and concept b,

LCS: Least common subsumer of concept a and b,

a, b: concept in UMLS,

depth (a) = shortest is-a path (root,a),

The value of depth and LCS are calculated from UMLS Semantic Network.

The semantic user model grows and modifies itself dynamically in accordance with system utilization. The user modeling system applies spreading activation mechanism to maintain the value in each node. When a consumer performs health information seeking, the user modeling system creates node(s) for new health topic and updates respective node(s) for recurring topic. After node creation/update, the system starts spreading activation process from the active node to its neighbors. The spreading process continues to activate the neighboring node and to update its value until the latest value of respective node is below the threshold or the maximum spreading distance is achieved. For the recurring health topic searching, the system also updates the familiarity level of the corresponding node. This approach enables the user model to be kept updated to its current attributes.

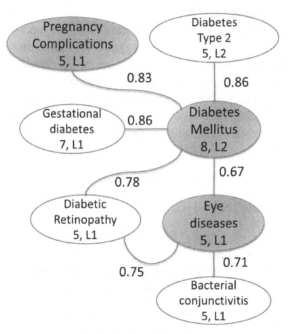

Figure 2 Portion of User Model

The example of user model portion is illustrated in Figure 2. Each node contains topic of interest label, interest score, and familiarity level classification. Node i = <concept$_i$, value (concept$_i$), familiarity-level (concept$_i$)>. Link between nodes represents semantic similarity and a higher score indicates more related concept. The shading in the node shows the hierarchy of medical concept based on UMLS reference. Shaded node contains more general concept, whereas the unshaded shows more specific concept. The familiarity level of health topic is denoted in L1 (introductory level in respective health topic), L2 (beginner level), or L3 (advanced level) classification.

6. Conclusion and Future Work

Health information seeking has distinctive requirements that distinguish it from conventional web search. Most consumers are not familiar with medical terminology, yet more and more people strive for online health information seeking. Personalization approach in health information retrieval system is necessary to assist consumers obtain relevant and understandable health information. In order to provide sufficient and effective personalization, the system must address two important attributes, the context attribute and the familiarity level with health topic.

This paper presented the design of personalization approach in health information retrieval system. The proposed system consists of user modeling and filtering module. Major features of the design are the user modeling mechanism and the semantic network based user model. The design of the proposed system is currently being implemented into a working system. For the next work, we aim to conduct experimental study to evaluate the accuracy of the semantic network user model and the performance of the proposed system.

References

1. A. B. Can and N. Baykal, *Computer Methods and Programs in Biomedicine.* 86, 1 (2007) 73–86.
2. A. Cawsey, F. Grasso, and C. Paris. Adaptive information for consumers of healthcare. In Brusilovsky, P., Kobsa, A., Nejdl, W., eds.: *The Adaptive Web: Methods and Strategies of Web Personalization.* Volume 4321 of Lecture Notes in Computer Science. Springer-Verlag, Berlin Heidelberg New York (2007).
3. P. Doupi and J. V. D. Lei, *Informatics for Health and Social Care* 27, 3 (2002) 139–151.
4. S. Gauch, M. Speretta, A. Chandramouli, and A. Micarelli. User profiles for personalized information access. In Brusilovsky, P., Kobsa, A., Nejdl, W., eds.: The Adaptive Web: Methods and Strategies of Web Personalization. Volume 4321 of Lecture Notes in Computer Science. Springer-Verlag, Berlin Heidelberg New York (2007).
5. G. Gentili, A. Micarelli, and F. Sciarrone, *Applied Artificial Intelligence.* 17, 8–9 (2003) 715–744.

6. M. R. Ghorab, D. Zhou, A. O'Connor, and V. Wade, *User Modeling and User-Adapted Interaction.* (2012) 1–63.
7. H. A. Hembrooke, L. A. Granka, G. K. Gay, and E. D. Liddy, *Journal of the American Society for Information Science and Technology.* **56**, 8 (2005) 861–871.
8. X. Jiang, and A. H. Tan, *Information sciences.* **179**, 16 (2009) 2794–2808.
9. C. Le Rouge, J. Ma, S. Sneha, and K. Tolle, *International journal of medical informatics* (2011).
10. G. Luo, C. Tang, H. Yang, and X. Wei, MedSearch: a specialized search engine for medical information retrieval. In *Proceedings of the 17th ACM conference on Information and knowledge management*, California, USA, (2008) 143–152.
11. G. Luo, Design and evaluation of the iMed intelligent medical search engine. In *IEEE 25th International Conference on Data Engineering* (ICDE'09), Shanghai, China, (2009) 1379–1390.
12. A. Micarelli and F. Sciarrone, *User Modeling and User-Adapted Interaction.* **14**, 2–3 (2004) 159–200.
13. K. Sugiyama, K. Hatano, and M. Yoshikawa, Adaptive web search based on user profile constructed without any effort from users. In *Proceedings of the 13th international conference on World Wide Web*, New York, USA, (2004) 675–684.
14. R. W. White, S. T. Dumais, and J. Teevan, Characterizing the influence of domain expertise on web search behavior. In Proceedings of the Second ACM International Conference on Web Search and Data Mining (WSDM09), Barcelona, Spain, (2009) 132–141.
15. B. M. Wildemuth, *Journal of the American Society for Information Science and Technology.* **55**, 3 (2004) 246–258.
16. Z. Wu, and M. Palmer, Verbs semantics and lexical selection. In *Proceedings of the 32nd annual meeting on Association for Computational Linguistics*, New Mexico, USA, (1994) 133–138.

LEARNING ENGLISH WORDS VIA ANIMATIONS AND MAKING SENTENCES USING AN ETYMOLOGICAL MEMORIZATION METHOD

KAORU SUMI

Future University Hakodate
041-8655 Hakodate, Japan

AYAKA KAZUHARA

Future University Hakodate
041-8655 Hakodate, Japan

A tablet PC system using an etymological memorization method with animations can enable Japanese children to memorize English words. The system specifically helps with memorization of compound nouns, which are combination of two simple nouns, for animals. For each noun it shows an animation with a narration produced by a voice synthesizer, followed by an animation showing the compound noun, again with narration. The system was experimentally evaluated by comparing the effectiveness of using animation, pictures, and text. We examined whether sentence construction by combining a compound animal noun with a simple verb, accompanied by animation, was effective for memorization after learning such nouns. The experimental subjects were 111 Japanese children in the fifth and sixth grades of elementary school. The experimental results were analyzed in terms of various subjects and conditions.

1. Introduction

English class for the fifth and sixth grades of elementary school became a compulsory subject in 2011 in Japan, although it has long been required in junior high school. As a result, the opportunity for primary school children to encounter English has increased. Since fiscal 2010 Japan's Ministry of Internal Affairs and Communications has been pursuing a research study, as part of its "Future School Promotion Project" [1], aimed at fostering cooperative education through information and communication technology (ICT). Ten public elementary schools have been selected as trial schools for the project. Some of these schools have tried to experimentally incorporate tablet computers such as iPads. Such tablet PCs can be used across a wide age group, including primary school children, because tablet PCs can be operated intuitively through tapping, dragging, and other gestures [2]. On the other hand, the phenomenon of "Englishphobia" [3] sometimes occurs when a child struggles to learn English at an early age. There is concern that such students might lose their motivation to learn English. Therefore, we have developed a system of iPad applications that is effective in enabling children to memorize English words yet enjoy themselves while learning English.

A compound noun is a combination of two or more simple nouns such that the meaning can be derived from the meanings of the simple nouns. We think that this concept is important for training English learners at an early age, because children come to understand the meanings of various words by considering etymology. Therefore, in our system we apply an etymological memorization method [4], which entails learning compound words by being conscious of the origin of each constituent word. For examples, "centipede" consists of "centi" (hundred) and "pede" (foot). The idea is that the learning effect should be increased by learning words via animations for understanding both compound nouns and their constituent simple nouns.

Our group has extensively researched content understanding through animation and shown that animations are effective for understanding content and vocabulary [5]. In general, animations have been shown to improve understanding and recall of text, making them an effective tool for promoting learning [6]. Research has also shown that animations increase motivation to learn [7]. This paper introduces our system and presents a comparative evaluation with elementary school students as subjects using the system with animations, pictures, and Japanese characters.

In addition, we think that after a student learns compound nouns, improvement in long-term memory is possible through the opportunity to use those nouns several times. For example, consider the case of building a simple sentence by combining a noun and a verb. Therefore, our system also has a function for sentence construction, in which the student combines memorized compound nouns and verbs and views corresponding animations.

In terms of English teaching materials for primary school children, the Microsoft Windows platform has a system for memorizing English words by viewing an English word and an illustration, such as "rice" or "milk" [8]. The problem with this system is the difficulty of its PC-based operation. In contrast, our system runs on the iPad, which can be operated more intuitively.

As for the effect of the etymological memorization method, research has verified its learning effect and indicated the advantage of being able to imagine the meaning of an unknown word by being conscious of etymology [9]. Another study [10] examined etymology learning by showing English words corresponding to Japanese words. This study involved changing the colors of the constituents of a compound noun and showing the whole noun, with a beneficial learning effect for some subjects. We thus adopt the technique in our system of separating English words by color according to etymology.

Various other techniques have also been tried for improving the effect of language learning. Presenting associated pictures with text improved learners' results on memorization tests [11]. Similar results were obtained by showing animations [12]. Furthermore, color pictures are preferred than monochrome pictures [13][14][15] and are effective in attracting the attention and interest of learners [16]. Other experiment shows that color pictures facilitate learning [17]. Systems for learning Japanese kanji characters improve motivation to learn when they use animations to show the stroke orders for writing characters [18]. On the other hand, an investigation into English word-learning software showed that most such software is of the test type [19].

The theme of learning support for children through games has been actively researched. Game is applied to wide-ranging use, because game has a power of attracting people and entertainment characteristics. Game based learning [20] or educational games are that games designed with educational purpose. Edutainment [21] is any entertainment content that is designed to educate as well as to entertain. Gamification [22][23][24] is the use of game thinking and game mechanics in a non-game context to engage users and solve problems. Persuasive game [25] is new initiative of that deliberately uses games as a rhetorical form to explore issues, or as a means of advocacy to encourage action, and persuading people to see the world differently.

As for the theme of learning English support, learning through games with visual content has been actively researched [26][27][28]. These [26][27][28] are researches of English learning games for children in developing countries. The theme of learning other language learning and other subjects through games also has been actively researched. [29] is context aware Chinese language learning software, and [30] is the learning software with an agent. Recently, in the area of children's learning, there are many studies being performed in order to make learning fun using games of cellphones or tablet PCs with visual representations. Our study also uses animations or pictures, and a tablet PCs. We discuss effects of visual representations by an experiment.

In this paper, we introduce our system of iPad applications using animation to help Japanese elementary school students learn English compound nouns for animals. The system includes the key functions of displaying animations and enabling sentence construction from learned compound nouns.

2. English Vocabulary Learning Applications

The system consists of four applications: "English Vocabulary," "Sentence Construction," "Vocabulary Quiz," and "Word Meaning Deduction Quiz." The "English Vocabulary" application operates in three different ways, using animations, pictures, or Japanese characters, to compare the effects of these three approaches. The picture and Japanese character approaches respectively show a freeze frame of a picture or Japanese characters representing a noun. In contrast, the animation approach expresses an explanatory state in which, for each noun, an animated animal appears and coalesces from a smoke screen, so that the application finally shows the animal corresponding to a compound noun.

We chose animal nouns as the target words because they are familiar to children. After learning compound animal nouns, students can use the Sentence Construction application to build sentences using the compound nouns while seeing animations of the corresponding animals. Students then use the Vocabulary Quiz and Word Meaning Deduction Quiz applications to confirm how many words they have memorized. The system keeps track of the current time, the class, the student number, the application, and the student's numbers of correct and incorrect answers.

All applications were developed using Adobe Flash Professional CS6, Adobe AIR for iOS, and ActionScript 3.0. All icons and pictures were created using Adobe Illustrator CS5. Sound for words in English was obtained from Google's speech synthesis system with words recorded beforehand in MP3 format. The system was designed to clearly express English words through pictures and animations and to support intuitive operation leveraging the benefits of the iPad.

2.1. *English Vocabulary Application*

As noted above, the English Vocabulary application operates in one of three ways, using animations, pictures, or Japanese characters. We chose compound nouns for ten kinds of animals (Table 1 and Figure 1-1, 1-2). The starting screen displays icons for these ten compound nouns. Touching one of the ten icons switches the screen to the corresponding learning screen for the compound noun. Touching the "?" button causes the animation (or picture, or Japanese character) corresponding to the word to be shown on the screen, with the sound of the word in English played at the same time. Similarly, touching the "=" button causes the application to show the animation (picture, Japanese character) and play the sound corresponding to the whole compound noun. Furthermore,

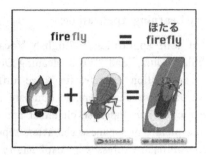

Figure 1-1. English Vocabulary application using animations or pictures.Touching the button causes the application to show the animation (picture) and play the sound corresponding to the whole compound noun.

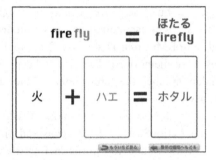

Figure 1-2. English Vocabulary application using Japanese characters. Touching the button causes the application to show the Japanese character and play the sound corresponding to the whole compound noun.

Table 1. Compound nouns and nouns.

Compound Nouns	Nouns
Firefly	fire + fly
woodpecker	wood + pecker
flatfish	flat + fish
anglerfish	angler + fish
catfish	cat + fish
anteater	ant + eater
pondskater	pond + skater
starfish	star + fish
seachestnut	sea + chestnut
turbanshell	turban + shell

Table 2.Verbs.

Verbs
read
run
rise
sleep
eat
sing
look
study
walk
stand

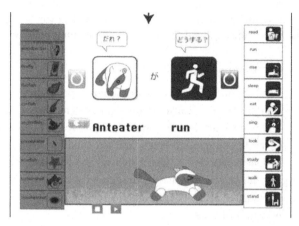

Figure 2. Sentence Construction application. Users can choice a noun (left) and a verb (right).

Figure 3. Correct answer screen. If a user selects the right answer, the application switches to a correct answer screen with a corresponding sound.

Figure 4. Final screen. One of six different screens is finally shown according to the number of correct answers, such as you are "Elementary school student level", "High school student level", "Teacher level", "Doctor level" and so on.

the animation shows the process of joining the two English words forming the compound together. The sound can be replayed by touching the icon.

2.2. Sentence Construction Application

The Sentence Construction application is designed to promote long-term word memorization through sentence construction. The student chooses a compound noun, which has already been learned, and a simple verb. The starting screen displays icons for the ten compound nouns and ten suitable verbs (Tables 1 and 2, and Figure 2). The compound nouns, listed on the left side, and the verbs, listed on the right side, can be selected by dragging each into the respective left or right part of the center area. The animation for the resulting sentence then appears in the lower part of the screen.

2.3. Vocabulary Quiz Application

The "Vocabulary Quiz" application is used to confirm whether a student was able to memorize the compound nouns. The application provides two kinds of quizzes, called Test 1 and Test 2. In both tests the student chooses an answer by selecting one of four icons to represent the compound noun upon seeing the corresponding characters and hearing the corresponding sound. In Test 1, the four answer choices consist of two of the compound nouns, including the correct answer, and two simple nouns. In Test 2, the four choices consist of three compound nouns and one simple noun. In our experiment we adopted Test 2 as words test, which is more difficult than Test 1, according to the results of a pre-test experiment with children.

The spoken compound noun can be replayed by touching the button next to the word. If the student selects the right answer, the application switches to a "correct answer" screen with a corresponding sound (Figure 3). Likewise, if the student selects a wrong answer, the application switches to an "incorrect answer" screen with a corresponding sound. Six different screens are finally shown according to the number of correct answers (Figure 4).

Note here that our system keeps track of the current time, the class, the student number, the application, and the student's numbers of correct and incorrect answers.

2.4. Word Meaning Deduction Quiz Application

This application is used to confirm whether the student can deduce the meaning of an unlearned compound noun from the etymology of English words. As in the Vocabulary Quiz application, this etymology quiz lets the student choose an answer by selecting one of four icons expressing a compound noun, upon seeing the corresponding character and hearing the corresponding sound. Because this test has a high difficulty level, the system shows hints in the form of pictures and characters for words with helpful etymology.

3. Experiment

We held an English learning workshop using our system with 111 children: 34 sixth graders (20 boys, 14 girls), and 77 fifth graders (38 boys, 39 girls) (Tables 3, 4, and 5). We analyzed the following issues: (1) comparison among media, in terms of which media are effective for memorizing nouns; (2) whether sentence construction is effective for memorizing English words; (3) whether the system differs in effectiveness depending on experience in learning English; (4) whether the system differs in effectiveness depending on cognitive style; (5) and whether, after learning nouns, students find sentence construction by combining a noun with a simple verb effective for memorization.

We used the Vocabulary Quiz application as a word test, and the Word Meaning Deduction Quiz application as an etymology test. To compare effectiveness, we also developed English vocabulary applications using pictures and Japanese characters, in addition to the application using animations.

The subjects were divided into five groups. Group 1 used the English Vocabulary application with animations and the Sentence Construction application. Group 2 used the English Vocabulary application with pictures and the Sentence Construction application. Groups 3, 4, and 5 used only the English Vocabulary application, with animations, pictures, and Japanese characters, respectively. We used the Group Embedded Figures Test (GEFT) for screening cognitive styles (Table 5). The GEFT involves looking for a specified figure from among various provided figures. It consists of seven practice questions as the first section (two minutes), and 18 real questions as the second section (five minutes) and third section (five minutes). We measured how many figures children could identify before running out of time. Then, we classified children with zero to nine correct answers as having a field-dependent cognitive style, and those with 10 to 18 correct answers as having a field-independent cognitive style. We translated the GEFT into Japanese because the original GEFT is in English.

3.1. *Comparing among Media*

Tables 6 and 7 list the average word test and etymology test scores, respectively. Analysis of variance showed no significant difference in scores after using the three different media $(F(2, \ 43) = 0.17, \ p < .05)$.

Table 3. Experimental subjects.

	Group 1		Group 2		Group 3		Group 4		Group 5	
Gender	Male	Female	Male	Female	Male	Female	Male	Female	Male	Female
Numbers	17	15	16	17	7	7	10	6	8	8
Total	32		33		14		16		16	

Table 4. Subjects categorized by English learning experience.

	Group 1		Group 2		Group 3		Group 4		Group 5	
Sub groups	1 - 1	1 - 2	2 - 1	2 - 2	3 - 1	3 - 2	4 - 1	4 - 2	5 - 1	5 - 2
English learning experience	No	Yes	No	Yes	No	Yes	No	Yes	No	Yes
Numbers	20	13	21	12	9	5	11	5	8	8
Total	32		33		14		16		16	

Table 5.Subjects categorized by cognitive style.

	Group 1		Group 2		Group 3		Group 4		Group 5	
Sub groups	1 - A	1 - B	2 - A	2 - B	3 - A	3 - B	4 - A	4 - B	5 - A	5 - B
cognitive styles	FD	FID	FD	FID	FD	FID	FD	FID	FD	FID
Numbers	16	16	18	15	8	6	9	7	10	6
Total	32		33		14		16		16	

Table 6. Average word test scores.

	Group1	Group 2	Group 3	Group 4	Group 5
Averages	7.28	7.70	7.36	7.75	7.31

Table 7. Average etymology test scores.

	Group 1	Group 2	Group 3	Group 4	Group 5
Averages	3.94	4.52	4.00	4.25	4.19

3.2. *Effectiveness of Sentence Construction*

As listed in Table 6, there was no significant difference in word test scores between Groups 1 and 2 (t = -0.75, df = 63, n.s.). On the other hand, there was a significant difference in etymology test scores between these groups (t = -2.56, df = 63, p < 0.05), as seen in Table 7. This suggests that presuming new English words was easier using the application with pictures than using the application with animations.

3.3. *Effectiveness Depending on Differences in English Learning Experience*

Table 8 lists the average word test scores, categorized by English learning experience. There was a significant difference in scores between Groups 1-2 and 2-2 (t = -2.35, df = 63, p < 0.05). That is, among the subjects with English learning experience, the application using pictures was more effective than that using animations, before sentence construction. There was also a significant difference in scores between Groups 2-1 and 2-2 (t = -2.96, df = 32, p < 0.05). This means that in the case of learning using the application with pictures, the subjects with English learning experienced performed better than did the non-experienced subjects.

Table 9 lists the average etymology test scores, also categorized by English learning experience. There was a significant difference in scores between Groups 1-2 and 2-2 (t = -2.22, df = 63, p > 0.05). That is, among the subjects with English learning experience, the application using pictures was more effective than that using animations. There was also a significant difference in scores between Groups 1-1 and 2-1 (t = -1.81, df = 17, p > 0.05). This means that among the non-experienced subjects, as well, the application using pictures was more effective than that using animations for deducing new English words. Lastly, there was a significant difference in scores between Groups 2-2 and 4-2 (t = 2.28, df = 47, p > 0.05). In other words, among the subjects with English learning experience, the application using pictures was more effective than that using animations for deducing new English words.

3.4. *Effectiveness Depending on Differences in Cognitive Style*

First, regarding differences in cognitive style, there were moderate differences between the word test and GEFT results (r = 0.51, p < 0.05), and between the etymology test and GEFT results (r = 0.47, p < 0.05).

Table 10 lists the average word test scores, categorized by cognitive style.

Table 8. Average word test scores, categorized by English learning experience.

	Group 1		Group 2		Group 3		Group 4		Group 5	
Sub groups	1 - 1	1 - 2	2 - 1	2 - 2	3 - 1	3 - 2	4 - 1	4 - 2	5 - 1	5 - 2
English learning experience	No	Yes	No	Yes	No	Yes	No	Yes	No	Yes
Numbers	7.39	7.14	6.86	9.25	7.56	7.00	7.55	8.2	6.75	8.13
Total	7.28		7.70		7.36		7.75		7.31	

Table 9. Average etymology test scores, categorized by English learning experience.

	Group 1		Group 2		Group 3		Group 4		Group 5	
Sub groups	1 - 1	1 - 2	2 - 1	2 - 2	3 - 1	3 - 2	4 - 1	4 - 2	5 - 1	5 - 2
English learning experience	No	Yes	No	Yes	No	Yes	No	Yes	No	Yes
Numbers	3.84	4.08	4.38	4.75	3.89	4.20	4.55	3.60	4.13	4.25
Total	3.94		4.52		4.00		4.25		4.19	

Table 10. Average word test scores, categorized by cognitive style.

	Group 1		Group 2		Group 3		Group 4		Group 5	
Sub groups	1 - A	1 - B	2 - A	2 - B	3 - A	3 - B	4 - A	4 - B	5 - A	5 - B
Cognitive style	FD	FID	FD	FID	FD	FID	FD	FID	FD	FID
Numbers	6.25	8.31	6.67	8.67	7.13	7.67	7.67	7.86	7.50	7.20
Total	7.28		7.70		7.36		7.75		7.31	

Table 11. Average etymology test scores, categorized by cognitive style.

	Group 1		Group 2		Group 3		Group 4		Group 5	
Sub groups	1 - A	1 - B	2 - A	2 - B	3 - A	3 - B	4 - A	4 - B	5 - A	5 - B
Cognitive style	FD	FID	FD	FID	FD	FID	FD	FID	FD	FID
Numbers	3.75	4.13	4.50	4.53	4.13	3.83	4.33	4.14	3.90	4.67
Total	3.94		4.52		4.00		4.25		4.19	

Table 12. Average word test scores a week later.

	Group1	Group 2	Group 3	Group 4	Group 5
Averages	8.86	8.57	7.84	7.00	8.14

There was a significant difference in scores between Groups 2-A and 2-B ($t = -2.54$, df = 32, $p > 0.05$). That is, the application using pictures was more effective for subjects with a field-independent cognitive style than for those with a field-dependent style. There was also a significant difference in scores between Groups 1-A and 1-B ($t = -3.22$, df = 31, $p > 0.05$). This means that the application using animations was also more effective for subjects with a field-independent style than for those with a field-dependent style.

Table 11 lists the average etymology test scores, also categorized by cognitive style. There was a significant difference in scores between Groups 5-A and 5-B (t = -2.23, df = 15, p > 0.05). That is, for deducing new English words using the application with Japanese characters, subjects with a field-independent cognitive style performed better than did those with a field-dependent style. There was also a significant difference in scores between Groups 1-A and 2-A (t = -2.20, df = 32, p > 0.05). This means that among subjects with a field-independent cognitive style, deducing new English words was more effective with the application using pictures than with that using animations. Lastly, there was a significant difference at the 10% level for etymology test scores between Groups 1-B and 2-B (t = - 1.55, df = 29). This indicates that among subjects with a field-dependent cognitive style, deducing new English words by using the application with pictures was more effective than by using that with animations.

3.5. Effectiveness of Sentence Construction for Memorization

Table 12 lists the average word test scores a week later. Comparing Groups 2 and 4, there was significant difference in scores (t = 1.93, df = 12, p > 0.05) That is, for the purpose of remembering new English words one week later, learning by using both the English Vocabulary application with pictures and the Sentence Construction application was more effective than learning by using only the vocabulary application with pictures. Similarly, comparing Groups 1 and 3, there was a significant difference in word test scores for the 10% level one-tail test (t = 1.44, df = 11) In other words, in the case of using the English Vocabulary application with animations, as well, the Sentence Construction application promoted better recall of new English words one week later.

4. Discussion

As described above, we have developed a system to help children memorize English words through an etymological memorization method with animations. The system consists of four iPad applications, namely, "English Vocabulary," "Sentence Construction," "Vocabulary Quiz," and "Word Meaning Deduction Quiz," designed to enable children to learn English in a fun way. To understand the effectiveness of our system, we conducted an experiment and examined the following issues: (1) comparison among media, in terms of effectiveness for memorizing nouns; (2) whether sentence construction is effective for memorizing English words; (3) differences in system effectiveness depending on English learning experience; (4) differences in system effectiveness depending on cognitive style; and (5) whether sentence construction by combining a noun with a simple verb promotes memorization after learning nouns.

Our analysis showed that the English Vocabulary application using pictures, rather than animations or Japanese characters, was the most effective for memorization. In particular, the system was effective for subjects with experience learning English. Moreover, the application using pictures was more effective for children with a field-independent cognitive style than for those with a field-dependent style. Another interesting result was that, for recalling memorized English words one week later, learning with both the English Vocabulary application (using pictures or animations) and the Sentence Construction application was better than learning only with the vocabulary application (using pictures or animations). This demonstrates the effectiveness of sentence construction for learning English vocabulary, thus confirming our hypothesis that building sentences with the "Sentence Construction" application after learning English words should have a learning effect, specifically for long-term learning.

Our hypothesis was that the learning effect would be enhanced by using animations for learning English words, and we thus expected that animations would have a higher effect on learning than would pictures or characters. The learning effectiveness of showing a picture or animation with text was demonstrated in studies by Cowen [11] and Peeck [12]. Additionally, because animation can express the process of combining two English words to create a compound noun, we thought that animation should produce better results than with pictures or characters. For example, the system can present an explanatory illustration such as an animation an animal noun appearing and coalescing beyond a smoke screen. We found, however, that such explanatory presentations through animation had little or no value and no relation to memorizing English words. It might be that unnecessary movement disrupts memory, or there might be a more suitable speed for presenting images to promote memorization. According to Levie & Lentz, visual representations contain cognitive function which facilitates learning from text by improving understanding and retention, and attentional function which attracts attention to the content. However, visual representations are possible to obstruct learning when the learner attracts attention to them, because visual representations itself contain mixed information [6]. This experimental result of animation condition is thought to be due to obstruct learning by attracting learner's attention to explanatory animations.

After the experiment we administered questionnaires to the subjects, offering the chance for free response, and gleaned the following opinions. For the question, "Were the positions and colors of screen icons easy to recognize?", there were many favorable comments. Examples include "The application was very colorful and characters were easy to recognize," "The icons for '? + ? =' were easy to comprehend," and "It was easy because of the sounds played with the words."

For the question, "Was the English learning fun?" there were also many favorable comments. In this case responses include "It was very fun, unlike learning from a textbook," " I have come to like English so far, though it was hard," "It was fun because of the Sentence Construction application," "I thought it was very good that I could learn English while playing a game, and it was fun," "I could learn English like a game and it was fun," "The Sentence Construction application was very fun," and "It was good to learn even with a quiz."

For the question, "Was the English learning easy?", as well, there were many favorable comments. Examples for this question include "It was easy, because the system spoke the words," and "It was easy, because the words were made up of other words.". Other comments include "Though it was difficult, it was fun," and "It was sometimes difficult and sometimes easy."

Finally, for the question, "Was it easy to learn English with this method?", there were also many favorable comments. In this case responses include "Because I understood the pronunciation by hearing it and the English was written, it was easy to learn," "Because I could hear the sound, it was easy," "I could learn English with this system rather than by having someone explain it," "It was easy to understand, because of the audio pronunciation," "It attracted everyone's interest that we could use an iPad system with sound," and "It was easy to learn more than usual, because we always learn English only by hearing."

The field of image psychology postulates that learning effects are determined by such factors as "variables in the image," "characteristic differences in the actor," and "the kind of problem." Here, "variables in the image" refers to media, such as animation. The phrase "characteristic differences in the actor" means the subject's ability. Finally, "the kind of problem" means the problem to be solved, such as learning English words. In this case, we investigated the problem of learning English words by using animations, pictures, and Japanese characters, for children who either do or do not have English learning experience and have either a field-dependent or field-independent cognitive style.

In our experiment, the child subjects could gain interest in English learning and learn in an enjoyable way via our iPad-based system. By using the system's applications to repeat the cycle of learning through memorizing, building sentences, watching animations, and taking a quiz, the elementary school children became more familiar with English, more aware of etymology, and more prepared for further English learning in junior high school.

5. Conclusion

In this paper, we have introduced an iPad-based system to help Japanese students learn English compound nouns while having fun. The system consists of four applications: "English Vocabulary," "Sentence Construction," "Vocabulary Quiz," and "Word Meaning Deduction Quiz." We conducted an experiment with our system and analyzed the results in terms of various subjects and conditions.

Acknowledgments

We thank Akagawa and Showa elementary school in Hakodate, and undergraduate students of Future University Hakodate, who help children's workshops.

References

1. http://warp.ndl.go.jp/info:ndljp/pid/3533060/www.soumu.go.jp/english/icb/
2. Tina J. Jayroe, & Dietmar Wolfram: Internet searching, tablet technology and older adults, Proceedings of the American Society for Information Science and Technology, Volume 49, Issue 1, pages 1–3, 2012
3. Subapriya, K.: English Phobia, BIN SAID: 82.
4. Bocheng, Zhang and Wei Han. "A Study on Presentation Models in English Vocabulary Teaching [J]." Foreign Languages and Their Teaching 4 (2004): 005.
5. Kaoru Sumi and Mizue Nagata: Interactive e-Hon as Parent-child Communication Tool, HCI 12, volume 6772 of Lecture Notes in Computer Science, page 199–206. Springer, (2011).
6. Levie, W. H., Lentz, R.: Effects of text illustrations: A review of research, Educational Communication and Technology Journal, 30, 195–232 (1982).
7. Lloyd P. Rieber: Animation, Incidental Learning, and Continuing Motivation, Journal of Educational Psychology, Vol. 83. No. 3, 318–328 (1991).
8. Mika Hatae: English Learning software FLASH WORDS, Shizuoka Kogyo Senmon School Journal, 44, 19–26 (2009).
9. Akio Kikuchi: An Attempt on Vocabulary learning using etymology, Hachinohe Kogyo Senmon School Journal, 46, 119–123 (2011).
10. Teruaki Suzuki: About learning Katakana-words and English abbreviations in ICT, IPSJ, 2011-CE-111(6), 1–4, 2011-10-07.
11. J. Peeck: Retention of pictorial and verbal content of text with illustration, Journal of Educational Psychology, 66, 880–888 (1974).

12. Cowen, P. S.: Film and text: Order effects in recall and social inference. Educational Communication and Technology Journal, 32, 131–144 (1984)
13. Samuels, S. J., Biesbrock, E., Terry, P. R.: The effect of pictures on children's attitudes toward presented stories. The Journal of Educational Research, 67, 243–246 (1974).
14. Winn, W., & Everett, R. J.: Affective rating of color and black-and-white pictures. Educational Communication and Technology Journal, 27(2), 148–156 (1979).
15. Chute, A. G.: Effect of color and monochrome versions of a film on incidental and task-relevant learning, Educational Communication and Technology journal, 28(1), 10–18 (1980).
16. Stone. V. L.: Effects of color in lmed behavior sequences on description and elaboration by Liberian schoolboys. Educational Communication and Technology Jornal, 31, 33–45 (1983).
17. Katzman, N. and Nyenhuis, J.: Color vs. black and white effects on learning opinion and attention, AV Communication Review, 20, 16–28 (1972).
18. Isao Miyaji, Yoshiki Nomura, Takashi Morita: Development of the Support System for Learning the Elementary School Chinese Character using animation, JSSE, 19(3), 7–10 (2005).
19. Setsuko Kondo: Learning English Vocabulary Software, Naruto English Research 7, 15–24 (1993).
20. Marc Prensky: Digital Game-Based Learning, Paragon House, 2007.
21. IE Hewitt: Edutainment — How to Teach English with Fun and Games, Language Direct; (2006).
22. Zichermann, Gabe: Cunningham, Christopher (August 2011). "Introduction" Gamification by Design: Implementing Game Mechanics in Web and Mobile Apps (1st ed.). Sebastopol, California: O'Reilly Media. p. xiv. ISBN 1449315399. Retrieved 2012-12-10.
23. a b Huotari, Kai; Hamari, Juho (2012). "Defining Gamification — A Service Marketing Perspective". Proceedings of the 16th International Academic MindTrek Conference 2012, Tampere, Finland, October 3–5.
24. Sebastian Deterding, Dan Dixon, Rilla Khaled and Lennart Nacke (2011). "From game design elements to gamefulness: Defining "gamification"". Proceedings of the 15th International Academic MindTrek Conference. pp. 9–15.
25. Ian Bogost: Persuasive Games: The Expressive Power of Videogames, The MIT Press, 2010.
26. Kam. M., Ramachandran, D., Devanathan, V., Tewari, A. and Canny, J: Localized Iterative Design for Language Learning in Underdeveloped Regions: The PACE Framework. CHI 2007 Proceedings, Designing for Specific Cultures. April 28-May 3, 2007.
27. Kam, M., Agarwal, A., Kumar, A., Lal, S., Mathur, A., Tewari, A. and Canny, J. (2008). Designing e-learning games for rural children in India: A format for balancing learning with fun. In Proceedings of the 7th ACM Conference on Designing interactive Systems (Cape Town, South Africa, February 25–27, 2008). DIS '08. New York, NY: ACM.
28. Anuj Kumar, Pooja Reddy, AnujTewari, RajatAgrawal,, Matthew Kam: Improving literacy in developing countries using speech recognition-supported games on mobile devices, CHI '12 Proceedings of the SIGCHI Conference on Human Factors in Computing Systems, Pages 1149–1158 (2012).

194

29. Edge, Darren, Searle, Elly, Chiu, Kevin, Zhao, Jing and Landay, James A. "MicroMandarin: Mobile language learning in context." Paper presented at the meeting of the CHI, 2011.
30. Ogan, S. L. Finkelstein, E. Mayfield, C. D'Adamo, N. Matsuda and J. Cassell, "Oh dear stacy!": Social interaction, elaboration, and learning with teachable agents; In Proceedings of CHI. 2012, 39–48.

A SERIOUS GAME STIMULATING CHILDREN'S INTEREST IN CHEMICAL BONDING

KAORU SUMI

Future University Hakodate
041-8655 Hakodate, Japan

KENTO KUDO

Future University Hakodate
041-8655 Hakodate, Japan

This paper describes a serious game for studying chemical bonding – a subject that does not exist in the regular Japanese elementary school curriculum. The system aims to induce children's interest in the unknown subject of chemistry. Using a system that shows atoms and molecules on a screen, children can perform chemical bonding virtually and produce virtual material objects by hand. The system uses the Kinect sensor for gesture recognition. It was evaluated in two experiments using test subjects. In the first experiment, the subjects were 37 children in the sixth grade. Most of these children became interested in chemistry, but there were some problems with the user interface. Accordingly, a second experiment was conducted to compare a modified interface and the initial unmodified interface. This experiment confirmed that the modified interface provided better operability and a more favorable user impression.

1. Introduction

The social issue of rikei banare or "flight from science" by students has become more serious in recent years. This issue is causing difficulty for human resources development, since there are fewer people with specialized knowledge and skills as a result of the increasing number of students who are unable to keep up with science or mathematics lessons. This paper describes a serious game for studying chemical bonding, even though chemistry is not included in the regular elementary school curriculum in Japan. Our serious game was developed for the upper grades of elementary school. It was designed to be fun and to give children a way to learn science by moving their bodies. We chose chemical bonding as a subject because even a child could learn to put atoms together like a puzzle. We also thought it would stimulate interest in chemistry for students to learn what kinds of atoms compose real materials.

Serious games are defined as simulations, of real-world events or processes, designed for the purpose of solving a problem. They are not intended solely for entertainment but also to train or educate users [1] [2] [3]. Games are applied over a wide range of uses, because they have entertainment characteristics and the power to attract people. Game-based learning [4] and educational games involve games designed with an educational purpose. Edutainment [5] means any entertainment content designed to educate as well as entertain. Gamification [6][7][8] is the use of game thinking and game mechanics in a non-game context to engage users and solve problems. Persuasive gaming [9] is a new initiative that deliberately uses games as a rhetorical form to explore issues, or as a means of advocacy to encourage action and persuade people to see the world differently. In this study, we developed a serious game for elementary school children to study chemical bonding in an enjoyable way. The game format should increase the desire to learn science.

We used the Microsoft Kinect to achieve intuitive manipulation in a virtual space, since this system would allow movement of virtual atoms by hand. The Kinect is a motion-sensing input device made by Microsoft for the Xbox 360 video game console and Windows PCs. It is equipped with an RGB camera, a depth sensor, and a multi-array microphone. It runs proprietary software that provides full-body 3D motion capture, facial recognition, and voice recognition capabilities.

Among natural user interface applications, Kinect is often modified for the nursing-care field. BallPool [10] is nursing-care support software enabling a user, represented by a virtual character, to throw virtual objects on the screen. It helps a patient's rehabilitation by letting the patient picture himself throwing on his own, even though he is not really throwing anything. Kiritsu-kun [11] is another example of nursing-care support software, in which the animation of a tree on the screen grows in response to a stand-up exercise performed by the user.

Children are said to become absorbed in a game because of three spontaneous motivations, which are challenge, imagination, and curiosity about the game [12]. According to a study on a learning-support game for mechanics, learning in a virtual space within a game is very effective, especially depending on the real world and how it links with the virtual space [12]. Our study here also aims to produce a serious game leading to real learning.

Alan Key's Squeak Etoys [13] is famous as an educational system in which programmable virtual entities live on the computer screen. Children can move the entities' pictures according to programming instructions that they create. As another example, Chemistry Quest is a card game for learning chemical formulas. Similarly, in this study we have developed a system intended to teach chemistry via intuitive operation and visualization of atoms.

2. Serious Game for Learning Chemical Bonding

Our system is designed for learning the concept of chemical bonding through the virtual experience of bonding to make a diamond, a ruby, and a pearl by using the hand to manipulate elements shown on a screen. To provide intuitive operation through gestures, we developed the system by using C# with Microsoft Visual Studio C# 2010 Express, Microsoft Windows SDK, and Microsoft Kinect.

Matter is composed of different elements. For example, carbon atoms form not only the graphite in pencil lead but also diamond. We want children to understand the fun of chemical bonding by using a familiar example of pencils and then showing how the same atoms can form diamonds by changing the bond structure.

To start the system, the user first stands in front of the Kinect camera and confirms that the mouse cursor moves in response to his hand movements. Then, he can choose an object and hover the cursor over the object for approximately one second. After choosing an atom, he can move it to the bonding zone when the palm shape of the mouse cursor becomes a grabbing hand shape. The number of atoms can be increased when the user takes them outside the game screen. In this case, the shape of the mouse cursor changes to a grabbing hand after an atom has been chosen.

This system provides three game modes, which we call Modes 1, 2, and 3. The modes have the following themes: "Let's produce a diamond from the atoms of an eraser!" for mode 1, "Let's produce a ruby from the atoms of aluminum and water!" for mode 2, and "Let's produce a pearl from the atoms of calcium and carbon dioxide!" for mode 3.

Game mode 1 involves producing a diamond from the chloroethylene (C_2H_3Cl) molecules of an eraser (Figure 1). Diamond is composed of eight carbon atoms. Thus, the combination succeeds when eight carbon (C) atoms are moved into the bonding zone (Figure 2).

Game mode 2 involves producing a ruby from aluminum (Al) atoms and water (H_2O) molecules. Ruby is composed of two Al atoms and three O atoms. Thus, the combination succeeds when two Al atoms and three O atoms are moved into the bonding zone.

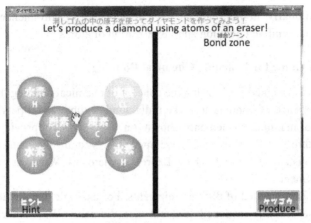

Figure1. Starting of model

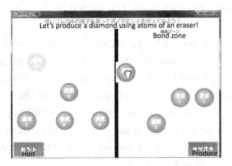

Figure 2. Moving an atom to the bonding zone

Finally, game mode 3 involves producing a pearl from calcium (Ca) atoms and carbon dioxide (CO_2) molecules. Pearl is composed of a Ca atom and a C atom. Thus, the combination succeeds when a Ca atom and a C atom are moved into the bonding zone.

The basic ideas of the system are (1) intuitive manipulation, which children can learn through direct operation by moving their bodies; (2) a hint display function, which compensates for differences in the individual abilities of children; (3) a collection function, which provides children with the motivation to attempt the game; and (4) experiential learning.

Because chemistry is not included in the Japanese elementary school curriculum, we considered how the game could work differently for different children. We developed a hint display function to compensate for individual differences in ability and to make it easier for a child to learn how to play the game. When a user learning the system does not know what to do and requests a hint, this function gives a hint in the form of a message from the system (Figure 3). When the user moves all the correct atoms to produce a jewel, the system shows the jewel and a message of success (Figure 4). To support learning, the system displays information about the jewel (Figure 5).

Figure 3. Displaying a hint message

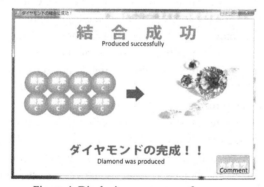

Figure 4. Displaying a message of success

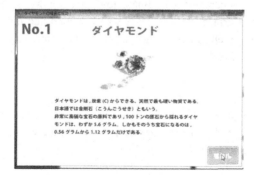

Figure 5. Displaying information about diamond

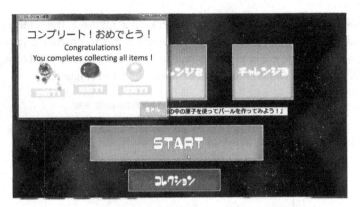

Figure 6. Message displayed by the collection function

The system's collection function strengthens the user's motivation to play the game. This function displays jewels as the user collects them, and it shows a message saying "Congratulations! You have finished collecting all the items!" when the user collects the jewels from all three modes (Figure 6).

The intuitive manipulation using Kinect enables operation with natural gestures and allows direct handling of atoms on the screen. This increases children's desire to manipulate atoms and interest in chemical bonding. We also designed the system as an experiential learning tool making it possible to visualize atoms on the screen and produce new materials.

At first, the system recognizes a hand after having recognized the joints of the whole body through the Kinect interface, and it gets the latest coordinates of the mouse cursor. To make the gesture interface operate like clicking controls, the system recognizes an object by using numerical values, namely, the stop time and threshold. The stop time is the time before recognizing an object, and the threshold is an acceptable coordinate tolerance for hand control. For our initial unmodified interface, the stop time was 1 second and the threshold is 15 pixels. For the subsequent modified interface, the stop time was 0.5 second and the threshold was 60 pixels.

3. Experiment

We conducted two different experiments: (1) an evaluation experiment at an elementary school, and (2) an experiment to compare the modified and unmodified interfaces.

3.1. *Evaluation experiment at an elementary school*

We conducted an experiment to investigate the system's effectiveness, operability, teaching potential, and effect of interest in chemistry. The subjects were 37 sixth-graders (18 boys and 19 girls) at Hakodate City, Akagawa Elementary School, on November 26, 2012. The subjects were divided into seven groups, each of which worked through modes 1, 2, and 3 for 30 minutes while using the system as a group. The students answered questionnaires afterwards.

It was the first experience for all of the students to operating a gesture-based system using Kinect, so they were very interested in the system. All groups read the hints prepared for the system, group members advised the student operating the system, and the members worked together as a team and finished each mode. Laughter sometimes ensued when a student became so absorbed in operation so that his body moved strangely.

According to the comments on the questionnaires, one learning outcome was that many students could specify the component atoms, such as "Rubies are composed of aluminum and oxygen." On the other hand, there were many comments about difficulties with the system, such as "Operation was difficult" and "It was difficult to catch an atom." It seems that the students had trouble operating the system. Therefore, we decided to improve its interface and carry out a second experiment.

3.2. *Experiment comparing the modified and unmodified interfaces*

The cause of difficulties in the system's initial operation was that the stop time was one second and the threshold was 15 pixels. This meant that a user had to stand still for one second without moving his hand after hovering the mouse cursor over the target object. There were problems in being unable to locate an atom smoothly in the bonding zone and unable to catch an atom when a hand moved. As a result, it was hard for users to operate the system. To improve the operation, we changed the stop time and threshold value and made it possible to place an atom in the bonding zone automatically. In contrast, for the unmodified interface, an atom entering the bonding zone was only placed after the system recognized that it had stopped in the zone. We changed the stop time to 0.5 second and the threshold to 60 pixels.

We next conducted an experiment comparing the modified and unmodified interfaces, with 20 undergraduate students (12 men and 8 women) from January 14 to 22, 2013. The subjects were divided into two groups: one group used the modified interface, and the other group used the unmodified interface. We then compared the results for these two groups. Each student worked individually through modes 1 to mode 3 and answered a questionnaire afterwards.

Figure 7 shows a comparison between the average values of the user impressions of the modified and unmodified interfaces. Figures 8 and 9 show the correlation coefficient matrices of the user impressions. Figure 10 shows a comparison between the average values for operability of the modified and unmodified interfaces. Lastly, Figures 11 and 12 show the correlation coefficient matrices of operability.

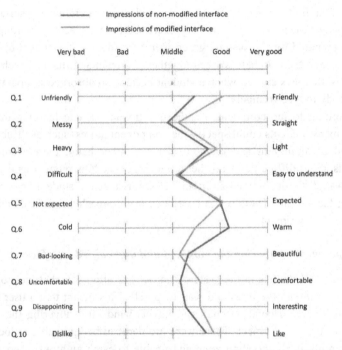

Figure 7. Average values of user impression for the modified and unmodified interfaces

	Q1	Q2	Q3	Q4	Q5	Q6	Q7	Q8	Q9	Q10
Q1	1									
Q2	0.265789	1								
Q3	-0.21272	0.587995	1							
Q4	-0.12659	0.320767	0.560112	1						
Q5	0.392232	0.225877	0.542326	0.322749	1					
Q6	-0.16575	0.229081	0.504184	0.218218	0.422577	1				
Q7	0.310087	0.607143	0.300123	0.153093	0.395285	0.534522	1			
Q8	0.310087	0.428571	0.085749	-0.35722	0	0.534522	0.375	1		
Q9	0.74796	0.301511	0.232689	0.184637	0.7151	0.040291	0.452267	0.075378	1	
Q10	0.66299	0.343622	0.297927	0.190941	0.633866	0.428571	0.467707	0.467707	0.765532	1

Figure 8. Correlation coefficient matrix of user impression for the unmodified interface

	Q1	Q2	Q3	Q4	Q5	Q6	Q7	Q8	Q9	Q10
Q1	1									
Q2	0.83181	1								
Q3	0.64147	0.480384	1							
Q4	0.457305	0.577101	0.469428	1						
Q5	0.51937	0.559038	0.533137	0.114848	1					
Q6	0.196875	0.238705	0.106479	0.079008	0.269191	1				
Q7	0.479349	0.551282	-0.0915	0.23763	0.462652	0.596762	1			
Q8	0.451292	0.458664	-0.08615	0.06392	0.254084	0.6742	0.700067	1		
Q9	0.594304	0.380304	0.82143	0.317999	0.210675	-0.18634	-0.22018	-0.30151	1	
Q10	0.72716	0.312255	0.458831	0.145908	0.441895	0.170996	0.404095	0.380443	0.315447	1

Figure 9. Correlation coefficient matrix of user impression for the modified interface

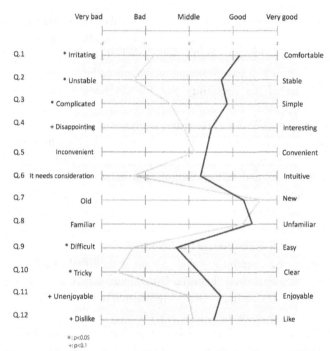

Figure 10. Average values of operability for the modified and unmodified interfaces

	Q1	Q2	Q3	Q4	Q5	Q6	Q7	Q8	Q9	Q10	Q11	Q12
Q1	1											
Q2	0.575302	1										
Q3	-0.31818	0.218218	1									
Q4	-0.26018	0.161917	0.0795	1								
Q5	-0.58004	-0.18389	0.210675	0.6508	1							
Q6	0.222681	0.356348	0.357217	-0.08655	0.098295	1						
Q7	0.037113	-0.08909	0.102062	-0.30292	0.098295	-0.25	1					
Q8	-0.36364	-0.76376	-0.375	0.053	-0.06019	-0.81237	-0.10206	1				
Q9	-0.29158	-0.17496	0.534522	-0.02833	0.193047	0.327327	0.327327	0.133631	1			
Q10	-0.03711	-0.35635	0.408248	-0.12982	0.147442	0.25	0.25	0.102062	0.49099	1		
Q11	0.117363	0	0.161374	0.136845	0.155417	0	0.263523	0	0.172516	0	1	
Q12	-0.03896	0.093522	0.071429	0.62086	0.498741	0.116642	0.116642	-0.07143	0.229081	-0.11664	0.73771	1

Figure 11. Correlation coefficient matrix of operability for the unmodified interface

	Q1	Q2	Q3	Q4	Q5	Q6	Q7	Q8	Q9	Q10	Q11	Q12
Q1	1											
Q2	0.312153	1										
Q3	0.88539	0.386441	1									
Q4	-0.46017	0.397026	-0.06574	1								
Q5	0.437877	0.387938	0.70441	4.95E-17	1							
Q6	0.20187	0.713451	0.321496	0.48118	0.557409	1						
Q7	0.366441	0.47541	0.312153	0.079405	0.091984	0.370272	1					
Q8	-0.08655	0.313625	-0.12982	0	-0.10599	-0.0288	0.209083	1				
Q9	0.176434	0.67213	0.50216	0.397028	0.597899	0.713451	0.47541	-0.20908	1			
Q10	0.163609	0.61482	0.472649	0.212718	0.246416	0.447573	0.59297	-0.14003	0.83441	1		
Q11	0.02833	0.581728	0.254967	0.497245	0.336011	0.622088	0.615947	0.49099	0.581728	0.389597	1	
Q12	-0.41548	-0.0388	0.09588	0.74796	0.216612	0.127602	-0.34744	-0.12309	0.154418	-0.15513	0.241747	1

Figure 12. Correlation coefficient matrix of operability for the modified interface

According to the user impression values for the unmodified interface, we found positive correlations between "Unfriendly/Friendly" and "Disappointing/Interesting," between "Unfriendly/Friendly" and "Like/Dislike," and between "Unexpected/Expected" and "Disappointing/Interesting. That is, the user impressions indicated the possibility that friendly impressions or designs are interesting and expected.

On the other hand, from the user impression values for the modified interface, we found positive correlations between "Unfriendly/Friendly" and "Messy/Straight," between "Unfriendly/Friendly" and "Heavy/Light," between "Unfriendly/Friendly" and "Like/Dislike," and between "Unfriendly/Friendly" and "Unexpected/Expected." We also found positive correlations between "Cold/Warm" and "Disappointing/Interesting," and between "Cold/Warm" and "Uncomfortable/Comfortable." That is, friendly impressions or designs may convey an image of straightforward operation.

According to the operability values for the unmodified interface, we found negative correlations between "Familiar/Unfamiliar" and "Unstable/Stable," and between "Familiar/Unfamiliar" and "Unintuitive/Intuitive." We also found positive correlations between "Unenjoyable/Enjoyable" and "Inconvenient/Convenient," and between "Unenjoyable/Enjoyable" and "Like/Dislike." These results suggest the possibility that an unstable user interface requires consideration.

From the operability values for the modified interface, in contrast, we found positive correlations between "Unstable/Stable" and "Difficult/Easy," between "Unstable/Stable" and "Tricky/Clear," between "Complicated/Simple" and "Irritating/Comfortable," and between "Like/Dislike" and "Disappointing/Interesting". Therefore, it is likely that a more stable interface made the system easier to use and clearer operation made it simpler and more comfortable.

There was great improvement from the unmodified to the modified interface in terms of the average values of items related to operability, such as "Irritated/Comfortable," "Unstable/Stable," and "Unintuitive/Intuitive." The unmodified interface generated many comments such as "It was difficult" and "irritating", but we obtained fewer such comments for the modified interface.

4. Discussion

In our evaluation experiment at the elementary school, there were not many students who considered science and arithmetic to be their weak subjects. In addition, there was little evidence of "flight from science" in their comments, which indicated that they knew science and arithmetic are important. Because all the children said the game was "very interesting" or "interesting," we may conclude that we were successful in creating a serious game. We were able to achieve our aim of stimulating the students' interest in chemistry, because 80% of the students indicated that they were indeed interested in chemistry. We think there was a learning effect, because students could give certain atom names even though they had never learned chemistry according to their comments in the questionnaires. On the other hand, we thought that we could build a better system by improving operability, because there were a great many answers indicating that the system's operation was difficult.

In the experiment comparing the modified and the unmodified interfaces, the operability was improved but the students' overall impression did not change, according to the questionnaires. This indicates that the design and idea behind a system, not its operability, determine the user's impression of the system.

Our data analysis indicated that a user-friendly design gave users a comfortable impression. The analysis also indicated that a mode of operation that feels familiar does not require consideration; that is, familiar operation gave the user an intuitive impression, because we found a strong negative correlation between "Familiar" and "Unintuitive." In addition, users felt that the system was convenient to operate and interesting, and they liked the system. Regarding the modified interface, its more stable operation gave users an impression that the system was easy to use, and they felt that its simple operation was comfortable. We think that it is difficult to have a good system when a user feels impatient with a more advanced interface and only considers it hard to use.

Because there was a significant difference between the modified and unmodified interfaces, the system's operability was certainly improved. The main factors creating the significant difference in operability were our improvement of the interface for moving atoms and our changing the stop time and threshold to make the system operate more smoothly. With the unmodified interface there were even cases where users knew the answer but could not catch an atom or move it to the bonding zone. With the modified interface, however, there was little waiting time for the result of placing an atom automatically in the zone. Thus, through our system improvements, users could move atoms to the bonding zone smoothly and learn about chemical bonding effectively.

5. Conclusion

We developed a serious game stimulating children's interest in chemical bonding through a gesture-based interface. In our initial evaluation experiment at an elementary school, the students experienced stress and did not accept the gesture-based operation at first. We improved the operability, however, by changing the system's stop time and threshold. We think that the system could successfully stimulate interest in chemistry among children who had not previously learned this subject.

Acknowledgments

We thank Akagawa elementary school in Hakodate, and undergraduate students of Future University Hakodate, who helpexperiments.

References

1. Abt, C.: Serious Games. New York: The Viking Press (1970).
2. Aldrich, Clark: The Complete Guide to Simulations and Serious Games. Pfeiffer. p. 576. ISBN 0-470-46273-6 (2009).
3. Reeves, Byron; Reed, J. Leighton: Total Engagement: Using Games and Virtual Worlds to Change the Way People Work and Businesses Compete. Boston: Harvard Business School Publishing (2009).
4. Marc Prensky: Digital Game-Based Learning, Paragon House, 2007.
5. IE Hewitt: Edutainment — How to Teach English with Fun and Games, Language Direct; (2006).
6. Zichermann, Gabe; Cunningham, Christopher (August 2011). "Introduction". Gamification by Design: Implementing Game Mechanics in Web and Mobile Apps (1st ed.). Sebastopol, California: O'Reilly Media. p. xiv. ISBN 1449315399. Retrieved 2012-12-10.
7. a b Huotari, Kai; Hamari, Juho (2012). "Defining Gamification — A Service Marketing Perspective". Proceedings of the 16th International Academic MindTrek Conference 2012, Tampere, Finland, October 3–5.
8. Sebastian Deterding, Dan Dixon, Rilla Khaled and Lennart Nacke (2011). "From game design elements to gamefulness: Defining "gamification". Proceedings of the 15th International Academic MindTrek Conference. pp. 9–15.
9. Ian Bogost: Persuasive Games: The Expressive Power of Videogames, The MIT Press, 2010.
10. "NAIST Ballpool" for NAIST, http://www.youtube.com/watch?v=LuNdc-Ejyjg
11. "Kiritsu-kun" for Medicus Shuppan, http://www2.medica.co.jp/topcontents/kirithu/

12. Kyosuke Miyawaki and Yuki Makihara: Analysis of What Makes Computer Games Fun on Grades and Sexes : Application and Future for Learning Environment of Science Education, Kagaku Kyoiku Kenkyu 17(2), pp.77–83, (1993). In Japanese.

13. Dan Ingalls, Ted Kaehler, John Maloney, Scott Wallace, Alan Kay: Back to the Future: the story of Squeak, a practical Smalltalk written in itself" by Paper presented at OOPSLA, Atlanta, Georgia, 1997.

DEVELOPMENT OF A VISUAL DEBUGGER FOR C IMPLEMENTED IN JAVASCRIPT

Akihiko Nagae

Graduate School of Engineering, Kagawa University,
2217-20 Hayashi-cho, Takamatsu, Kagawa 761-0396, JAPAN
s12g472@stmail.eng.kagawa-u.ac.jp

Koji Kagawa

Faculty of Engineering, Kagawa University,
2217-20 Hayashi-cho, Takamatsu, Kagawa 761-0396, JAPAN
kagawa@eng.kagawa-u.ac.jp

It is difficult for programming novices to correct a program when it does not behave as they intended. Although it is possible for novices to use a debugger, its installation can cause initial obstacles. Even after a successful installation, it can be difficult to choose appropriate actions. Therefore, a debugger is needed that needs no installation and provides features and information that match a beginners' proficiency. This paper discusses the design of a visual debugger for C that runs in Web browsers. The system is constructed using HTML + CSS + JavaScript, and therefore can be customized easily by a teacher. It offers information such as animations adapted to the state of a program's execution. It is difficult to execute C programs in Web browsers because the C language is usually compiled into a machine-language form. The proposed system therefore uses an interpreter for a subset of C implemented in JavaScript.

Keywords: Web; Programming, C

1. Introduction

It is difficult for programming novices to fully understand computer-oriented concepts and the behind-the-scenes behavior of programs. It is therefore not easy for them to correct programs when the result of their execution is different from what they expected. Debuggers exist to remedy this situation. For example, stepwise execution in a debugger can enable a novice to follow the execution of a program, to notice changes in the values of variables, and to understand the control flow.

However, it can be troublesome for programming novices to use debuggers in the early stages. Debuggers have many features, which may require the user to learn about the debugger before being able to use it. Moreover, for most novice learners, it is a considerable obstacle simply to install and configure the debugger.

If we could circumvent these problems, debuggers could become much more helpful tools for novice learners. In this paper, we discuss the design of a Web-based debugger for novices.

In many computer science departments in Japan, C is a popular choice as the first language for introductory programming courses. This is probably because C, especially its syntax, has affected many other languages, including Java, JavaScript, PHP, Perl, and Python, and because it is still important in industry, particularly in the development of embedded applications. The authors' own department is one of those using C as the first language. We therefore chose C as the target language for our Web-based debugger. There are, however, few existing environments that can run C programs in Web browsers. In this study, we implement an interpreter for (a subset of) C. The target users of the debugger are novice learners of the C language. Their teachers are expected to be able to customize the debugger appropriately.

Existing debuggers for C include the GNU Project Debugger (GDB), the Data Display Debugger, which can behave as a graphical front-end for GDB, and Microsoft Visual Studio. They each have a variety of features for debugging. Accordingly, they have many commands and menu items, which users are expected to become familiar with before being able to use the debuggers effectively.

In most debuggers, users must specify breakpoints in terms of line numbers. It is not possible to specify these points in terms of syntax. This is undesirable whenever teachers wish to customize the behavior of the debugger. Instead, it would be preferable to specify breakpoints by saying "the conditional expression of the inner for-statement" or "the conditional expression of the seventh if-statement."

These debuggers must be installed in advance as they are provided as native application packages.

Furthermore, learners can have difficulty making good use of the information obtained from debuggers. This is because existing debuggers are not good at presenting information that is intuitive for novice learners.

Therefore, desirable features for the proposed debugger are as follows:

- it should have low installation cost,

- it should provide information appropriate to the proficiency of learners and the progress of classes,
- it should present visual information targeted at novice learners.

To adapt the provision of information for a variety of learners, it should hold much information internally. It should then be accompanied by a built-in interpreter for executing programs interactively, rather than offering simply a visualization of trace information.

To achieve these goals, our proposed system is designed as a Web-based system constructed from HTML + CSS + JavaScript. The advantages of Web-based systems for learners are as follows:

- they do not need to install software in advance.
- they need only Web browsers to execute the system and do not need to open multiple windows,
- they will always be using an up-to-date version.

The advantages for teachers are as follows:

- they can customize the contents according to the progress of classes by simply editing HTML/CSS/JavaScript files in a text editor,
- they can provide usage information as ordinary Web pages,
- they can readily update the system.

There are two feasible approaches to implementing a Web-based debugger. One is to execute programs on the server side and then send information to the client side. For such a system, the simplest design would send the trace information obtained after finishing the execution of programs to the client side. However, this system would lack flexibility. For example, we would not be able to change the value of a variable during the execution of a program. It might be possible to suspend execution of a program on the server side and let the client side send commands such as step/continue to the server side. This would, however, involve heavy consumption of server-side and network resources.

The second approach, which we adopt, is to execute programs on the client side using a Web-friendly language platform such as Java or JavaScript. Of course, it is not feasible to port existing debuggers such as Visual Studio and GDB. Therefore, we develop a new interpreter for (a subset of) C in JavaScript. It performs some preprocessing such as parsing on the server side and executes the programs in a Web browser. The interpreter receives abstract syntax trees from the server side and executes the programs in a stepwise fashion.

We prefer JavaScript to Java because we would like to make it easier for teachers to customize the user interface of the debugger and the user interface is already implemented in JavaScript. If we wrote the interpreter as a Java Applet, we would have to design the interface between the Java Applet component and the JavaScript component very carefully.

For parsing, we use the parser component of the eXperimental ANSI C Interpreter (XCI),[1] which is a C interpreter written in C. It can parse C source programs and output their abstract syntax trees in an XML format. Our JavaScript-based interpreter executes the program by traversing the abstract syntax tree and evaluating subexpressions recursively. Using abstract syntax trees, rather than intermediate language codes, is expected to provide a more fine-grained stepwise execution, and to present information that is adapted to the proficiency of learners.

The remainder of this paper is structured as follows. First, Section 2 explains the design of the proposed system. Then, Section 3 discusses related work. Finally, Section 4 gives a summary.

2. The Proposed System

The proposed system targets programming novices. Therefore, we deal with a subset of C that includes primitive types such as `int`, `char`, and `double`, control structures such as `if-else`, `while`, and `for`, function calls, and function definitions. In particular, we exclude pointers, structures, unions, enums, `typedef`, and type qualifiers such as `const` from the subset.

The proposed system is a debugger executable on Web browsers. Users access a page offered by our system, enter the source code for a program written in (the proposed subset of) C and execute the program stepwise. The system comprises three major components (see Fig. 1), namely the server-side component that processes the source code, the interpreter that

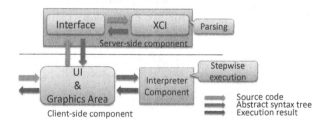

Fig. 1.   Structure

(stepwise) executes the programs, and the client-side component acting as the user interface.

2.1. *The Server-side Component*

The interpreter component requires an abstract syntax tree for stepwise execution. Therefore, the system must parse the textual source code edited by learners before execution. The server side plays this role.

It would be advantageous if we could locate the parser component on the client side. However, it would be very tedious to implement a parser of C in JavaScript. Theoretically, it would be possible to port the parser component written in C to JavaScript using tools like Emscripten (as explained in Section 3.2). This approach is left for future work.

The server-side component is a Web application currently implemented as a PHP script. It invokes XCI to parse the source code submitted by the Web browser, and produces an abstract syntax tree in a JSON-based format from the XML-based format returned by XCI.

It reports an error and stops if it encounters syntactic forms outside the language subset supported by our system. This is done during the XML-to-JSON conversion phase.

2.2. *The Interpreter Component*

To support stepwise execution based on abstract syntax trees, we implement an original interpreter for a subset of C in JavaScript. It handles both global variables and automatic variables allocated in the stack area and maintains a variable table to enable variable values to be observable from the outside. The units of its stepwise execution are the nodes in the syntax tree. It traverses the tree structure and executes a step in terms of a transition from one node to another. For example, the code given in Fig. 2 is parsed into the abstract syntax tree shown in Fig. 3.

By using abstract syntax trees, we expect that we will be able to specify breakpoints in terms of CSS-selector-like expressions rather than by line

```
int main(void) {
  puts("Hello, world!");
  return 0;
}
```

Fig. 2. An example of C source code

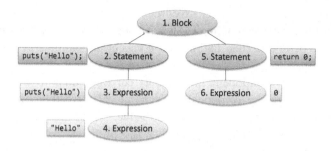

Fig. 3. Abstract Syntax Tree

numbers. For example, we would like to designate a breakpoint by saying "the conditional expression of the first **if** statement in any **for**-loop." This is useful when teachers send messages asking learners to use the debugger, because wrong answers often have common patterns even though their line numbers may vary.

2.3. *The Client-side Component*

This component is a graphical user interface directly manipulated by learners and is written in HTML + CSS + JavaScript, which enables it to be customized by teachers to match the proficiency of learners.

It provides a user interface with VCR-like buttons and a source code editor, as shown in Fig. 4. It also submits the textual source code edited by learners to the server side and controls the interpreter.

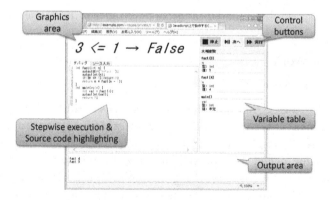

Fig. 4. User Interface

To show a component being executed in a stepwise execution, it produces a DOM tree corresponding to the abstract syntax tree of the program being executed. It can then highlight the execution component, as shown in Fig. 4.

The client-side component has a table corresponding to the variable table of the interpreter component. Each row of the table contains the variable name, its scope, its type, and its value.

To provide information that matches the proficiency of learners, the client-side component has an area for graphical representation. It uses the `canvas` component in HTML5 to enable various drawings, including

- animation for bitwise operations,
- animation of a call tree of (recursive) functions,
- graphical representation of a state in the middle of an iteration.

This component can be customized by teachers.

In general, it is difficult to provide information that matches the proficiency of learners and the progress of classes using existing debuggers. The proposed system enables teachers to customize the interface at various points and to limit the information to that necessary for learners. Specifically,

- teachers can set breakpoints by specifying the type of abstract syntax tree nodes,
- teachers can add built-in functions such as turtle-graphic functions.
- teachers can implement original functions for displaying information in the graphical representation area.

The latter two can be achieved in terms of JavaScript functions.

3. Related Work

3.1. *C Interpreters*

There are several C interpreters, including CINT (http://root.cern.ch/drupal/content/cint), Ch (http://www.softintegration.com) and XCI. Of these, XCI[1] provides an API that outputs abstract syntax trees in an XML format called ACML. XCI can also interpret programs based on abstract syntax trees. Because XCI is written in C, it is not feasible to port the whole of XCI to JavaScript. We therefore use just the parser component and the ACML producer in the server component of our system.

3.2. *Emscripten*

Emscripten is an LLVM-to-JavaScript compiler.[2] Using Emscripten, we can compile various program languages with compilers that have LLVM as their target into JavaScript.

Because we want to manipulate the abstract syntax trees directly, we do not adopt LLVM for our debugger. It would, however, be possible to provide library functions that are not followed by debuggers using LLVM and Emscripten. This would be advantageous in terms of efficiency.

3.3. *Jeliot*

Jeliot is a pedagogical integrated development environment for Java.[3] It interprets users' Java source code using DynamicJava (http://sourceforge.net/projects/djava/) and produces graphical representations from the trace information. We will be able to use its representations for reference purposes. However, in our system, we want to make the interpreter component and front-end component more loosely coupled, to enable teachers to customize the graphical representations easily.

3.4. *WappenLite*

WappenLite[4] is a Web-application framework for the programming environments for various programming languages, developed by our research group.

Because WappenLite is mainly designed for languages based on Java virtual machines, WappenLite is not directly relevant to the proposed system. However, it would be desirable for WappenLite and the proposed system to share some graphical user interface components to reduce both the learning cost for teachers and cognitive cost for learners.

3.5. *Scala-based Monitoring Server*

Our research group is developing a Scala-based monitoring server for Web-based programming environments for learning programming.[5] It is a customizable Web server-side application designed for Web-based programming environments. It can, for example, send a message to learners when they submit a program that meets some condition specified by a script.

The proposed Web-based debugger could be a typical application used in this server-side application. For example, it may send a message to a learner such as "Click this link to start a debugger, execute the program until the breakpoint and make five further steps to see the problem in your submitted program."

4. Summary

In this paper, we have discussed the design of a visual debugger for C that is targeted at programming novices. The system is currently under development and its implementation status is shown in Fig. 5.

Because it is troublesome for novices to install and learn how to use debuggers, we have designed a debugger as a Web-based system implemented in JavaScript. Moreover, it is hard for learners to acquire mastery of a debugger if its many features are introduced without guidance. To remedy this situation, we have made the system customizable by teachers. In particular, the user interface component is written in HTML + CSS + JavaScript, enabling teachers to customize the menus and the debug information provided to learners easily.

The main features of our debugger are stepwise execution, highlighting of source codes, syntax trees, and variable tables, and the graphical representation area. These are all customizable by teachers to some extent. Using stepwise execution, teachers can specify various conditions that will halt the program if one of them is met during the previous step. Teachers can also control the highlighting of the source code and the variable table. Similarly, teachers can devise alternative visualizations of the result of stepwise execution, as displayed in the graphics area.

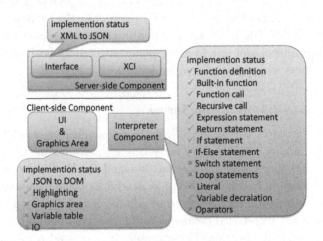

Fig. 5.   Implementation Status

Acknowledgment

The authors would like to thank the anonymous reviewers of WCTP 2013 for their helpful comments.
This work is supported by Kakenhi 23501152.

References

1. K. Gondow and H. Kawashima, Towards ANSI C program slicing using XML, in *2nd International Workshop on Language Desciptions, Tools and Applications (LDTA02), Electronic Notes in Theoretical Computer Science* **65** 2002.
2. A. Zakai, Emscripten: an LLVM-to-JavaScript compiler, in *Proceedings of the ACM international conference companion on Object oriented programming systems languages and applications companion*, SPLASH '11 (ACM, New York, NY, USA, 2011).
3. A. Moreno, N. Myller, E. Sutinen and M. Ben-Ari, Visualizing programs with Jeliot 3, *Proceedings of the working conference on Advanced visual interfaces*, 373 (2004).
4. K. Kagawa, WappenLite: a Web application framework for lightweight programming environments, in *9th International Conference on Information Technology Based Higher Education and Training (ITHET 2010)*, April 2010.
5. K. Kagawa, Design of a Scala-based monitoring server for Web-based programming environments, in *Theory and Practice of Computation*, eds. S. Nishizaki, M. Numao, J. Caro and M. Suarez, Proceedings in Information and Communications Technology, Vol. 7 (Springer Japan, 2013) pp. 143–150.

FLASH CODE WITH DUAL MODES OF ENCODING

Michael Joseph Tan[1.1], Proceso Fernandez[2.1], Nino A. Salazar[2.2],

Jayzon Ty[2.3] and Yuichi Kaji[1.2]

[1] *Graduate School of Information Science*
Nara Institute of Science and Technology,
8916–5 Takayama, Ikoma, Nara, 630–0192 Japan
E-mail: [1.1]*joseph-t@is.naist.jp,* [1.2]*kaji@is.naist.jp*

[2] *Department of Information Systems and Computer Science*
Ateneo de Manila University,
Loyola Heights, Quezon City, 1108 Philippines
E-mail: [2.1]*pfernandez@ateneo.edu,* [2.2]*oh_ninja_nas@yahoo.com,*
[2.3]*jayzonkid_21@yahoo.com*

This paper proposes a novel coding scheme which can extend the lifespan of flash memory. Flash memory has a number of advantages against conventional storage devices, but it must be noted that the flash cells which constitute a flash memory accommodate, not a small, but limited number of operations only. A flash code provides a clever way to represent data values in flash memory so that the number of operations over flash cells becomes as small as possible, and this contributes to extend the lifespan of flash memory. Several flash codes have been studied so far, and this paper proposes a novel coding scheme which makes use of two different modes of encoding. Computer simulation shows that the proposed coding scheme shows much better average-case performance than existing codes. Besides the computer simulation, the paper also gives detailed analysis of the performance which justifies the advantage of the proposed code from a more theoretical viewpoint.

Keywords: flash memory, flash code, binary-indexed, dual-mode encoding

1. Introduction

Flash memory is a non-volatile memory that consists of an array of floating-gate cells which are grouped in uniform sized blocks. Each cell can store at most $q - 1$ levels of electric charge which is represented as an integer value. A peculiar characteristic of a flash memory is the asymmetric relationship between the two operations over the cell values. It is simple to raise the level of one cell, but due to physical constraints, reversing the procedure is not allowed. The only way to lower a cell level is through a *block erasure* which completely removes the charges, bringing the cell level to zero, in an entire *erase block* of flash memory cells. The continuous use of a block erasure is not favorable because it is slow and inflicts physical damages to the cells. Practical flash memory often employs a wear-leveling mechanism which contributes to extend the lifespan of flash memory by equalizing the damages of cells evenly. Despite these efforts, the limited lifespan is still a significant issue of flash memory.

One option to extend the lifespan of a flash memory is to improve the coding scheme that updates and interprets the data stored in a flash memory. Such coding scheme is called *flash code* and it is the target of this study. Flash codes can be considered as a generalization of coding scheme for write-once memories and this coding scheme has been studied since 1980s.[1,7] The framework for flash code itself was only introduced in 2007.[3] In this framework, we consider to store a k-bit data in an erase block which consists of n flash cells, and the performance of a flash code is evaluated in terms of *write deficiency* which can be regarded as a quantitative measure of the overhead of the code. For small n and k, Jiang et al. proposed good flash codes which give more number of operations (and hence less write deficiency) than naive simple coding scheme.[3] In,[4] investigations are made to enlarge the parameters n and k. Mahdavifar et al. improved the idea of,[4] and proposed the index-less indexed flash code (ILIFC).[6] In ILIFC, cells in an erase block are grouped into smaller sub-blocks which we call *slices*. Each bit of the k-bit data is assigned with one slice, and the slice is used to remember the current value of the corresponding bit. ILIFC is a simple and powerful coding scheme, but the problem with ILIFC is that the size of a slice must be k or more. This restriction degrades the flexibility of the code construction, and furthermore, affects the performance of the code in a direct manner.

There are two areas of discussion with regard to the performance of flash code. In papers such as,[3,4,6] they discuss on lowering the worst-case write deficiency of flash codes. Other papers such as[2,5] discuss the importance of constructing flash code that has a low write deficiency in the average-case scenario. Both scenarios are equally important. The worst-case scenario depicts the durability of the flash code. On the other hand, the average-case scenario shows the practicality of a flash code which should also be considered since flash memory is intended to be mass produced and be used by people in their daily lives.

Based on the above described observations, the authors have proposed several flash codes which can be regard as improvements of ILIFC.[8,9] Those codes surely show smaller write deficiency than ILIFC, but the use of slices in constructing flash codes seems to bring a certain overhead. To mitigate the issue of using slices, we propose in this paper a new approach in constructing flash code by integrating two modes of encoding. Each mode of encoding is a flash code on its own, but by integrating them we are able to capitalize on their advantages and mitigate their disadvantages. The proposed code shows a much smaller write deficiency than existing flash codes in terms of average-case discussion, and allows accommodating a large data in one fixed-size block.

2. Preliminaries

A *block* in a flash memory consists of some fixed number n of cells, and this can be represented by a vector $C = (c_0, c_1, \ldots, c_{n-1}) \in A_q^n$ with $A_q = \{0, \ldots, q-1\}$. Each element c_i of C indicates the amount of charge of the corresponding cell. A cell with a charge 0 is said to be *empty* while a cell with a charge $q-1$ is said to be *full*. A cell that is neither empty nor full is said to be *active*. This concept is extended to a group of cells which is analogously classified as *empty* (if it is $(0, \ldots, 0)$), *full* (if it is $(q-1, \ldots, q-1)$) or *active* (neither empty nor full). For two states $C = (c_0, \ldots, c_{n-1})$ and $C' = (c'_0, \ldots, c'_{n-1})$, we write $C \preceq C'$ if $c_i \leq c'_i$ for $0 \leq i < n$ and $C \prec C'$ if $C \preceq C'$ and $C \neq C'$. A state can transit from C to C' only if $C \prec C'$.

The information stored in a single block is a k-bit data $D = (d_0, d_1, \ldots, d_{k-1})$, where $d_i \in \{0, 1\}$ and $k \leq n$. The value of the data is updated through a *write operation* which inverts the binary value of a single bit in the data D. A flash code F bridges together the physical state of a block with the logical interpretation of the data that the block contains.

Formally, a flash code consists of a pair of functions $F = (\mathcal{E}, \mathcal{D})$. The encoding function $\mathcal{E} : \{0, 1, \ldots, k-1\} \times A_q^n \to A_q^n \cup \{E\}$ is invoked at each write operation, and $\mathcal{E}(j, C)$ provides the rules on how to write a new state (possibly a block erasure E) to the block given the index $j \in \{0, 1, \ldots, k-1\}$ of the data bit d_j to be changed and the current state $C \in A_q^n$ of the block. The decoding function $\mathcal{D} : A_q^n \to \{0, 1\}^k$ interprets the contents of the block into the corresponding k-bit data value. Furthermore, if $\mathcal{E}(j, C) = C'$ where $C' \neq E$ and j is the index of the bit given by a write operation, then value of $\mathcal{D}(C)$ and $\mathcal{D}(C')$ are the same except for j-th bit position.

A flash code increases at least one cell level for each write operation, and therefore, the maximum number of write operations allowed for a block is $n(q-1)$. This value is used to define a metric for flash codes, called the *write deficiency*:

$$\delta(F) = n(q-1) - t \tag{1}$$

where t is the number of write operations that the flash code F is able to accommodate before a block erasure. Flash codes are usually compared against one another in both the average-case and worst-case performances using the write deficiency metric, and a smaller value of $\delta(F)$ is more favorable. To normalize this metric, we further divide the write deficiency by $n(q-1)$, to produce the write deficiency *percentage* which we use for the average case performance analysis in later sections.

Among several constructions of flash codes, the authors are especially interested in those suitable for large parameters of n and k. In this aspect, the *index-less indexed flash code* (ILIFC)[6] seems promising because it is simple and scalable in nature. The key idea of ILIFC is, the authors consider, the use of *slices* which is a small group of flash cells. Through clever encoding rule, a slice is able to store both of the index and the value of a bit of the data. This mechanism assigns more number of cells to more frequently written bits, and contributes to reduce the write deficiency. The problem with ILIFC is that the size of a slice is fixed to k, which requires that $k \leq \sqrt{n}$ and some degradation of write deficiency. To overcome this problem, the authors have studied encoding techniques such as the *binary-indexed* slice encoding and its effective uses.[8,9] The flash code which is discussed in the following sections can be regarded as the extension of those studies of the authors.

3. Dual-Mode Flash Code

In this study, we propose a new flash code which we refer to as *dual-mode flash code* (DMFC). This flash code incorporates two modes of encoding; stacked segment encoding (SS encoding) which is introduced in this study, and the binary-indexed slice encoding (BS encoding) which has been developed in a previous study.[9] SS encoding works fine if all data bits experience almost the same numbers of write operations, but its efficiency is degraded if some data bits are written more frequently than others. To get around this problem of SS encoding, we consider to temporally switch to BS encoding, and accommodate excess write operations for those frequently written bits. The use of BS encoding brings a certain overhead, but the BS encoding is able to incorporate the "non-uniform" situation in which some bits are written more frequently than others. In the following, we first introduce the two encoding schemes which are used in the proposed flash code.

3.1. Stacked Segment Encoding

A simple encoding rule, which we call *stacked segment encoding* (SS encoding), is introduced in this section. A *segment* is a group of k cells in an erase block, and a *stack* of segments is an ordered collection of segments. Let h be the number of segments contained in a stack, and let $S_i = (c_{i,0}, \ldots, c_{i,k-1})$ with $0 \le i \le h - 1$ denote the i-th segment in the stack. In this encoding, the value $c_{i,j}$ is managed in such a way that $c_{i,j}$ is not empty only if all of $c_{0,j}, \ldots, c_{i-1,j}$ are full. In a sense, h cells $c_{0,j}, \ldots, c_{h-1,j}$ are stacked over, and used from the bottom of the stack. Those h cells form a single *virtual cell* whose value can be $h(q-1)$ at the maximum, and represents the value d_j of the j-th bit of the data by $d_j = (\sum_{i=0}^{h-1} c_{i,j}) \bmod 2$. The encoding operation is obvious; to flip the value of d_j, we determine the smallest integer i such that $c_{i,j}$ is not full, and increase the value of $c_{i,j}$ by one. If all of $c_{0,j}, \ldots, c_{h-1,j}$ are full, then we allocate a new segment, push that new segment on the top of the existing stack, and raise the value of $c_{h,j}$ in the newly stacked segment. A block erasure is called if we cannot allocate a new segment in the erase block.

This SS encoding works fine if all data bits experience almost the same number of write operations. However, we need to retain many active segments, which results in large write deficiency, if there is a big difference among the numbers of write operations for data bits. To mitigate this issue, we include another mechanism for recording excess write operations, and invoke that mechanism if we already have too many active segments. To implement a trigger mechanism for that switch, a slightly modified encoding function is defined and denoted by $\mathcal{E}_{S,m}$ with m an integer parameter. The function $\mathcal{E}_{S,m}$ works almost the same way as the above explanation, but $\mathcal{E}_{S,m}$ refuses to allocate a new segment and issues a *failure* signal if the stack already has m active segments. We use $\mathcal{D}_{S,m}$ to denote the decoding function of this encoding.

3.2. Binary-Indexed Slice Encoding

The *binary-indexed slice encoding* (BS encoding) is an encoding scheme which is similar to (the first-phase of) ILIFC but makes use of smaller slices than ILIFC. A *slice* is a set of s cells where $s = k$ in ILIFC, and s is the smallest even integer which satisfies $s \ge \lfloor \log_2(k + 1) \rfloor + 1$ in this

BS encoding. An active slice $S = (c_0, \ldots, c_{s-1})$ represents a bit index $i(S)$ and a bit value $v(S)$ by itself. The value d_j of the data is regarded as one if and only if the erase block contains an active slice S with $i(S) = j$ and $v(S) \bmod 2 = 1$. In the BS encoding, slices are operated through the "binary-indexing" rule which is reviewed in this section. See[9] for a more detailed explanation of the rule. We also assume that readers are familiar with the principle of the index-less indexed encoding in.[6]

The binary-indexing encoding rule consists of four phases. The phase-1 rule is used only when an empty slice $S = (c_0, \ldots, c_{s-1})$ is "activated", that is, the slice is assigned an index j. In this phase, cell values are set so that $(c_0 \cdots c_{s-1})_2$ becomes the binary representation of $j + 1$ (i.e., $j + 1 = c_0 2^{s-1} + \cdots + c_{s-1} 2^0$). Cells having the value of 1 after this operation are called *type-1* cells, and cells having the value of 0 are called *type-0* cells. Note that a slice contains both of type-0 and type-1 cells because $1 \le j + 1 \le k$, and therefore the Hamming weight of $(c_0 \cdots c_{s-1})_2$ is more than 0 and less than s. Further encoding operations are defined so that type-0 cells and type-1 cells are always distinguishable, and we can find that $i(S) = j$ by identifying the types of cells.

The phase-2 rule is applied as far as we have a type-1 cell which is not full. In this phase, the encoding function selects a type-1 cell that has the lowest value among all type-1 cells, and raises the value of the selected type-1 cell by one. The types of cells are distinguishable because all type-0 cells are empty while all type-1 cells are not.

The phase-3 rule is applied if the criteria of the phase-2 does not hold and there is at least one type-0 cell whose value is less than $q - 2$. The rule in this phase-3 is similar to that of the phase-2, but the encoding function selects a type-0 cell that has the lowest value, and raises the value of the selected type-0 cell by one. Note that the cell cannot be full because the value of the selected type-0 cell was less than $q - 2$. Therefore, all type-0 cells remain not full, while all type-1 cells are full.

The final phase-4 rule is used if the values of cells in the slice are either of $q - 2$ (for the type-0 cells) or $q - 1$ (for the type-1 cells). In this phase, all cells are filled up and the slice is brought to full.

Figure 1 illustrates the change of the state for the case of $s = 4$, $q = 4$ and $j = 4$. In this case, $j + 1 = 5 = (0101)_2$ and the second and the fourth cells are type-1. Type-1 cells are operated in the phase-2, and type-0 cells are operated in the phase-3. Remark that type-0 cells are never filled-up in the phase-3, and the type of cells in an active slice are always distinguishable.

224

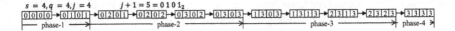

Fig. 1. The operation of cell values in binary-indexing rule.

The bit value $v(S)$ is defined as the number of operations that the slice has experienced so far, that is, $v(S) = (\sum_{i=0}^{s} c_i - w_j + 1) \bmod 2$, where w_j is the Hamming weight of the binary representation of $i(S) + 1$. We denote the encoding and decoding functions of BS encoding by $\mathcal{E}_B$ and $\mathcal{D}_B$, respectively.

3.3. Dual-Mode Flash Code

To accommodate both of the SS encoding and BS encoding in one erase block $(c_0, \ldots, c_{n-1})$, we consider to allocate segments of SS encoding from the beginning of the erase block, and slices of BS encoding from the end of the erase block. The allocation is done in an adaptive manner. If $\mathcal{E}_{S,m}$ requests the i-th segment, then the segment is allocated at $(c_{ik}, \ldots, c_{(i+1)k-1})$. If $\mathcal{E}_B$ requests the i-th slice, then the slice is allocated at $(c_{n-1-(i+1)s+1}, \ldots, c_{n-1-is})$. In both cases, the allocation fails if the erase block does not contain enough number of empty cells. To prevent a possible collision of the allocation of segments and slices, we consider to keep s or more cells empty between the region of segments and the region of slices. By scanning slices from the end of the block, we can precisely identify the region of slices. The region of segments are then easily identified because the two regions cannot overlap.

The encoding function $\mathcal{E}$ of the *dual-mode flash code* (DMFC) is described by utilizing the encoding functions $\mathcal{E}_{S,m}$ and $\mathcal{E}_B$. Given a bit index j and a current state C, $\mathcal{E}(j, C)$ first invokes $\mathcal{E}_{S,m}(j, C)$ and tries to record the write operation by the SS encoding. If $\mathcal{E}_{S,m}(j, C)$ successfully records the change, the encoding completes. If, unfortunately, $\mathcal{E}_{S,m}(j, C)$ issues the failure signal, then $\mathcal{E}(j, C)$ invokes $\mathcal{E}_B(j, C)$ and tries to record the write operation by BS encoding. In case $\mathcal{E}_B(j, C)$ cannot accommodate the write operation, $\mathcal{E}(j, C)$ returns E and requests a block erasure. The decoding function $\mathcal{D}$ is simply defined as $\mathcal{D}(C) = (\mathcal{D}_{S,m}(C) + \mathcal{D}_B(C)) \bmod 2$.

Figure 2 illustrates how the cell values are raised in the encoding of DMFC. Consider the case when $n = 100$, $k = 5$ and $q = 4$. Here, we let $m = 2$ (which means that only two segments can be simultaneously active) and each slice consists of $s = 4$ cells. We illustrate using an array of $q - 1 = 3$ boxes to correspond to a cell, and the boxes represent the use of cell levels.

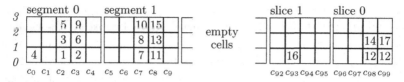

Fig. 2. A demonstration of the encoding process of DMFC.

If 17 write operations are performed on bits in the following sequence,

$$2, 3, 2, 0, 2, \quad 3, 2, 2, 3, 2, \quad 3, 2, 3, 2, 3, \quad 3, 2$$

then the cell levels are used as illustrated in the figure. Up to the 11th write operation (counting from 1), the writes are recorded in segments by using the SS encoding. The 12th write, on the bit 2, is not accommodated by the SS encoding because it requires a third active segment which is not allowed, and we switch to the BS encoding. A slice 0 is allocated, and the third and the fourth cells in the slice become type-1 because $2 + 1 = (0011)_2$. Meanwhile, the writes on the bit 2 is accommodated by the BS encoding, but it has the chance to switch back to the SS encoding when more write operations are performed and the segment 0 becomes full.

4. Results and Analysis

4.1. *Four Factors of Write Deficiency*

The write deficiency of DMFC is contributed by four factors. The first and the second factors are the write deficiencies made by active segments and active slices, which we denote by δ_1 and δ_2, respectively. The third factor δ_3 of the write deficiency is the contribution made by full slices.[a] It is shown in[9] that one full slice contributes $s - 2$ write deficiency. If we can determine the number θ of full slices, then $\delta_3 = \theta(s - 2)$. The fourth factor δ_4 is made by cells which do not belong to any segments or slices. Using the number ϕ of such cells, we can write $\delta_4 = \phi(q - 1)$.

4.2. *Worst Case Write Deficiency*

Depending on the parameters n, k, q and m, there are two different scenarios which result in the largest write deficiency.

The first scenario is such that write operations are made only on one bit until the block erasure occurs. In this case, the SS encoding accommodates

---

[a]Different from slices, full segments makes no contribution to the write deficiency, and we can ignore full segments in the analysis of write deficiency.

the first $m(q-1)$ write operations, and the other write operations are all made through the BS encoding using binary-indexed slices. At the time of block erasure, we have m active segments which occupy mk cells, no active slice, $\theta = \lfloor (n - mk)/s \rfloor - 1$ full slices, and $\phi = n - mk - \theta s$ cells which do not belong to any segments or slices. Each active segment contains one full cell and $k-1$ empty cells, and therefore one such segment contributes $(k-1)(q-1)$ write deficiency each. We have $\delta_1 = m(k-1)(q-1)$, and the write deficiency in this scenario is given by

$$\delta_1 + \delta_2 + \delta_3 + \delta_4 = m(k-1)(q-1) + 0 + \theta(s-2) + \phi(q-1). \quad (2)$$

In the second scenario, the number of active slices is maximized. One way to construct this is to have $m(q-1)+1$ write operations for each of the $k-1$ data bits, and then, have the succeeding write operations solely to the remaining one bit until the block erasure occurs. This pattern of write operations results in m full segments, m active segments, $k-1$ active slices, $\theta = \lfloor (n - 2mk - (k-1)s)/s \rfloor - 1$ full slices and $\phi = n - 2mk - (k-1+\theta)s$ cells which do not belong to any segment or slice. Similar to the previous scenario, each active segment contributes $(k-1)(q-1)$ write deficiency. The active slice is used only once, and each active slice contributes $s(q-1)-1$ write deficiency. Consequently,

$$\delta_1 + \delta_2 + \delta_3 + \delta_4 = (k-1)((m+s)(q-1)-1) + \theta(s-2) + \phi(q-1). \quad (3)$$

There is no particular order between the values of (2) and (3); the former can be larger than the latter for some specific parameters, and the converse is true for some other parameters. In an asymptotic "big-O" notation, however, (3) gives the worse (larger) write deficiency because (2) is in $O(qk+n)$ and (3) is in $O(qk \log k + n)$.

The write deficiency of DMFC contains $O(n)$ factor, and is therefore worse than ILIFC. However, as we see in the next section, DMFC shows remarkably superior write deficiency in the average case.

4.3. Average Case Write Deficiency

Computer simulation was performed in order to estimate the average case write deficiency of DMFC against ILIFC and some other flash codes. It should be noted that ILIFC in its original form[6] consists of two main phases, but we only implemented the first phase of ILIFC since, as observed in [5], the contribution of the second phase is not significant in a non-asymptotic discussion. For the simulations, we fixed the values of $n = 2048$ and $q =$

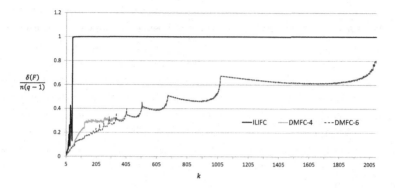

Fig. 3. Write deficiency percentage of ILIFC, DMFC-4 and DMFC-6.

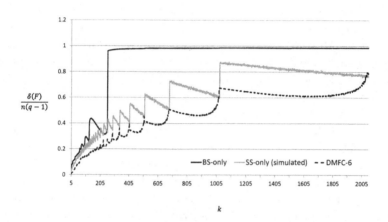

Fig. 4. Write deficiency percentage BS-only, SS-only (simulated) and DMFC-6.

8, and investigated the results at different values of k. For each k value, 30 experiments were run, and the average write deficiency percentage was gathered. It is assumed that all k data bits have equal probability to be selected by write operations.

Figures 3 and 4 shows the average write deficiency percentage of several flash codes including ILIFC and DMFC. DMFC-4 and DMFC-6 stand for DMFC with $m = 4$ and $m = 6$, respectively. To understand the contribution of the dual-mode encoding, the graph also shows the performance of "single-mode" flash codes; SS-only (simulated) shows the write deficiency of a flash code that makes use of the SS encoding technique only (the number of active segments is not bounded in this case), and BS-only shows the

228

write deficiency of a flash code that makes use of the BS encoding technique only. We can see that DMFC shows the smallest write deficiency among all flash codes compared. Unlike ILIFC and BS-only encoding, DMFC and SS-only encoding do not have a degeneration point where the write deficiency percentage shoots up close to 1. This favorable characteristic is due to the use of segments which allow us to start encoding by assigning only one cell to each bit. This is not possible in a pure slice-based flash code, and DMFC inherits the advantage of the segment-based encoding. We can also see that DMFC shows better performance than SS-only encoding. This is because DMFC makes use of slices whose size is much smaller than segments. Consider for example that, after several encoding operations, we have $k - 1$ empty cells in an erase block. The space is too small to accommodate a new segment, but sufficient to accommodate several slices. In this sense, DMFC inherits the advantage of the slice-based encoding. The effect of the parameter m is not clear in these experiments. For small values of k, we can see that DMFC-6 shows better performance than DMFC-4. For large values of k, the difference of m makes little sense because, if k is large, then an erase block is able to accommodate a limited number of segments.

We have seen that the write deficiency of DMFC is contributed by four factors. Figure 5 shows the contribution of each factor on the write deficiency. The graph shows that the contribution of δ_3 and δ_4 are almost negligible. The major factors of write deficiency are δ_1 and δ_2 which are made by active segments and active slices, respectively. Figure 5 shows that the value of δ_2 changes regularly according to the value of k. This phenomenon can be explained in terms of the number of slices. Except for very small values of k, the DMFC tends to allocate as many segments as possible in the erase block. This means that only $(n \bmod k) - s$ cells are used to

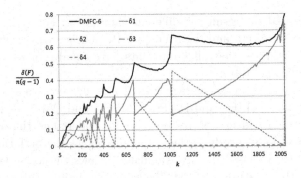

Fig. 5. An analysis of the different factor of write deficiency of DMFC.

accommodate slices, and the number of slices is about $((n \bmod k) - s)/s$. These slices are once assigned, but not used so much. Almost all cell levels in the slices are left unused, which implies that δ_2 is approximated as

$$\delta_2 = \frac{(s(q-1) - 1)((n \bmod k) - s)}{s}. \tag{4}$$

Even though this discussion is quite harsh, the formula well explains the experimental result in Figure 5.

For the estimation of δ_1, we consider the number of segments which are used in SS-only encoding. Even though DMFC and SS-only encoding are different, the estimation result on the SS-only encoding helps in analyzing DMFC also. In Section 3.1, we saw that cells in a stack of segments consti-tute a virtual cell, and we have k virtual cells in a stack of segments. Let X_w^t with $w \geq 0$ and $t \geq 0$ be a random variable denoting the number of virtual cells whose values are w or more after t write operations. Obviously $X_0^0 = k$ and $X_w^0 = 0$ for $w > 0$. With one write operation, one of virtual cells is selected and its value is increased by one. If a cell with value w is selected at the t-th write operation, then $X_{w+1}^{t+1} = X_{w+1}^t + 1$. This event occurs with probability of $(X_w^t - X_{w+1}^t)/k$, and therefore the expected values of X_w^t satisfy

$$E[X_{w+1}^{t+1}] = E[X_{w+1}^t] + (E[X_w^t] - E[X_{w+1}^t])/k. \tag{5}$$

If we regard that the h-th segment is allocated when $E[X_{(h-1)(q-1)+1}^t] \geq 1$, then (5) defines a certain relation between t and h. Figure 6 shows the growth of the number of segments obtained from (5), and those gathered from computer simulations for DMFC-6 and SS-only encoding. We can see that the recursive relation (5) accounts for the number of segments used in DMFC. Let $h_{max} = \lfloor n/k \rfloor$ be the maximum number of segments which can

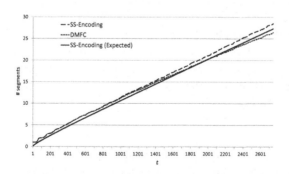

Fig. 6. The growth of the number of segments.

230

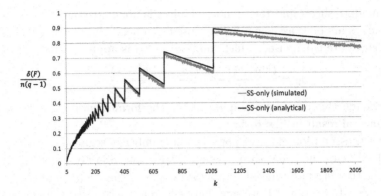

Fig. 7. Write deficiency percentage of SS-only for simulated and analytical.

be allocated in an erase block, and let t_{max} be the smallest integer such that $E[X^{t_{max}}_{h_{max}(q-1)+1}] \geq 1$. The value of t_{max} can be regarded as the estimation of the number of write operations accommodated by SS-only encoding. Unfortunately t_{max} is not derived by a closed-form formula, but we can determine t_{max} by a computer search. The curve of SS-only (analytical) in Figure 7 shows the value of t_{max} for each value of k. The analytical values are slightly larger than the values gather by computer simulation, but give good approximation of the average write deficiency of SS-only encoding. Using the value of t_{max}, $v_w = E[X^{t_{max}}_w] - E[X^{t_{max}}_{w+1}]$ can be regarded as the expected number of virtual cells whose values are w. A virtual cell with value w contributes $m(q-1) - w$ write deficiency, and the value of δ_1, which is the write deficiency contributed by active segments, is given as

$$\delta_1 = m(q-1)k - m(q-1)(E[X^{t_{max}}_{m(q-1)}]) - \sum_{w=0}^{m(q-1)-1} v_w w. \qquad (6)$$

Because δ_3 and δ_4 are negligible, the average write deficiency is approximated as $\delta_1 + \delta_2$, which is computed by using (4) and (6). We have clarified all four factors of the write deficiency of DMFC, though some computer search is needed to determine the value of δ_1.

5. Conclusion

In this paper, a new flash code, called dual-mode flash code (DMFC), is proposed. DMFC inherits the advantages of the stacked segment encoding and binary-indexed slice encoding, and shows remarkable write deficiency in the average case. The paper also investigates the average write deficiency of DMFC, and proposes an analytical estimation of the write deficiency. Further studies can focus on providing a more rigorous discussion of the average performance, and the derivation of a closed-form formula of the write deficiency. Furthemore this paper introduces a new method for constructing a flash code. Further research can also involve investigating combining different modes of encoding to create new flash codes.

References

1. Fiat, A., and Shamir, A.: "Generalized Write-Once Memories," *IEEE Trans. Inform. Theory*, vol. 430, pp. 470-480, September 1984.
2. Finucane, H., Liu, Z., and Mitzenmacher, M.,"Designing floating codes for expected performance," *Proc. 46-th Allerton Conf. Communication, Control and Computing*, pp. 1389-1396, Monticello, IL, September 2008.
3. Jiang, A., Bohossian, V. and Bruck, J.: "Floating codes for joint information storage in write asymmetric memories," *Proc. IEEE Intern. Symposium on Information Theory*, pp. 1166-1170, Nice, France, June 2007.
4. Jiang, A. and Bruck, J.: "Joint coding for flash memory storage," *Proc. IEEE Intern. Symposium on Information Theory*, pp. 1741–1745, Toronto, Canada, July 2008.
5. Kaji, Y.: "The expected write deficiency of index-Less indexed flash codes," IEICE Trans. Fundamentals of Electronics, E95-A, December 2012.
6. Mahdavifar, H., Siegel, P.H., Vardy, A., Wolf, J.K. and Yaakobi, E.: "A nearly optimal construction of flash codes," CoRR, abs0905.1512, 2009.
7. Rivest, R.L. and Shamir, A.: "How to reuse a write-once memory," *Information and Control*, vol. 55, pp. 1–19, December 1982.
8. Tan, M.J. and Kaji, Y.: "Uniform-compartment flash code and binary-indexed flash code," IEICE Technical Report, IT2012-13, pp. 25–30, July 2012.
9. Tan, M.J. and Kaji, Y.: "Flash code utilizing resizable-clusters," IEEE Intl. Conf. on Electro/Information Technology, May 2013.

RANKING ANALYSIS OF BATTLE RESULT OF BOARD GAME STRATEGY IN JAVA PROGRAMMING EXERCISE

KOHEI YAMADA

Faculty of Engineering, Kagawa University,
2210-20 Hayashi-cho, Takamatsu City, 761-0396, Japan

HIROYUKI TOMINAGA

Faculty of Engineering, Kagawa University,
2210-20 Hayashi-cho, Takamatsu City, 761-0396, Japan

We propose an applied Java programming exercise with board-game strategy for problem-solving learning. In the study, we use the Gogo game, a variation of Gomoku. During implementation of move methods of the game, students learn the realization of an idea as algorithms and revisions through trial and error based on execution results. In addition, we have developed a support system called WinG, which consists of the local review package LA and the contest management server CS. The server maintains a preliminary and a final league, which decide the scores of students based on the results of round-robin matching. We performed several educational practice sessions in 2011. By introducing three levels of index strategies as the standard of strength, the number of student submissions increased. A weighted winning degree was introduced for more precise strategy ranking and rating. We analyze the relations and tendencies of the rankings in both leagues, and also discuss the efficiency of the process in round-robin matching and an approximate ranking method for immediately response.

1. Introduction

In information engineering colleges, a programming exercise is regarded as a required subject. Several related subjects are prepared in a systematic and complementary curriculum. In particular, knowledge of C language is very important for entrant students in the course. Introductory exercises to C programming mainly consist of basic grammar, operation of data structures such as stacks and queues, and algorithms such as sort and search. Advanced exercises tackle object-oriented programming using C++/Java language, and software engineering methods such as development styles, system design, data models and testing. Applied exercises deal with practical programming for information processing with respect to databases and networks and programming as problem-solving techniques for several specific fields. For example, they are mathematical simulations, knowledge information processing, Web systems, and device controls.

However, if the subjects in the field of study are too removed far from a student's interest, it is difficult to illustrate concrete images and to pursue the goal of programming. Moreover, a student does not develop the attachment to a software product that he/she creates and has to maintain. In the field of knowledge information processing, game strategy programming is focused on as an attractive exercise subject. It incorporates a competitive learning approach by adopting a contest or competition style among students, who play against each other. A student feels these exercises to be voluntary attempts rather than the imperative tasks of a teacher. This approach is expected to increase motivation and bring about educational effects.

2. Programming exercise with abstract board game strategy

2.1. *Abstract board game Gogo*

In this research, we propose an applied Java programming exercise with abstract board-game strategy for problem-solving learning [1][2]. We adopt the Gogo game as the subject, the basic rules of which are based on Gomoku, which is a well-known traditional board game in Japan. The additional rules are similar to Pente, which is a variant of Gomoku [3]. We have made some rearrangement of the rules to achieve an affordable subject for a programming exercise, viz the board has 169 cells in 13 square sizes instead of intersection points.

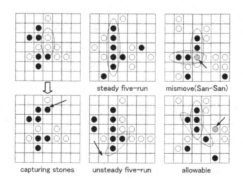

Fig. 1 The rules of Gogo

Players place a stone of his/her color (white or black) in a cell on the board alternately. The aim is to make a connected run of five stones in a straight or diagonal line. In addition, if your stone and another stone pinch two opponent's stones, you remove and capture the opponent's stones (Fig. 1). There are two ways of winning: creating a "steady" five-run, or capturing five pairs (ten stones). As an "unsteady" five-run has removable pairs, you can break the run the next turn and the game does not finish. Moreover, if you obtain a fifth pair in this situation, you win as a come-from-behind victory. A run of more than five stones does not constitute a win. Making a double run of three (San-San) when putting a stone down is a penalty move that results in a loss, while removing a pair of stones is allowed.

Gogo is so challenging a game that removing stones cause a significant change in the situation on the board, and there are surprising turnovers to the game aspect. When thinking of strategy, you must consider two aspects (Fig. 2). One is a tendency to aim at connecting or capturing stones, and the other is tendency to choose attack or defend. The strategy policy has a lot of variations with diverse evaluation functions. Although the rules are simple, a beginner shows his/her individuality with the preference and attitude. As documentation on the rotes of Pente is scarce, the student must research good strategies himself/herself.

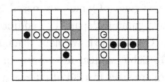

Fig. 2 Aspects of strategy policy

2.2. *The outline of our proposed programming exercise*

Our proposed exercise has the following problem setting. We offer a board game execution library for Gogo as Java API (Fig. 3). After downloading it from the server, a student starts programming for implementation of a strategy by using a text editor or integrated programming environment such as Eclipse. He/she overrides a hand method in his/her subclass inherited Computer Player class. The method receives a current state as an argument. It returns a next move. The state, as an instance of State class, consists of a board situation for stone placement and two pockets for captured stones. An instance of Master class manages game progress according to the rules.

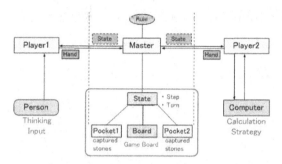

Fig. 3 Java API of game execution library in WinG

A match consists of two game sets, with players taking it in turns to go first and second for fairness. A player is given winning points by winning or losing. If the result of two sets is one win and one loss, the outcome is decided on points based on the sum of captured stones. The score for a strategy is determined based on the total winning points of a battle league with round-robin matching. The ranking of all strategies is open for the results of the exercise. An evaluation of each student is decided by the score and a summary report, in which he/she analyzes the process and the result.

2.3. The steps of strategy design and support system WinG

The overview of strategy design in Gogo is shown in Fig. 4. In the first step, you con-sider the outline of a strategy idea and decide a tactics policy. Each tactic is almost described by if-then rules in knowledge-information processing. The left-hand side of a rule as the second step is pattern recognition of stone placement on a board. You realize various matching algorithms of stone placement such as a four-run, double runs and multiple capturing. You may refine more detailed patterns and find specific patterns for a winning process. The right-hand side as the third step is an assignment of an evaluation value for every cell by a heuristics function. The evaluation value must be revised by trial and error by game execution. In the fourth step, you consider the global board situation and an adjustment of the priority of the rules. You may adopt a look-ahead searching algorithm and probability approach. In the last step, a cell with the maximum value is selected as the hand.

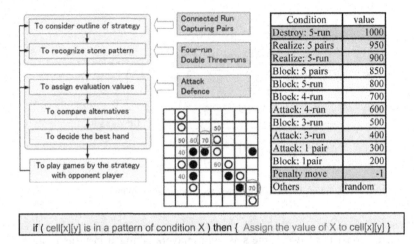

Condition	value
Destroy: 5-run	1000
Realize: 5 pairs	950
Realize: 5-run	900
Block: 5 pairs	850
Block: 5-run	800
Block: 4-run	700
Attack: 4-run	600
Block: 3-run	500
Attack: 3-run	400
Attack: 1 pair	300
Block: 1pair	200
Penalty move	-1
Others	random

if (cell[x][y] is in a pattern of condition X) then { Assign the value of X to cell[x][y] }

Fig. 4 Overview of strategy design in Gogo

In the exercise, we show a sample source code of a prototype program with comments about the guideline of implementation. A student begins implementation of simple rules with typical patterns as basic practice, and he/she states an analysis and original strategy. To realize the exercise, we developed the support system WinG [2]. The configuration of WinG is shown in Fig. 5. It contains a local side WinG-LA and a server side WinG-CS. WinG-LA is a package of review tools. It offers a game execution library as Java API and contains four modules for examination of a strategy. It also prepares various samples as test cases for debugging. WinG-CS is a contest management server. It executes a large number of games from among uploaded students' programs. It maintains a preliminary and the final period for battle league.

The concept of WinG is based on the competitive learning approach. For educational purposes, WinG aims to increase student motivation to continuously refine the strategy program and to promote student activity in the exercise. We have carried out several educational practice sessions since 2005 in applied programming lessons. We analyzed the results in previous practice sessions, and as a result of feedback, we revised the support system and improved the exercise style. In this paper, we introduce the recent version of WinG and report on the situation of educational practice in 2012.

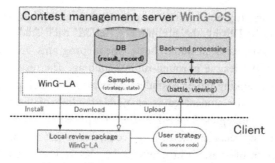

Fig. 5 Configuration of support system WinG

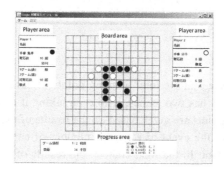

Fig. 6 GUI of WinG-LA

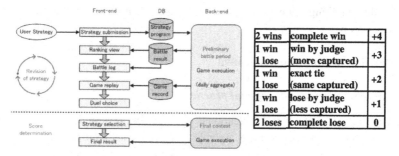

Fig. 7 Preliminary period and final contest for battle leagues

3. A preliminary period and the final contest for battle leagues

3.1. *A preliminary league*

While the evaluation of each strategy is based on the final contest, we also include a preliminary period (Fig. 7). It is important for a student to revise his/her incomplete program continuously through trial and error based on the feedback of results. During the preliminary period, each student may upload candidate programs as a personal best. These programs from all students participate in a battle league in round-robin matching. The results of the battles are exhibited as a ranking table. A student knows his/her own position and that of rivals, by which the student gains an understanding of the tendencies and features of his/her strategies. This stimulates competitive volition and increases activity motivation because there is a concrete target. It also shows the temporary situation of exercise progress in the classroom for a teacher. At the end of the preliminary period, each student chooses his/her best strategy. After that, these selected strategies participate in the final contest in round-robin matching.

3.2. *The final contest*

The final result is based on the total winning points of each strategy. A match between two strategies has two games, with each taking it in turn to move first or second. Winning points are given based on the results of two games as shown in the table below. In the event of a tie, the number of captured stones in two games is very important. In the final contest, the results of the final league are exhibited in the final result page. The ranking table is the same as in the preliminary league, but the ranking order is based on the winning points. Each cell in the matching table shows a winning point of the battle and a link to the battle replay page.

4. Revision of contest management

4.1. *Several previous educational practices*

We have carried out several educational practice sessions since the 2005 term based on our proposed exercise style [1], which is an applied programming subject for third-degree students in an information and electronics engineering college. Programming using board-game strategy is one of the themes of the exercise. Each practice session lasts about four weeks. The learning contents are related to "Knowledge Engineering" and "Object-Oriented Programming with Java" as precondition subjects. However, because of the reform of the curriculum, the exercise has not been a required subject since the 2008 term. Therefore, the number of participating students decreased. The result of previous practices showed that while upper-level students studied very hard, middle-level and lower-level students did not work hard and did rather poorly. In particular, the number of submissions in the early stages of the contest was not enough.

4.2. *Preparation of index strategies in three strength levels*

We have prepared several strategies for the index of strength levels since 2011. These strategies are uploaded to the server by a teacher as dummy students at the start of the exercise. These are crisp targets in the ranking table to promote early submission. We set three levels for these strategies. The weak level has the same strength as the given prototype strategy. It shows the guidelines for creating a simple strategy by a skeleton code. If a strategy is weaker than this, it may have some errors and bugs. The middle level has implemented basic functions in the prototype. It is a minimum requirement to overcome as a first sub-goal. The strong level is selected in the upper-level strategies of the previous exercises. It is the final target to conquer.

4.3. *Introduction to a winning degree for the ranking*

We have introduced winning degree instead of winning percentage for the ranking since 2011 in the preliminary league. A simple winning degree is the value of the sum of winning points divided by the number of battles. The degree is a relative value that is not dependant on the difference in the number of battles. It distinguishes an "out-right win" from a "win by decision." The preliminary and final leagues use the same measure. However, in the preliminary league, the ranking may be influenced by a tendency of the main strategy group during a period. At the beginning of the period, very weak strategies by incomplete programs are included. A high winning degree by these does not show exact strength. While a few aggressive students upload many similar strategies, deviation of strategies causes inaccurate or unfair result with ill-suited battles.

On the other hand, the process of battles in round-robin took many plays and this delayed the reflection of the result in the ranking page. Because the system could not perform all battles in the round-robin in time, it exhibited the ranking table by partial results. In 2012, we adopted WWD, which is a weighted winning degree by each rating of opponents as more stable measurement of strength. The objective of WWD is to avoid a biased or false result and to introduce a thinning method for the number of battles from the round-robin. WWD is a real number in interval $[0,1]$ and is calculated by recurrence. The initial value $V0$ is just a simple winning degree, which is the sum of winning points Pk for each opponent strategy u. The $(n+1)$-th value $Vn+1$ is the sum of a product of winning point Pk and $Vn(u)$ for each opponent k. $Vn(u)$ is also a rating degree of strategy u. To prevent the value from shrinking to zero, V is normalized by division by the maximum value in all strategies. The process is repeated until the difference of Vn and Vn+1 is less than the given threshold. Actually, the process may stop until the ranking is stable.

In WWD, while a winning point from a weak strategy has a low contribution, a winning point from a strong strategy is very important. WWD estimates the quality of each winning point. By using WWD, the influence of deviation in strategies decreased. In particular, the difference of strength of strategies in the middle level became clear.

5. Educational practices and the result

5.1. *Educational practice and the result in 2011*

An educational practice in 2011 was reintroduced as a required subject only for the information engineering course in our college. The target learners were 35 students. The period was five weeks including a short vacation. Submissions in the preliminary period were much increased because of the index strategies. The number of student strategies was 277. The average was 8 and the maximum was 46. The number of battles included in the index strategies was more than 40,000s.

We classified submitted strategies into four groups based on the ranking position of the index strategies according to each level in the final contest. The upper-level 18 students whose strategies overcame the middle-level strategy submitted about 20 times. They revised their programs frequently to challenge the strong-level strategy. The top 4 students in the upper group succeeded in overcoming the strong-level strategy. They showed very affirmative activity. The middle 10 students also submitted about 10 times. They are upsides with the middle level strategies. The lower 7 students submitted several times just before the deadline, and were only the same strength as the weak strategies. Initially, in the preliminary period, one-third of the students were in the lower level. But, finally, 80% of all students exceeded the winning ration percentage.

Here we look at the best strategies of each student. Fig. 8 shows the correlation of winning percentage in the preliminary league and winning points in the final league. In the upper group in the upper right area, both orders in two leagues are almost the same. Strategy as to which values are in large difference is influenced by battle results with strategies that are not the best in the preliminary league. Fig. 9 shows the correlation between winning points and percentage in the final league. The stretch of distribution in the horizontal line as the same winning percentage is caused by difference of winning point. Strategies on the right-hand side of the standard line along the diagonal line have many battle results of "outright win" and "lose by decision." Strategies on the left-hand side have many battle results of "win by decision" and "outright lose." Some strategies in the upper group received a rather inflated evaluation by winning percentage. Because the result in the preliminary league uses the selection of the best strategies of each student in the final league, the difference is not desirable.

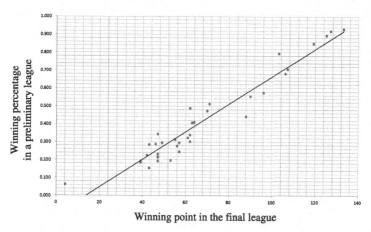

Fig. 8 Correlation between preliminary and final result in 2011

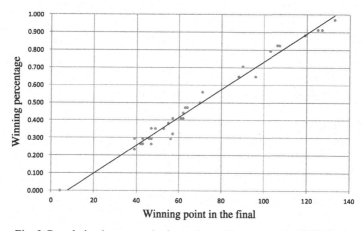

Fig. 9 Correlation between winning point and percentage in 2011 Final

5.2. *Educational practice and the result in 2012*

An educational practice in 2012 was carried out by 44 students over 8 weeks. We prepared 5 index strategies for 3 strength levels in the preliminary period. Fig. 10 shows the cumulative frequency of submissions in the preliminary period. At the beginning of the period, early submissions were carried out mainly by aggressive students. After 2 weeks, the number of submission increased constantly. In the 2 weeks before the deadline, the number of submission increased sharply. The number of strategies was 824. The average was about 19 and the maximum was 95. The number of executed battles in actuality was about 210,000 against the total number.

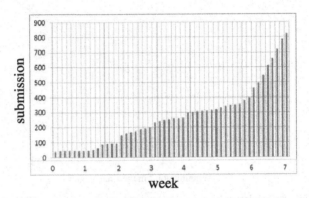

Fig. 10 Cumulative frequency of submission in 2012 Preliminary

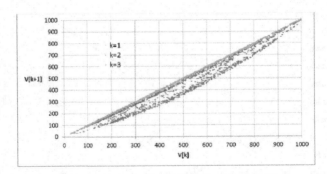

Fig. 11 Convergence situation of WWD in 2012 Preliminary

Fig. 11 shows the convergence situation of WWD in the preliminary league. It is a scatter diagram of plotted points <V0, V1>, <V1, V2> and <V2, V3> for each strategy. Vn is the value of winning degree under recurrence calculation. As the diagonal straight line means fixed points, the V3 series almost converge. Fig. 12 shows the correlation between SWD and WWD in the preliminary league. To observe plotted points along a vertical line in the graph, strategies that have almost same values in SWD often differ in values in WWD. A strategy that has lower values in WWD than in SWD shows a facade of strength by assisting weak opponents. The shape of distribution in the graph is a downward convex, which indicates that the difference of strength of strategies in the middle level became clear.

Fig. 13 shows sorted WWD values of the best strategies of each student in the final league. The 5 horizontal lines are the WWD values of index strategies. The top 2 strategies are outstanding and the WWD values almost equal the past best record. About a half of the strategies have WWD values over index strategies in the middle level. The low 8 strategies could not exceed the index strategies of the weak level in WWD values. Some students gave up halfway or could not finish implementations due to bugs.

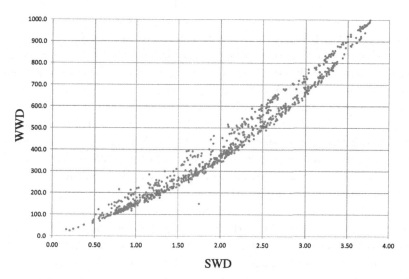

Fig. 12 Correlation between SWD and WWD in 2012 Preliminary

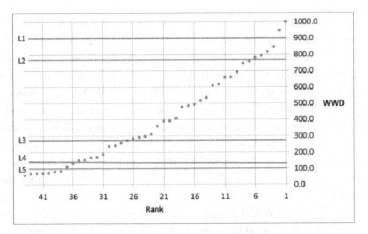

Fig. 13 Ranking and WWD in 2012 Final

6. Conclusion

We proposed a Java exercise with strategy programming of an abstract board game. The exercise is an applied subject of knowledge information processing and for problem solving exercise. According to competitive learning approach, we adopt a preliminary period and the final contest for battle leagues. We developed a support environment WinG, which consists of local debugging support tool WinG-LA and contest management server WinG-CS.

After carrying out several educational practices until 2010, we improved the contest management. In 2011, we prepared index strategies for three strength level. They were uploaded at the beginning of preliminary period. The weak level strategies role the first targets and easily reachable goals. The middle level ones work as standard targets to examine the minimum required specification. By these strategies, the number of submissions much increased. And the quality of implementation was improved. The strong level ones are powerful enemies to overcome. They stimulated competitive volition of excellent students.

On the other hand, the process of battles in round-robin took many times and it delayed the reflection of the result in the ranking page. Moreover, in the preliminary league, very weak strategies caused battles of little value and confused the ranking. In 2012, we adopted WWD, which is a weighted winning degree by each rating of opponents as more stable measurement of strength. By WWD, influence of deviation of strategies decreased and the difference of strength of strategies in the middle level became clear.

In future work, after more detailed analysis, we must consider a thinning method in the number of battles from round-robin in order to exhibit the result immediately.

References

1. H. Ozaki, H. Tominaga, T. Hayashi, and T. Yamasaki, Support System for Java Exercise with Strategy Programming about Board-Game Gogo, *Proceedings of ITHET 2007*, pp. 530–535 (2007).
2. K. Yamada, and H. Tominaga, Support System WinG and an Applied Programming Exercise with Board-Game Strategy, *Proceedings of ITHET 2012*, PS9, pp. 1–6 (2012).
3. Pente Net, http://www.pente.net/.

DISTRIBUTED INFERENCE TO SUPPORT INTER-SUBJECTIVE EMPATHIC COMPUTING

Masayuki Numao

The Institute of Scientific and Industrial Research,
Osaka University, 8-1 Mihogaoka,
Ibaraki, Osaka, 567-0047, Japan
E-mail: numao [at] sanken.osaka-u.ac.jp

We usually prove logical formulas by rewriting them step by step. Reduction machines have been proposed for functional programming languages to make an inference based on such a rewriting scheme. However, it has not been efficient in distributed environment, since they rewrite a logical formula on a memory by using processors. A computer network has many switches, and transfers packets to their destinations. We propose to rewrite a formula in logic or algebra on distributed switches and state memories with higher-order meta-rules. Although such inference seems similar to one by a production rule in expert systems, it utilizes distributed working memories and self-optimizing properties in their inference with meta-rules. We show this mechanism is appropriate for weight-based learning for controlling its inference, and inter-subjective formalization for a sensor network in Empathic Computing.

1. Introduction

In Artificial Intelligence research, the target has been extended many times due to the progress, with which researchers are pursuing various images of intelligence. Its research started in 1950s. Until 1960s, its target had been mainly puzzles or games, where their goal search was an intelligent process. At this stage, the resolution principle was proposed as the foundation of inference. In 1970s, increases in computer power had made possible to apply search and inference to various fields, and to construct domain knowledge in a computer. Knowledge Engineering had been systemized to propose several knowledge representations for storing knowledge. Many companies for Knowledge Engineering were launched to implement the technology. From the viewpoint of computer science, knowledge representation is a higher form of conventional high-level programming languages. Declarative programming is such a higher form that does not specify each computing process, but describes only a piece of declarative knowledge, which can be reused in multiple programming situations. Predicate logic, for example, describes such general declarative knowledge, which automatically derives several procedures. In an intelligent agent, we set up knowledge representation, whose element is assumed to have a correspondence with an object, i.e., a thing or an affair outside.

However, after we develop an expert system equipped with knowledge representation, its external world changes continuously, and we have to update and to modify the knowledge representation as well as its contents, which requires everlasting maintenance. Winograd and Flores[1] discussed this difficulty based on phenomenology in Philosophy. Things or affairs in the external world are not objective, but inter-subjective. After a group of people have talked many words each other, they feel plausibility that there exists an object. This belief spreads around and gradually becomes an established object in the society. This story explains why the external world seems continuously changing from (rather subjective) viewpoint of people in the society. A piece of knowledge can be a belief in some levels of communities, e.g., in a person only, a small group, an expert community, or the whole world on earth. Although a piece of knowledge is usually assumed to be objective, it is rather subjective, plausible, and even empathic in a community. Saijo[2] proposed reconstruction of human science by allowing various beliefs, which may interests researchers in Artificial Intelligence. The conventional knowledge representation and expert systems cannot keep various beliefs simultaneously for proper processing, are inflexible and brittle, and have imposed the limitation on Artificial Intelligence.

To overcome this limitation, there should not be only one knowledge representation in an intelligent agent. A group of agents should exchange candidates of their belief, and construct their inter-subjective knowledge dynamically. We already have such multi-agent systems, constructed in an ad hoc manner. We can assume that sensors in a sensor network exchange candidates of belief to detect an object outside. Websites in a Semantic Web exchange a tagged description, which does not directly correspond to an object (called *anchor*[3] in Situation Theory), but to only each different phenomenon experienced by its user. Therefore, websites in a network has to exchange and modify candidates of belief in the form of tagged description to reach a common belief.

To adopt this scenario, we propose a distributed inference mechanism for describing interaction. Logic programming paradigm has assumed an inference of Horn logic as an execution of a procedure by a processor. Our paradigm considers an inference as a flow of information controlled by a (packet) switch in our distributed inference engine. From the viewpoint of its programmer, it infers by rewriting terms, where the flow of information determines the precedence of term rewriting rules.

2. An Approach Towards a Flexible Symbol

Logic programming was founded and established based on the procedural interpretation of Horn clause by Kowalski in the early 1970s. This interpretation was well matched to the relatively simple computing environment then. As is well known, logic programming language *Prolog* has been adopted as the base language in the fifth generation computer project in the 1980s. In that era, microprocessors had been more popular by LSI technology; computer had decentralized steadily from a minicomputer to a workstation, a personal computer, an embedded system and ubiquitous computing. A system does not run on a single CPU now, but on a distributed network. The mainstream is currently cloud computing. Although the fifth generation computer project was in success as a research program, logic programming languages have not generally spread. The reason is that, although it supports parallel computation, it has no advantage in computing in a distributed network. When the logic programming language is parallelized, its designer emphasized the procedural interpretation, while its programmer tends to ignore its declarative interpretation, and impairs the merits based on logic. In the viewpoint of fallacy of logic programming, logic is an abstract description, and it is better to write a procedural program based on a specification in logic. People suspect that logic is not suitable for a high-level language. It is still hard to write a program by using a conventional programming language in a distributed environment. However, even in logic programming, we emphasize its procedural interpretation, and tend to suppress backtracking. Even in the case of a logic program, we have to trace execution of each literal (sentence) one by one, when we debug a program based on procedural semantics. Its hardness is similar to that in procedural programming languages in distributed environment. We feel no advantage over conventional programming languages, if we employ the procedural interpretation. We should rather try to find a niche for logic programming, and develop a new way of programming that compliments procedural programming languages.

We usually prove logical formulas by rewriting them step by step. Reduction machines have been proposed for functional programming languages to make an inference based on such a rewriting scheme. However, it has not been efficient in distributed environment, since they rewrite a logical formula on a memory by using processors. A computer network has many switches, and transfers packets to their destinations. We propose to rewrite a formula in logic or algebra on distributed switches and state memories with higher-order meta-rules. Although such inference seems similar to one by a production rule in expert systems, it works without intermediate working memory and utilizes self-optimizing properties in their inference with meta-rules.

3. An Inference that Supports an Empathic Symbol

The author proposed a method for the first-order logic in a distributed system,[4] which does not adopt the procedural interpretation of Horn clause, but logical interpretation of general clauses. It rewrites a clause to reduce a literal for resolution. A set of clauses is represented in a graph that a small number of micro rules reduce.

The author introduced one-arc reduction scheme for distributed rewriting of a graph.[4] In this scheme, a rewriting rule is divided into small rules by introducing an intermediate step as shown in Figure 1, where the

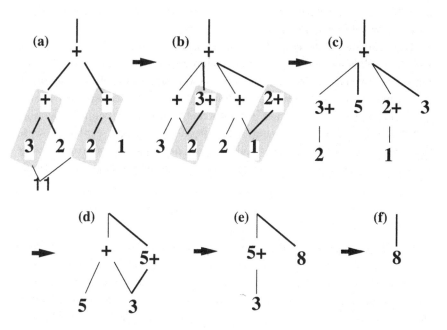

Fig. 1. One-arc reduction

left-hand-side of each rule only contains an arc and two nodes that it connects. It does not directly reduces $3 + 2$ into 5, but first rewrites a graph $3 + 2$ into nodes $3+$ and 2, which is reduced into 5. Although it seems complicated, it reduces a graph locally in adjacent two nodes and an in-between arc, making distributed reduction easier.

However, the author assumed to represent a graph by pointers, and to implement the scheme at the level of software, where a complicated mechanism was necessary to handle two adjacent nodes allocated in two processors. It handled only the first-order logic, which limited its applications.

The author is planning to describe the distributed inference mechanism at the hardware-level, e.g., Field-Programmable Gate Array (FPGA). The goal is to perform distributed inference of higher-order predicate scheme:

$$L_1, \ldots, L_m \leftarrow R_1, \ldots, R_n \tag{1}$$

where each literal L_i and R_i is $< A_1, \ldots A_p >$. A_1 is a predicate, for which we may assign a variable to represent a higher-order scheme. We define various logics or algebras by using this scheme, e.g., natural deduction. Although this scheme seems similar to a production rule in expert systems, by directly unifying the left-hand side of a rule with the right-hand side of another, it works without working memory that memorizes intermediate data, suppressing generation of extra copies.

The first step is to convert a higher-order rule into a graph, where a packet switch constitutes each arc to exchange rewriting messages. We simulate logic by placing its meta-interpreter on the system, based on which we discuss its consistency and completeness. Its mechanism has a *self-optimizing property*, which enables that a meta-interpreter competes against a direct interpreter in efficiency. This mechanism might explain how to represent a symbol by using a collection of neurons. We control message passing to put priority on applying a rule to introduce stochastic relational learning.

4. Conclusion

Although popularization of personal computers and smart phones makes our communication easier, consideration for other people's feeling is conspicuously lacking in these stressful times. The fields of artificial intelligence and knowledge engineering are formed before the popularization of information technology, and rather accelerate the crises it is causing. Towards Empathic Computing,[5] the author is trying to cultivate empathy for artificial intelligence, e.g., a machine that feels empathy for its user, and that makes its user feel empathy for it. In contrast to *Affective Computing*, we emphasize to analyze such relationships or contexts in empathic computing, where inter-subjective formalization and inference are quite important.

Acknowledgment

JSPS KAKENHI Grant-in-Aid for Challenging Exploratory Research: *Distributed Inference to Support Inter-Subjective Formalization*, Grant Number 25540101 is supporting this project from this year (2013).

References

1. T. Winograd and F. Flores, *Understanding Computers and Cognition — A New Foundation for Design* (Ablex Publishing, 1986).
2. T. Saijo, *Structural-constructivism — the principle of next generation human science (in Japanese)* (Kita-oji Shobo, 2005).
3. J. Barwise and J. Perry, *Situations and Attitudes* (The MIT Press, Cambridge, MA, 1983).
4. M. Numao, S. Morita and K. Karaki, A learning mechanism for logic programs using dynamically shared substructures, in *Machine Intelligence 15*, (Oxford University Press, 1999) pp. 268–284.
5. M. T. Suarez, M. Numao, B. the Duy and M. T. Rodrigo, 4th International Workshop on Empathic Computing, a workshop in IJCAI-13 (2013).

AUTHOR INDEX